MOTIVATION

Psychological Principles and
Educational Implications

Chandler Publications in

EDUCATIONAL PSYCHOLOGY

David G. Ryans, *Editor*

MOTIVATION

Psychological Principles and Educational Implications

MELVIN H. MARX

University of Missouri

TOM N. TOMBAUGH

Carleton University, Ottawa

CHANDLER PUBLISHING COMPANY

124 Spear Street

San Francisco, California 94105

 Science Research Associates, Inc., 259 East Erie Street, Chicago, Illinois 60611
A Subsidiary of IBM   Distributors

To   Stella and Salina Marx
     Si and Marie Tombaugh
     who provided our education

CONTENTS

PREFACE

The purpose of this book is to present for the undergraduate student in psychology and educational psychology an outline of the major efforts thus far made by psychologists to explain the multifold facts of what is commonly called "motivation." As will become evident in our discussion, the problem of motivation has been attacked by psychologists using a variety of different methods and differing widely in their theoretical approaches. Our experience has been that the typical student is familiar with the most "popularized" motivational accounts and has been exposed to various of the other theoretical accounts which are largely concerned with personality, but that he is practically void of any knowledge of the empirical data relevant to motivation. The typical beginning psychology student will tend to define such words as *ego, drive,* and *aggression* in lay terms. The professional psychologist, however, depends for his definition on the original meaning of the term as defined by the theorist or experimenter. This text, it is hoped, will provide the student with a scientific explanation of the origin of these terms and will provide some understanding of the empirical and theoretical methodology of the professional psychologist.

Within the last decade psychologists, particularly experimental psychologists, have tended more and more to question the essentially nonempirical positions of the orthodox theorists on the problem of motivation. The result of this movement has been twofold. First, theoretical attempts to explain motivation have become more limited in scope. Instead of attempting to relate motivation to all facets of behavior, as was done in the past, psychologists now concentrate on analyzing the motivational components of limited segments of behavior. Second, the current approach is largely oriented toward gathering and analyzing empirically grounded facts rather than merely speculating on the principles underlying motivated performance. It is this goal of an empirically grounded motivational approach with which we are most sympathetic, and we have attempted to emphasize empirically grounded explanations as much as possible.

The plan of the book is as follows:

The first chapter discusses the basic concepts and problems attendant upon explaining motivation and lays the groundwork for understanding experimental data presented in subsequent chapters. Chapters 2 and 3 describe the classic theories of motivation. These classic positions are presented not only because they are important in their own right but also because they form the background against which much of the more recent and more critical work has been done. Some evaluations of their adequacy, however, will be included throughout this book.

The remaining chapters are organized around the different experimental approaches which have been used to investigate the parameters of motivation. Chapter 4 is concerned with the problems of motivation as they relate to the interpretation of personality, and Chapter 5 with the physiological basis of motivated behavior. The book is completed by discussions of the relationships between learning and motivation (Chapter 6) and between motivation and education (Chapters 7 and 8).

This last topic is of course the most relevant for any student of education, and of the learning process as it relates to education. It is our deep conviction that the problem of motivation is central to the problem of education and that it has *not* been adequately treated in either the educational literature or educational curriculum. We have, therefore, included in Chapter 8 a discussion of proposed methods to alleviate this problem and we would urge students to prepare themselves adequately to perform appropriate research in this area.

A number of persons have assisted us in the preparation of this book. We wish to thank Jo Tombaugh for her help with the first draft. We are especially indebted to Charles Cole, who gave the entire manuscript a very critical reading and whose perceptive commentary proved invaluable to us in revising the text; and to Kathleen Marx, who searched the literature, criticized the manuscript, and supervised the technical details involved in preparation of the final copy. Thanks are due to Ronald Press and the Responsive Environments Foundation, Inc., and to authors Neal Miller, Pauline Sears, and O. K. Moore, for their kind permission to reprint materials.

M. H. M.
T. N. T.

September, 1966

MOTIVATION

Psychological Principles and
Educational Implications

Chapter 1

PROBLEMS AND METHODS

The concept of motivation has long been a key one in attempts to explain or interpret behavior. Although precise uses of "motive" have not been common, the term has referred to presumed internal activating and directive forces. That is, there has been a strong tendency to assume some kind of motive as an explanatory factor in behavior, particularly when no controlling environmental stimuli are clearly present and effective.

As an example of this point, consider the classroom situation in which two children, sitting side by side and exposed to almost exactly the same environmental stimulation, nevertheless behave quite differently. One of them responds readily and correctly to the teacher's questions while the other fails to do so. If we have reason to believe, from past performances, that the ability and knowledge levels of these two pupils are now essentially the same, then we will tend to attribute the present performance difference to differential internal activating conditions. Prominent among these conditions are what are typically called "motives"; the first child may be said to be strongly motivated, the second child weakly motivated—at least with regard to the educational task at hand.

The same basic kind of contrast can also be pointed up by comparing the performance of two laboratory animals, each thoroughly trained on some particular response such as pressing a bar, which in the past has regularly been followed by the presentation of food. If we now allow the first animal unlimited access to food while depriving the second animal of food in the usual manner, then it is hardly surprising that we observe the first to barpress only sporadically when given the opportunity while the second performs in the normal manner. But to an observer who knows only the past training history of the two animals (and not the immediately prior differences in food accessibility), the differential performance will seem mysterious indeed—just as does the differential classroom performance of the two children described above when one does not know the differentiating motivational conditions.

Motives are most generally attributed when one or both of the two following conditions hold: (1) a variety of otherwise apparently unrelated behaviors can be systematically related, being subsumed under a single fundamental rubric (as hunger or curiosity); and (2) the same stimulus conditions produce, on different occasions, different behavioral results, either within a single subject or between subjects (for instance, food is presented to a deprived and a satiated animal, as described above, with strikingly different results).

HISTORICAL OVERVIEW

Historically, there are two major types of attitudes toward the concept of motivation.

ORTHODOX POSITION

The oldest and most orthodox of these attitudes, deriving directly from the common lay usage of the concept, is that motives represent the causal mainsprings of behavior. Prime examples of this approach are the psychoanalytic position developed by Freud, with its emphasis that much behavior can be explained by assuming strong unconscious forces of a directive sort, and the functionalistic position developed by Carr (1925), that a motive is a strong and persistent internal stimulus around which behavior is organized.

These classic approaches to the problem of motivation have been increasingly and justifiably criticized by certain of the more "tough-minded" members of the scientific community for their essentially "literary" character. That is, such free and easy assumption of motives has been insufficiently buttressed by controlled scientific evidence of the sort ordinarily required before scientific propositions are accepted. Moreover, the proponents of the classical positions have often been disinclined to attempt experimental verification. Such a practice is scientifically danger-ous and misleading in that it gives the appearance of an explana-tion when in actuality the proponent does not know the effective antecedent factors producing the behavior. The causal use of a scientifically untested concept has the effect of cloaking ignorance or merely substituting one kind of ignorance for another.

Apart from the failure to contribute in any positive manner to the understanding of behavioral phenomena, the misuse of moti-vational concepts as described above has two unfortunate conse-quences. First, it tends to discourage the active search for effective antecedent factors in behavior. Until such factors can be isolated and experimentally manipulated it will be difficult, if not impos-sible, to obtain lawful relationships in behavioral science.

Second, there is a very serious danger of overinterpretation of motivational constructs, particularly in the sense that they are no longer treated, properly, as constructs—that is, as inferences de-pendent upon observations—but are treated instead as though they were actual entities within the person. This criticism of reification can be made against many popular and some scientific motivational interpretations. Perhaps the best known and most controversial of these interpretations is the Freudian psychoana-lytic system. Freudian concepts such as the "id," "ego," and "superego" are often regarded as though they actually exist, in some substantive manner, within the organism. When such think-ing occurs we tend to lose sight of the essentially inferential basis for all such constructs, which cannot be—or at least have not been—directly identified.

POSITIVISTIC POSITION

The second major position on motives has largely developed from the criticisms just described. The motive concept is held to be scientifically unnecessary because behavioral variations can be accounted for satisfactorily in terms of stimulus-response associa-tions. There has been a strong trend away from the use of the term "motivation" or any of the usual substitutes for it such as "drive." Certain theorists (as, Farber, 1955; MacCorquodale,

1955; Bindra, 1959) have raised serious questions about the necessity of such a concept for many important behavioral relationships, pointing out that the habit construct—the association between stimulus and response—may be sufficient and that the evidence for the necessity of a motivational construct is weak. Other theorists take an even more extreme position. The more avid positivists, for example, have tended to ignore or to deny the concept and generally to reject the "vernacular."

Primarily, what these critics are opposing is the idea of some sort of driving internal force—some "little man" within the organism—to supplement the eliciting powers of external stimulation. This combination has been referred to as the "push-pull model," a term which takes account of both the presumed internal driving conditions and the external stimulus attractions.

It would be unfortunate indeed if the serious questioning of the motivational concept by this positivistic position is permitted to retard the badly needed research on motivational problems, however these may be verbally identified. Our own position is that neither of these extreme views is essentially correct. The first position is too broad; certainly much of the behavioral variation casually attributed to motivational factors in the absence of sound scientific evidence can be explained on associative grounds. The second position is too limited; although a good case can today be made for the importance of strictly associative factors, many changes in performance appear to vary directly and immediately with incentive manipulations and so are fundamentally motivational, rather than associative.

Fortunately, we are not bound to select one of these two historical positions. A more attractive alternative appears to be quite feasible, and perhaps more productive of research. This would involve a rigorous scientific (as opposed to a primarily speculative) attack directly upon the motivational problem. Three major facets of this kind of approach are: (1) conceptualization, the scientific posing of the problem; (2) experimentation, the obtaining of adequately controlled data; and (3) theory construction, the development of integrating general principles. At the present time the first two of these facets appear to be most immediately necessary, with theory playing a research-directive role. The ultimate scientific objective of integrating principles (theory) can be achieved only after a sound empirical basis is established.

The following sections are concerned with each of these three major divisions into which scientific research on motivation can be divided.

CONCEPTUALIZATION OF MOTIVES

Though the psychological literature has seen a great deal of emphasis upon the critical role that motives play in behavior, there has been, as was suggested above, a paucity of systematic, analytic attempts to deal with the problem of motives directly— that is, as behavioral processes in their own right. The suggestions outlined in the following paragraphs illustrate the kinds of considerations that might well be generated by such a direct investigation. Thus the present approach is distinctly programmatic; it attempts merely to point to some ways in which thinking about motivation may profitably turn. Some of the major dimensions of motives thus considered will be treated as illustrative of this kind of direct approach to the problem of motivation.

CHARACTER OF MOTIVES

A number of dichotomies have been suggested as characteristic of motives. One of the more common of these is the primary-secondary distinction. As usually presented, this dichotomy categorizes motives in terms of their biological role. That is, motives that are essential to life, either ontogenetically or phylogenetically (eating, drinking, breathing, sex activity), are considered *primary,* and motives not essential to life (taking courses, playing games, making money) are considered *secondary.* In a related vein, motives that deal more or less directly with biological functions (eating, drinking, and the like) are termed primary, whereas motives for which the related biological functions are more obscure are termed secondary. Sometimes the terms "viscerogenic" and "psychogenic" or "innate" and "learned" are used to classify these two types of motives and to indicate their presumed origin.

From the present point of view there is nothing intrinsically wrong with these usages. But there is some danger that they will divert attention from what seem to us to be the more significant aspects of motives; categorizing motives as primary or secondary on some bases such as those mentioned hardly advances our knowledge of how motives operate. On the contrary, if we wish to look more closely at motives, as worth investigation in their own right, then all motives may, in this sense, be considered primary. That is, motivated behavior can be investigated directly, as a given, rather than simply related to other phenomena such as learning or perception. Experimental analysis of motives thus construed is needed in psychology to supplement the highly speculative and theoretical considerations that they have typically been accorded.

It is also possible to characterize motives in terms of their consummatory-instrumental and their appetitive-aversive nature. The consummatory-instrumental continuum distinguishes between activities which are goals, objectives, purposes of motivated behavior—as indicated objectively by the cessation of ongoing behaviors when the goals are attained—and instrumental activities, which precede and presumably make possible these consummatory behaviors. Common laboratory examples of consummatory activities are eating and drinking; of related instrumental activities, running and barpressing. Common everyday-life examples of consummatory activities are passing a course and winning a political contest; of related instrumental activities, writing examinations and making speeches. This particular distinction has often been made in the literature but seldom utilized in theory development (for one such attempt, see Marx, 1966).

The distinction between appetitive or approach behavior and aversive or avoidance behavior is commonly made in the literature. It is generally presumed that appetitive behavior is elicited or occasioned by positive, rewarding goals and that avoidance or aversive behavior is elicited by negative, punishing situations.

These suggestions exemplify the kind of reordering that can be attempted in the welter of overlapping categorizations that exist, mainly in implicit form, among motivational concepts. Explication of the basis of other similar kinds of categorization is an important function for motivation theorists if significant clarification of the terminology and conceptualizations used is to be achieved. An illustration of how this dichotomy has been utilized in the analysis of complex behavior is provided by Miller's (1944, 1959) conceptualization of conflict behavior, which is described in Chapter 3.

TEMPORAL FACTORS IN MOTIVES

Some of the more interesting variations in motivated behavior concern their temporal relationships. The immediacy of motives varies enormously, as all of us learn; "good intentions" pave certain roads very well indeed!

A somewhat less obvious facet of motives is their dormancy; many motives are latent and are sporadically expressed as salient behavior (for example, phases in a childlike negativism, playing with dolls or guns, and the like). The temporal pace of motives comprises a continuum of expression from the impulsive ("emotional") to the deliberate or suspended mode. Finally, the strength, persistence, and duration of a given motive vary. Some of this variation is cyclic (as in hunger and sex rhythms, biologically controlled to a great extent) and some is in accordance with external environmental conditions (for instance, the amount of time spent in study is a function of the stage of the course, grade standing at the time, and the like).

SCOPE OF MOTIVES

Motives quite obviously vary widely in their scope, or degree of comprehensiveness. To take one particular chain of motives as an illustration, let us consider a student who is motivated, in increasingly broad scope, (a) to answer some specific question on an examination, in order (b) to pass the course, in order (c) to obtain his A.B. or B.S. degree, in order (d) to pursue some professional career, and so on. This oversimplified account suggests the chaining and interrelatedness of motives as well as the variability in scope of motives.

Note also that a single motive, instrumental or consummatory, may entail varying numbers of associated responses, and that a single response may have a number of associated motives.

To illustrate the former relationship (single-motive,

multiple-response) , consider the single motive *to earn money;* this motive may be implemented by all sorts of behaviors, such as teaching, selling magazines, or entering contests. To illustrate the latter relationship (multiple-motive, single-response) , consider the single behavior of teaching school; this behavior may be activated by a variety of more or less clearly separable motives, such as to earn money, to influence students, to gain prestige, to maintain an intellectual challenge, and/or perhaps to stay out of some other less desirable activity.

The varying scope of motives may also be illustrated by the way in which their generality differs. For example, a student may leave home in the evening merely to "go out" or to see some particular movie or be with some particular person. A child's shoe-tying behavior may represent a highly generalized "do it self" motive or merely a specific motive to tie shoes.

DEVELOPMENT OF MOTIVES

One of the more sadly neglected aspects of behavioral science is the problem of the origin of motives. The classic theories offer some suggestions. Thus Freud looked to "libido" (basic life energy) and "cathexis" (emotional attachment) . More recently Miller, Galanter, and Pribram (1960, p. 64) have suggested a similar answer, which epitomizes the same sort of grand solution: "the nature of life itself." Lewin (1936) offered "valence." These gross categories, themselves poorly defined or identified, raise questions beyond the ones associated with the original problem and leave us no closer to a satisfactory answer to that problem.

The standard solution in Hullian S-R reinforcement theory was primary drive, which was somehow elaborated by learning into secondary drives. Thus the love of money, or power, was assumed to develop from basic drives such as hunger or thirst. Unfortunately, however, the mechanism by which this elaboration is accomplished has never been satisfactorily demonstrated, even in theory.

Rather than attempt to answer this question on the basis of some grand theoretical solutions, such as those mentioned above, it might be well to ask a number of pointed and much more specific questions. For example: What is the role of the exteroceptors as contrasted with internal, "drive" factors (see Harlow, 1953; White, 1959) ? When a child sees a toy or other goal object there is apparently a very direct exteroceptive motivational effect. It would be worth while to investigate this motivational effect in respect to the above question.

A similar question may be raised about the role of the brain. What neural functions underlie a motive, in contrast to a perception or a response as such? As an example of the kind of thinking that could be done on this problem, one may inquire as to whether there might not be a neural counterpart to the spontaneous development of muscular action in a developing organism.

Questions of this sort may also be asked about the role of cognitive and "rational" factors (see Bruner, 1964). Their relationship to motives is especially in need of analysis.

Finally, there are questions to be raised concerning (a) biologically determined needs and (b) personal-social needs. The latter are of special interest. Culturally or individually acquired, they seem to underlie many types of consummatory motives without logical relationship. That is, their role can be appreciated only on historical bases. But the question of the extent of this role, and also of their formation, will require intensive investigation.

Once initiated, motives develop and are modified. Problems bearing on this process also need energetic investigation. The question of functional autonomy, early raised by Allport (1937), remains unanswered. "Functional autonomy" refers to the persistence of some behavior after the original motivating factors are no longer present; apparently the behavior has developed an intrinsic motivational basis—become functionally autonomous. Classic examples of such behavior are the old sailor who continues to go to sea, although he no longer needs the pay, and the bus driver whose holiday is spent in riding buses. The same problem, in a somewhat different form, was early tackled by Woodworth (1918), who proposed that "mechanisms become drives." More recently, Woodworth (1947) has made the important point that visual perception, typically considered a mechanism serving an information-gathering function, can also be viewed as a process with important rewarding (reinforcing) properties of its own. A direct confirmation of this proposition was later provided by

Butler (1957), who showed that monkeys would readily learn an instrumental task in order to obtain visual stimulation (specifically, a brief look into the laboratory from their visually shielded cage). This whole problem of the development and modification of motives is a most important one desperately in need of experimental and conceptual analysis.

SOME REDEFINITIONS

If motivational phenomena are simply assumed to occur as behavioral phenomena in their own right they may be studied directly rather than merely treated as determinants of, say, learning or emotion. In this more direct approach to the analysis of motivation a first step is the careful redefinition of the key concepts.

A vast array of terms has been at one time or another applied to motivation. In their dictionary, for example, English and English (1958, p. 330) list 33 separate terms under the general rubric of motivation.

The three central terms of our proposed redefinition are *motive, purpose,* and *intention.* These will be briefly characterized.

The term *motive* is the most general, and applies to behavioral situations of widely varying scope and comprehensiveness. It involves two components: (1) a habit, or associative factor, and (2) a drive, or activating (energizing) factor. A motive is thus seen as a kind of activated habit.

Much of the recent argument about the term *motive* has stemmed from semantic (definitional) differences. If a motive is defined as a broad and complex process or state, including both directive and energizing functions, at least some clarity may be achieved. For example, a person may be said to have high academic motivation. This kind of motive would subsume a very large number of instrumental tasks (studying for examinations, writing reports, and the like) as well as the presumed internal energizing processes that initiate and activate such behavior.

The term *purpose* emphasizes the goal-directedness of behavior. As used here, a purpose is a complex, generally long-range kind of motive, with a more or less distinct beginning and end-point, somewhat in the manner conceptualized by Tolman (1932) and Muenzinger (1942).

Much of the resistance to the purposive formulations of these psychologists arose from the fear of so-called teleology. In brief, "teleology" refers to any explanation of behavior in terms of its consequences, or ultimate utility, in the absence of direct evidence that consequences and utility actually are effective determinants. For example, consider the case described by Carr (1925). The larval forms of certain insects typically move up the tree trunks on which they are produced. This behavior has the consequence of placing them in position to eat the tender leaf shoots as these develop and so has considerable utility. But to consider such behavior "purposive" is to overlook the simpler (that is, more parsimonious) interpretation that light directly attracts the larvae (positive phototropism). If this behavior is said to be purposive with regard to obtaining food, then the label "teleology" may properly be applied, since there is no evidence that this particular utility is in any way a direct stimulating or causal factor. Our use of the term *purpose* is intended to be strictly ateleological; "purpose" is a fully objective concept based upon observed behavioral relationships to particular goals or goal objects.

The term *intention* refers to a special kind of motive—one in which a particular instrumental task or consummatory action is either explicitly stated or implicitly indicated. It thus involves not only a more specific motivational situation but also the addition of some kind of verbalization about the motive. Intentions as critical factors in adult human behavior have been emphasized, especially by Allport (1947, 1955), but without empirical research.

An excellent example of a relevant research program is the ingenious experimentation instigated and supervised by Kurt Lewin (1935, 1936) while he was at the University of Berlin in the 1920s. He postulated the existence of an active tension system (another name for what we are calling "intention") and designed experiments to demonstrate and investigate it. By "tension" Lewin meant an internal energy system somehow acting to stimulate the organism to behave in a particular manner. This tension was held to be initiated by a particular objective, or goal, and dissipated only by the achievement of the goal.

The two best-known researches performed within this framework were doctoral dissertations under Lewin's supervision by Zeigarnik (1927) and Ovsiankina (1928).

Zeigarnik demonstrated that tasks not completed by human subjects, and so presumably still represented within the organism by active tension systems, were reliably better recalled than comparable tasks which the experimenter allowed the subjects to complete (and so presumably to dissipate the tension system). Her results have been amply verified with a number of interesting follow-up experiments (see Alper, 1952, for a review of the basic work).

Ovsiankina showed that children would return to those activities which had been interrupted, when offered an appropriate opportunity, more readily than to otherwise comparable activities which they had been allowed to complete. Here again an interpretation in terms of tension systems and their maintenance or dissipation is quite plausible.

One of the difficulties in developing this kind of direct experimentation upon motives is that of defining the stimulus conditions. If a motive is viewed as an intervening variable—as *whatever* it is within the organism that mediates the referent behavior in a specified stimulus situation—then we need to know as precisely as possible what the stimulus conditions are. This need points up the necessity of carefully controlled experimental situations, since in everyday life the stimulating conditions, as well as the responses, are too complex for careful identification. For this reason children and infrahuman animals are considered to be especially good subjects.

Animal subjects obviously offer the best conditions for exact control of the environment but are also obviously deficient in behavioral complexities (see Chapter 6 for a more complete discussion of the use of infrahuman subjects). Nevertheless, the extent to which generalizations can be made from their behavior to that of humans is entirely an empirical problem. That is to say, one cannot determine on an a priori basis the amount of modification and elaboration needed when behavioral principles based on research with animals are applied to humans. This problem can be solved only by the accumulation of a great deal of empirical data. Moreover, quite probably a very wide range of elaborations will be required; some principles will require relatively little in the way of transformation while others will be virtually useless and so will need to be completely redone.

Children subjects offer greater simplicity than adults, with underlying motivational mechanisms that seem to be much closer to the behavioral surface. Children also offer the advantage, as compared with lower animals, of affording a readier (although still not completely reliable) source of intentions, via their verbalizations, with a lesser danger of an overlay of rationalization than is present in adult subjects.

There is today a need for research programs emphasizing instrumental-consummatory relations and motivational conditions other than the usual viscerogenic ones (deprivation of food and water or of sex activity) that have been used with animal subjects. The early dependence of psychological experimenters and theorists on food and water motivation has been increasingly questioned. Most mammalian behavior is clearly activated by such other kinds of factors as curiosity and exploration. Motivation experiments need to be performed on a wide range of mammalian organisms from rats to humans. Although a start has been made, especially with rats and monkeys, the research thus far reported is just sufficient to indicate the importance and feasibility of the program; definitive principles await the development of data on a scale comparable to that already achieved with motivation manipulated through deprivation of food and water.

SCIENTIFIC METHODOLOGY

This section is concerned with two major facets of the general problem of applying scientific methods to motivational phenomena. First, we briefly review the general nature of the experimental method, which has been the key to the success of modern science. Second, we review some of the particular techniques that have been developed to measure motivation and then discuss one of the persistent methodological problems that have plagued many such attempts—the problem of test reliability and validity.

THE EXPERIMENT

Science as an empirical method of obtaining knowledge is marked by its dependence upon the *experiment*. An experiment is, briefly, a contrived situation. It is contrived by the investigator in a way that maximizes the probability of his obtaining as data (records) the best possible answer to some question (such as, "Is learning more efficient in small discussion groups or in formal lectures?" "In a live classroom situation or by means of a televised presentation?"). It should be recognized that any question admits of varying degrees of refinement. As a matter of fact, the continuing effort to answer more and more refined questions is what marks, in essence, the advance of a science.

All science is concerned with *variables* and their functional relationships. A variable is some factor or condition the magnitude of which is measurably different under differing circumstances (examples include age, intelligence, and rate of performance).

Three fundamental types of variables may be identified. An *independent variable* is one whose magnitude is manipulated in an experiment. It is that condition whose effect upon behavior is of interest. For example, an experimenter might be interested in determining how the time lapse between completion of an examination and provision of knowledge of results affects students' subsequent performance. Time lapse would then be his independent variable, and he would choose two or more levels or values of the time variable to use in the experiment. He might choose three values, say 1 day, 1 week, and 2 weeks. He would then have three groups in his experiment: a group given knowledge of results 1 day after the test, a group given such knowledge 7 days after, and one given it 14 days after the test.

A *dependent variable* is one which is observed and measured. In psychology it is ordinarily some measure of performance. In the above example, scores made on a second test over the same material that had been covered in the first test might be used as the dependent variable. The task of the investigator is to discover the nature of the relationship between independent and dependent variables so that this relationship may be codified in some sort of formal statement (for instance, "There is an inverse relationship between time lapse until knowledge of results and later performance on a retest"). Such a formal statement, when based on and supported by experimental results, may attain the status of a scientific "law."

In the process of making this kind of experimental determination a third kind of variable, not itself specified directly in the lawful relationship, is nonetheless of critical importance. This is the *controlled variable*. It is so called because its influence is *eliminated* and thereby "controlled" in the experiment proper. Most commonly this elimination is achieved by holding the variable constant across treatment groups. That is, in order to determine the effects of the independent variable all other relevant conditions must be kept the same for all groups. Unless they are, it is impossible to specify whether the results are a function of the independent variable or are due to the influence of some other, uncontrolled variable. (In the above example, the experimenter would have students of approximately the same intelligence, ability, and age in all groups, to control the influence of these variables).

It would be difficult indeed to overemphasize the importance of this kind of control in science. Control may be seen as the hallmark of research in all sciences and as the major characteristic that distinguishes science from other kinds of human enterprise in which knowledge is an objective (see Marx and Hillix, 1963, Chapter 1). Without control, the researcher cannot pinpoint the particular variables whose action is influencing the dependent variable. Reliable estimates of the relationship between the manipulated (independent) and the measured (dependent) variables cannot be established unless the effect of other variables is eliminated.

Let us consider three cautions with regard to this all-important principle of control. First, it is not absolute. That is, there are degrees of control, often progressively achieved in experimentation. In general, experimentation becomes more effective as control of variables increases, but obviously other determinants of scientific success must be considered (among them the ingenuity

of the investigators in forging useful questions, developing promising techniques of test, and so on). Second, the choice of the
variables to be controlled and those to be manipulated or measured is itself an arbitrary procedure. That is to say, in a given
experiment one may wish to control the variable sex, or age, or
intelligence, whereas one or more of these same variables may be
manipulated (that is, be used as independent variables) in the
next experiment. As a matter of fact, it is just this constant
shifting of experimental attention that is characteristic of a dynamic science, and, furthermore, it is the *interactions* of variables
which become the object of investigation as a science advances.
Third, there are other ways of introducing control into observations besides the experimental (for example, in the passive observations of the kind typically made in astronomy or in clinical
psychology), but these are only used when the more active,
experimental procedures are not feasible.

Although it is generally agreed that the best kind of control is
that achieved through experimental operations, utilizing direct
observation, there are several different methods of instituting
control. The two major techniques are refinement in apparatus
and statistical analysis of the data. An illustration of control
by apparatus is the use of soundproofing to void extraneous
(nonmanipulated and therefore unwanted) auditory stimulation; an illustration of control by statistical techniques is the
use of the analysis of variance, in which the influence of some
particular variable may be isolated or excluded by statistical
rather than by experimental means. Each of these two commonly
employed and important types of control may be regarded as a
kind of extension of experimental control, with the same objective; but they involve different operations and so to that degree
may be considered different from experimental control although
in no sense incompatible with it.

Finally, we would like to take note of a common confusion in
terminology which results from the same word, "control," being
used to refer to two basically different procedures. The control
which we have been discussing is a control *of variables,* with the
purpose of reducing ambiguity in relating results to antecedent
factors. The other use of "control" relates to a more practical

objective, the management of things and events. In this latter sense we speak of controlling crime, or weather, or social movements. In this control our purpose is not the accumulation of knowledge, nor the reduction in ambiguity of conceptualized relationships among variables, but rather the manipulation of practical events themselves. Since such manipulation is an important objective of science, and has been widely regarded as such, the confusion between the two meanings of "control" is easy to understand. This latter meaning is represented in the common statement that the objective of science is to "describe, predict, and control." Here "control" refers to management, and the principle of control utilized in experimentation would be necessarily involved in one or both of the two earlier processes, description and prediction.

TECHNIQUES OF MEASUREMENT

There are four general methods of inducing motivation, by means of manipulation of independent variables, in order to make possible measurement of motivation. These are, briefly: (1) withholding from the subject over a specified period of time some kind or class of goal object (frequently food and water, as biologically necessary goal objects) ; (2) presenting to the subject a noxious stimulus (as electric shock or verbal censure) ; (3) stimulating the subject with symbolic representation of a goal object or situation (as praise for good work) ; and (4) giving a standardized test to a human subject.

Each of these methods depends upon prior assurance of an empirical nature that the goal objects or conditions utilized are in actuality effective ones. That is, the experimenter must be certain that the incentive is one which the organism under the circumstances of the test will work to obtain or to avoid. Once such empirical evidence is available there is no need to renew it on each experimental occasion. But the investigator, if he is questioned, should be able to show empirical evidence in support of his assumption that the incentives he uses have motivating power; for him merely to state such a conclusion or assumption is insufficient.

A number of specific techniques for measurement of motivation may be identified (following Marx, 1960). Nine of these are described:

1. The *obstruction* technique, mainly relevant for infrahuman subjects, employs a block of some type placed between the appropriately motivated subject and the goal. The usual measure applied here is the number of times that an organism will cross such an obstruction (say, an electrified grid) to obtain the goal, or the amount of noxious stimulation (again, say, electric shock of measured intensity) that the organism will take.

The possibility of adapting this technique to children, dispensing with the noxious character of the block, is suggested by certain interesting results (Margolin and Bunch, 1940) which indicate that shock is not necessary even with rats as subjects. In this research essentially the same results were obtained with albino (laboratory) rats when merely the number of (unelectrified) grid crossings was utilized as the experimental measure.

2. *Choice* techniques involve offering the organism an opportunity to select one of two or more relevant incentives. Although this technique has been mainly used in dietary studies with rats (see Young, 1961), there seems to be no good reason why it could not be systematically applied to human research and especially to children subjects.

3. Measures of *general activity* have been made, with animal subjects, in three major kinds of apparatus: (a) the rotating drum or squirrel cage, with number of revolutions per unit of time counted; (b) the stabilimeter or tilted cage, in which slight vertical tilt or motion of the floor is sensitively measured, thus affording a quantitative record of practically all body movements; and (c) an open area with clearly marked spatial units (such as squares painted on the floor) where amount of free locomotion can be quantitatively observed.

The latter technique especially could be readily adapted for use with young children but does not seem as yet to have been so utilized.

4. State of *specific activity*, such as eating and drinking by infrahuman animals or crank-turning by children, has also been measured by appropriately constructed devices.

5. *Neurophysiological* measures, such as direct electrical or chemical stimulation of selected areas of the brain, have been recently developed and applied to animal subjects with exciting prospects for the future (see Olds and Milner, 1954; Miller, 1961). These are described in Chapter 5.

6. *Specific learned responses,* such as are typically involved in learning studies, may be measured as a function of variation in motivational conditions (offering of greater monetary or other incentive, and the like).

7. Selected *personality* tests, such as the Manifest Anxiety Scale (MAS) of Taylor (1953), may be administered to human subjects to produce indicants to motivational states. Manipulation of other variables in conjunction with the analysis of this kind of score has revealed a number of interesting relationships, such as that between anxiety (so defined by the scale used) and complexity of task. (See Farber, 1954, and Taylor, 1956, for a review of the early work on this problem. See also Spence, 1964, and Spence and Spence, 1966, for reviews of more recent work.)

8. *Projective* techniques, which utilize an analysis of imaginative materials produced by human subjects, have long been utilized for clinical purposes. Their application has more recently been extended to problems of motivation. In addition to the original Rorschach test, utilizing "ink blots" as test material, there is Murray's (1943) thematic apperception test (TAT) and its recent modification by McClelland and his colleagues (1953) with emphasis on various kinds of achievement motivation. For children, doll play may be useful (Sears, 1951), and human subjects of all ages may be used in psychodrama techniques (Moreno, 1946).

9. *Experimental* procedures of the kind introduced by Lewin for the study of "tension systems" (described briefly above, more fully in Chapter 3) are among the most promising techniques available. The possibilities here are limited only by the ingenuity and motivation of the investigators.

Special problems are associated with techniques 7 and 8. These mainly revolve around the problems of reliability and validity. Although these characteristics are necessary in any test, they may be particularly troublesome in tests from which motivational variables are to be estimated.

VALIDITY AND RELIABILITY

"Validity" refers to the degree to which a test measures what it says it measures. We may distinguish two general types of validity: *predictive* validity and *item* validity. The former is concerned with the degree to which the test items measure what the test purports to measure. Item validity is used here in its broadest sense and refers to both the stimuli (test items) and responses (answers to these questions).

Several methods may be employed to ascertain item validity. Three are commonly used. The test responses may be compared with the behavior of other individuals or against clinical diagnoses; they may be compared with tests which have previously been validated for a similar content and evaluated with respect to the degree of statistical correspondence; or they may be validated by reference to individuals known to possess the characteristics the test is trying to measure. These and other criteria are most easily applied to aptitude and achievement tests, and are more difficult to apply to tests assessing the "underlying" attributes of personality. Consequently, the validity of many such tests (for instance, projective tests) is frequently suspect.

Predictive validity is measured by studies that explicitly test the predictions made by the test. In this way the predictions are directly confirmed or disconfirmed. For example, if a test measuring anxiety predicts that in a given situation the person will display anxious behavior, and he displays it, the test result is evidence of high predictive value. If the prediction is not substantiated the test result is evidence of low predictive value.

"Reliability" refers to the extent to which a test consistently measures the same thing. Several of the factors with which any reliability determination must contend are age, interval between different administrations of the test, and degree of test sophistication. The last of these is becoming more important because of the undue amount of emphasis placed upon test scales in modern-day educational systems—not only are many children becoming very "test wise" (knowledgeable as to the most efficient way to take a test) but they are sometimes coached by teachers and parents prior to the administration of the test. As a consequence, many tests are being restandardized.

"Reliability" may refer to the internal consistency of the test items—the degree of correspondence among the individual test items within a given test. Thus, internal reliability addresses itself to the question: "Are the different questions homogeneous?" Obviously the greater the homogeneity of the test items, in respect to the characteristic being measured, the greater the reliability. A further consideration must be noted lest we oversimplify the concept of internal consistency—the matter of representative sampling of the test items. Not only is it desirable to have a homogeneous set of items, but the items selected must be representative of the attribute measured (assuming necessarily that what is being measured is homogeneous).

A second type of reliability is test-retest reliability. It refers to results derived by administering the test on two different occasions separated by a predetermined duration of time. Test-retest reliability is important in that if a test does not produce comparable results on repeated administrations it is of limited usefulness. There are other ways of determining this type of reliability besides using the same test twice. For example, equivalent forms of the test may be used or the test may be divided into two parts by using the odd-numbered questions for one form and the even numbered questions for the other. This latter design is usually referred to as the split-half method.

Although validity and reliability have been treated separately, they are in practice coextensive and a good test must have both. If a test is valid, it is necessarily also reliable, but a reliable test is not necessarily valid.

THE ROLE OF THEORY

Although we must emphasize that science is based upon empirical foundations, and fundamentally differs from other human enterprises in its dependence upon controlled data, a strictly empirical science is seldom encountered in practice. Indeed, the prime objective of most scientists is not to obtain the data for themselves, but rather to achieve the ordered interpretations, or understanding, that the data make possible. In working from the data to interpretation there are certain difficulties, usually surmounted by utilization of abstract concepts, or constructs, in relationships which are generally called "theoretical." Some mention will therefore be made here of the role of theory in scientific work.

A theory may be broadly defined as a statement or series of statements expressing the relationship between various abstract concepts or constructs. Specifically, four major types of theories are employed in scientific work: model, deductive theory, functional theory, and inductive theory (Marx, 1963). However, the difference between the deductive and functional types of theory is largely a matter of degree and for our present purpose they may be combined under the heading of deductive theory.

THE MODEL

A model is a more or less formal conceptual structure from one field of investigation that is applied to another field in an effort to guide data collection. For example, the telephone switchboard has often been used as a model of the human nervous system; recently, the telephone switchboard has been replaced by the computer as an analog of human thinking and problem solving. A model may be characterized as an "as if" statement. That is, the computer is viewed "as if" it were actually representative of the nervous system. Characterization of the model as an "as if" statement is useful because it emphasizes the fact that a model is *not* intended as an actual representation of the phenomena, but it is merely a conceptual analog used to suggest or provide the guidelines for empirical research. Its major function is found in its heuristic or tool value. An investigator who uses a model is not primarily concerned with modifying the model but rather employs it as a tentative guide for generating research and collecting data. If the investigator is interested in developing and modifying the model he is then utilizing one of the other types of theories. That is, one of the characteristics of the model is that data are not fed back into it; in other words, a model is not self-corrective.

DEDUCTIVE THEORY

A deductive theory consists of a set of logically interrelated principles by means of which formal predictions or hypotheses of empirical outcomes are made, with the explicit intention of modifying the propositions in accordance with empirical outcomes. The best example of this type of theory is probably Hull's behavior system (1943) which is described in Chapter 3. The principle underlying such an approach is that a deduction is made from an original set of postulates or principles. The prediction is then tested under experimental conditions and the results are fed back into the theory, forcing modification and revision of the theory when necessary. Then further deductions are made and the cycle begins again.

The major value of such an approach is found in its ability to direct research and its quality of self-perpetuation and modification through empirical research. The directive aspect found in both the model and the deductive theory has disadvantages as well as advantages. Some critics of the theoretical approach state that *too much* direction is provided by theories, which tend to blind investigators to alternative views, data, and methodologies. This point of view has been instrumental in the development of the inductive types of theory in psychology.

INDUCTIVE THEORY

An inductive theory is qualitatively different from the other types of theory. It contains a minimum of inferential commitment and deductive logic. An inductive theory begins by "asking a question," such as "What is the relationship between rate of response and hunger?" rather than by starting from a series of interrelated postulates and then deducing a hypothesis or prediction. Such an approach emphasizes that a theory should be nothing more than a series of empirical relationships or summary statements. That is, it utilizes no active attempt to develop theory for itself but rather depends upon the accretion of sound empirically verified relationships ("laws") for the development of orderly interpretations. This kind of "theory" is thus presumed to occur naturally as the result of the gradual accumulation of laws rather than as the result of purposive intervention. It is best illustrated in psychology by Skinner's (1938, 1959) brand of positivism. This type of theory, which is by far the least "theoretical" of the various forms, is characteristic of the positivistic or empirically oriented emphasis in science.

The difference between "asking a question" (inductive theory) and "testing a hypothesis" (deductive theory) in many cases is nothing more than a problem of semantics. The translation between question and hypothesis is typically very simple— often being in essence a matter of verbal shifts—and there need be no real difference in the actual experimental operations employed. For example, one may ask the question: "Is there a relationship between amount of fear and learning efficiency?" Or one may test the hypothesis, "There is a negative (or positive) relationship (of this sort)." Thus, to some extent one's selection of the positivistic or the more theoretical types of procedure is a matter of personal preference. This point is important and often overlooked in view of the emphasis laid upon the distinction by proponents of one side or the other. Critics of the inductive approach (proponents of the deductive approach) state that while some danger may exist in the tendency toward overdirection of deductive theory, an equally serious potential danger of underdirection exists in the inductive approach.

It should be evident that no approach is without its drawbacks and potential pitfalls. The important point is to realize that dangers as well as advantages do exist, and that, therefore, one needs to develop a tolerance and appreciation for the various alternative types of approach.

HYPOTHESIS AND LAW

The difference between these two terms is largely a matter of degree of empirical confirmation. A *hypothesis* may be loosely defined as any conjecture that states a relationship among variables. There are different types of hypotheses, such as the *statistical* (referring to a specific prediction in terms of some kind of analysis of data) and the *experimental* (referring to the predicted outcome of an experiment). Experimental hypotheses range from fully formalized ones, generated logically on the basis of a theory of some sort, to very informal ones, based on little more than a hunch or a guess. The term *law* has come to refer to an empirical demonstration of the relationship between two or more variables. It tends to have a more concrete or "proven" (that is, tested) character than a hypothesis. However, a law may be, in essence, an empirically confirmed hypothesis.

OPERATIONISM

When the more theoretical propositions are employed, the specification or definition of the constructs used as elements of theories is often an important issue. It is in this connection that the physicist P. W. Bridgman (1927) initiated a movement known as *operationism*. Briefly, it holds that the meaning of a concept is identical with a corresponding set of operations. That is, the concept of "drive" (or of physical "length" in Bridgman's context) may be defined in terms of a particular set of operations or procedures—for example, hunger drive may be defined in terms of the number of hours since a subject last ate. It is obvious that when a definition is specified in terms of observational referents there can be little doubt concerning what the term means. This clarification of terminology is the objective of operationism.

Psychology is replete with such vague and variably defined concepts as "frustration," "anxiety," and the like. Much argument within psychology has been based upon semantic or definitional differences rather than on differences of substance. When these terms are defined in relation to empirical or observational referents, that is, defined operationally, then the meaning of the concept is clear and there is reduced opportunity for ambiguity of interpretation.

Frustration, for example, is frequently defined as a condition which results when a subject is blocked from reaching a goal. This definition may be different from what another person means by *frustration,* such as an emotional state of some sort or the other. Without operational clarification, a third person may assume that the term refers to a single concept when in actuality it refers to two different concepts.

Moreover, if two different concepts relate to the same set of operations, then a single concept exists rather than two. As long as attention remains focused upon the set of operations, regardless of what term is attached to these operations, there is little possibility of semantic confusion; it is only when this attention is neglected that clarity of communication begins to break down. In this respect it is difficult to see how any scientifically oriented person can deny the usefulness of operationism, although there are many procedural questions (such as the problem of generalization of concepts) that are not easily answered.

IN CONCLUSION: A PARADOX

This introductory discussion of the general problems attendant upon the development of psychological explanations of motivation can be pointed up by an interesting paradox. There is a striking discrepancy between the almost universally high degree of interest evidenced in the problem, within educational and psychological circles, and the relatively small amount of empirical work *directly* expended upon motivational phenomena.

The lack of empirical work has been noted by Ryans (1942) and more recently by Marx (1960). Empirical checks of the contents of education textbooks and journals revealed disappointingly small percentages of space devoted to the problem of motivation. In the 1955–1957 issues of two important education research journals, for example, the number of pages on motivation was found to be 0 per cent and 2 per cent of the totals.

A similar result has been obtained for educational psychology. We have examined the 1951–1955 and the 1961–1965 volumes of the *Journal of Educational Psychology*. The total number of pages devoted to motivational topics, very broadly interpreted, was less than 2 per cent for the 1951–1955 set and was 4.4 per cent for the 1961–1965 set. Although the increase in percentage is somewhat encouraging, three of the ten years had no articles at all on this general problem. A check of popular textbooks in the field of educational psychology was also made. Of the 12 "leading textbooks" listed by Ripple (1964), 6 were examined. The mean number of pages in these texts concerned with motivational problems, again broadly interpreted, was less than 5 per cent of the total. The range was from something less than 2 per cent to almost 10 per cent. These figures, though extremely imprecise, do suggest that insufficient attention is being paid, in educational-psychology textbooks as well as in the journal literature, to what we see as a focal problem in education and training.

Within psychology proper, a more substantial portion of the literature seems to be devoted to motivational topics. For example, a check of the 1951–1955 and 1961–1965 issues of the *Journal of Experimental Psychology* and the *Journal of Comparative and Physiological Psychology* showed 6.5 per cent and 4.8 per cent of the former and 11.5 per cent and 8.6 per cent of the latter devoted to motivational topics. The mean number of pages concerned with motivational problems in six leading introductory psychology textbooks was found to be just slightly less than 10 per cent, approximately double the percentage of pages similarly counted in the educational-psychology textbooks examined. The range of percentages for individual general psychology textbooks was 7.4 per cent to 15.8 per cent. Thus there does seem to be some empirical basis for our presumption of more attention to the problem of motivation in the literature of general psychology as compared with that of education and educational psychology.

It is nevertheless true, as is emphasized above, that the theoretical and experimental emphasis on motivation within psychology has until relatively recent times been concentrated upon the distinctly biological motivational conditions, particularly those associated with deprivation of food and water in animal subjects. The turning of attention to motivational processes involving curiosity and exploratory behavior, conditions much more directly relevant not only to educational problems but also to much everyday primate behavior, is a relatively recent development (see Fowler, 1965). It may be expected that continued research upon this kind of motivation will ultimately bear fruits of greater utility for educational theorists and practitioners as well as for those concerned with other facets of behavior.

If educational theorists and practitioners are to benefit adequately from such basic research, however, they must themselves be prepared to design appropriate investigations upon distinctly educational problems. We do not mean to suggest that pure research is not of immense value. Quite to the contrary, we feel that pure research should hold a prominent position. But pressing problems of immediate concern must also receive experimental attention. As we point out in more detail in Chapter 7, these problems cannot be left solely to the general psychologist. Basic principles of motivated behavior by themselves are not sufficient. Their implications for education, for child development, or for personality analysis may be suggestive, but their full value cannot be developed without research directly related to the particular issues of a given subject matter. This proposition is another way of saying that educational psychologists cannot depend entirely upon psychologists for help in the solution of their problems. In particular they cannot do so with regard to theories described in Chapters 2 and 3. Educational psychologists can certainly look for research leads and suggestions from general psychological research, and especially from some of the newer kinds of such research—those involving motivations like curiosity and exploration. But the detailed working out of psychological problems involved in education will need to be done by persons working more directly on the educational problems themselves. For this reason, students in the field of educational psychology should not only be fully familiar with behavioral research techniques and results but should also recognize the need to apply comparable techniques to their own problems.

Suggested Readings

Atkinson, J. W. 1964. *An introduction to motivation.* Princeton: D. Van Nostrand.

Cofer, C. N., and M. H. Appley. 1964. *Motivation: Theory and research.* New York: John Wiley and Sons.

Haber, R. N., ed. 1966. *Current research in motivation.* New York: Holt, Rinehart and Winston.

Marx, M. H., and W. A. Hillix. 1963. *Systems and theories in psychology.* New York: McGraw-Hill Book Co., pp. 3–19.

Chapter 2

CLASSICAL THEORIES
OF MOTIVATION:
PSYCHOANALYTIC
AND INSTINCTIVE
THEORIES

The purpose of this chapter and the next is to provide the reader with an overview of the major classical theoretical orientations toward the concept of motivation. The selected theories were chosen as representative of theoretical efforts in each of the following four major areas: psychoanalysis and instinct theories, covered in this chapter; cognitive (field) theory and stimulus-response (S-R) learning theory, covered in Chapter 3. The most detailed account is devoted to Freud, not because we feel his psychoanalytic theory is the most adequate but because Freudian thinking has been enormously influential and has provided the impetus and foundation for many of the later theories. In addition to a summary of each theory, most sections contain a sample of the methods used to collect data and illustrative experiments. Salient criticisms are also described.

Since these chapters do not cover all of the theories dealing with motivation, we have included at the end of each chapter references related to more detailed accounts as well as critical reviews and analyses of the different motivational theories.

The classical theories in this chapter and the next are presented because of their historical importance as well as their contemporary influence. However, two cautions concerning them should be kept in mind. First, the day of the "grand theory" in psychology is clearly past, as Koch (1959) among others (for instance, Marx and Hillix, 1963) has emphasized. Today psychological researchers are concentrating more on small-scale theoretical attempts to resolve a few specific problems, rather than attempting to resolve in one theory a large number of specific problems. Such a resolution is to be achieved by means of the accumulation of many smaller theoretical successes. This refocusing of theoretical effort, described briefly in Chapter 1, means that the classical theories, which tend to be on a "grand" scale, are becoming less important.

Second, the hope that theories constructed within the field of psychology can be transferred more or less directly to help solve practical problems in other fields such as education is increasingly questioned. This doubt does not mean that psychological theory has nothing to offer education; it does mean, rather, that simply to transfer theoretical propositions from one field to another is not feasible without a considerable amount of empirical research in the new field. We develop this notion at some length in the final chapter of this book, where motivation and education are considered.

One implication of these restrictions on classical theory is that theoretical disputes are becoming of less significance, even though they will no doubt continue to rage, within psychology as well as without. Less significant, also, is the question as to which of the several major psychological theories or types of approaches to behavior is the "best" single one for, say, education to adopt. Although we would certainly not say that this kind of question has no relevance whatsoever for education, or for any other practical subject matter, we do say that other and more important ways are now indicated for uses of psychological theory in attempts to solve practical problems. For this reason we deliberately avoid discussion of certain of the well-established notions that have been hotly debated (such as treating of the "whole" child, or emphasizing the automaticity of learning à la Pavlov and Thorndike); we concentrate instead upon a more or less straightforward description of selected motivational theories of the classic mold.

FREUDIAN PSYCHOLOGY

Sigmund Freud (1856–1939) never made any attempt to amalgamate his many different papers, books, and ideas under a single cover. Therefore, any systemization of his work is achieved by reading either the totality of his original publications (1955 collection and translations) or such excellent secondary sources as Brill (1956), C. S. Hall (1954), and Ernest Jones (1953, 1955, 1957). However he investigates, the reader soon realizes that Freud's theory was not full blown at conception but developed slowly over the years; and often his later formulations, with which we are here concerned, bear little resemblance to his earlier ones. A detailed exposition of Freud requires too much space for this book. Therefore, we have selected for discussion those propositions which are most relevant for the understanding of his theory.

THE PSYCHIC APPARATUS

Every organism possesses a finite amount of physical energy, which serves to maintain its metabolic functions. From this physical energy, according to Freud, a supply of psychic energy is derived. Freud believed that the precise specification of how this energy was transformed was a job for the physiologist rather than the psychologist and consequently did not attempt to suggest how the transformation occurred. Initially, the psychic energy was deposited within a single system, known as the *id* or primary process. The id can be best understood if it is viewed as a kind of mental manifestation of all the physiological processes. That is, physical needs such as thirst, hunger, and sex are all represented in the id. The id serves as the reservoir from which is drawn all of the energy necessary for the different psychic functions. Moreover, the other two systems or components of the personality, the ego and the superego, develop from the id. In short, for Freud the id is the prime source of motivation.

The major function of the id is to reduce tensions which arise from unsatisfied needs. These tensions produce an increase in the amount of energy, an increase which sometimes exceeds the id's capacity or tolerance limits. In an attempt to reduce the tension a proportion of the energy is discharged to form a mental image or images of a need-reducing object. The realization of such an image removes the tension and lowers the energy below the tolerance limit. At birth, the images represent innate objects (water for example), but as the individual matures they may refer to previously experienced or learned objects (for example, a specific type of liquid such as "Coke" or beer). The general principle which Freud assumed to govern this process was called the *pleasure principle*—the seeking of pleasure and the avoidance of pain. "Pleasure" in this context is not synonymous with the term *enjoyment* but more appropriately refers to maintaining the energy level within its required limits. Pain results when these limits are exceeded. Thus, the removal of the pain (hunger, thirst, sex excitement) constitutes pleasure.

The dominant feature of the primary process and one which becomes increasingly important as the other systems develop is the id's demand for the immediate discharge of tension. When tension develops it must be dissipated—the appropriate image must be obtained irrespective of the consequences that might result. Thus, if hunger develops the id demands that the appropriate image or object be produced. In a word, the id "sees" the world as it wishes it to be.

The unique characteristic of this process is the inability of the id to distinguish between an image and its corresponding external object. They are the same, they have *identity of perception,* so that the image of food reduces the tension just as effectively as does real food.

Frequently, the id is referred to as the seat of the instincts. The reason is that the psychic energy is divided between two great classes of instincts—the life (eros) and death (thanatos) instincts. The term *instinct,* as used by Freud, does not signify a complex set of unlearned responses (which is the usual psychological meaning). Viewed simply, Freudian instincts are psychical drives which arise from specific needs and attempt to seek objects which will satisfy these needs. Any specified "instinct" is simply a name given to a particular type of energy doing a particular type of job.

The life instincts include any mental activities and corresponding motivations related to the basic biological drives necessary for life (such as thirst). The energy which is in the service of these instincts is called the *libido*. Sex is the most important of the life instincts and is emphasized to such a degree that Freudian theory is often called a pansexual theory. Sex is emphasized for two reasons: (1) in modern civilization this instinct is the one most frequently thwarted and thus utilizes the majority of an individual's available energy in an attempt to reduce the corresponding tension; (2) it is the only instinct which can remain unsatisfied without causing the death of the organism. It is necessary to recognize that Freud's interpretation of sex is far more encompassing than the common usage; it includes numerous meanings, as will be evident in the section concerning sexual energy, beyond the ordinary meaning associated with the male and female reproductive organs. When a particular instinct begins to control the majority of psychic energy, perseveration upon a particular need-reducing object occurs. Thus, a person in love finds it difficult to think of anything else and a person dying of thirst becomes obsessed by the thought of water.

The death instinct is the tendency of an organic structure to return to an inorganic state; in Freudian thinking it is actually an attempt to destroy its own organic structure. The energy which is invested in the death instinct was never specifically named by Freud but is sometimes referred to as the *mortido*. The agent of the death instinct is the *primary death wish,* an intense motivation to return to a state of equilibrium regardless of the cost. It is manifested in suicide and in the heroic deeds of military men. Criticisms of the construct of "death instinct" and "primary death wish" are probably those most often advanced by both Freud's sympathetic and unsympathetic critics.

Since the human organism cannot exist on mere images and the id is unable to discriminate between mental images and objective reality, another process evolves that enables the organism to survive. This process is the *ego,* or *secondary process.* It is governed by the *reality principle,* whose function is to postpone the immediate discharge of energy until an adequate tension-reducing object is produced or discovered in the environment. It attempts to identify a mental image with its corresponding physical object which produces physiological satisfaction. This process of finding appropriate physical objects is called *reality testing*. Whenever an object and its corresponding mental image succeed in reducing tension, there is a higher probability of their being used again when the same drive recurs—a "habit" develops. The more efficiently the ego reduces tension, the more energy it obtains from the id. Eventually the ego achieves more than enough energy to reduce the existing tensions, and the surplus is used for developing different psychological processes such as attending, perceiving, and learning.

The ego has several other major characteristics: it eventually obtains the majority of the original psychic energy; it *can* withstand tension and postpone immediate satisfaction for long-range goals; it is rational and mature; and it is in contact, not only with the id, but also with the superego and the environment—it serves the "executive" function of the organism.

The *superego* develops from the ego when a child begins to assimilate the parental standards of "good" and "bad." By internalizing these values, the child comes to have his own inner authority or value system. This inner authority is the superego. It is the moral or judicial branch of the psychic structure and strives toward the ideal rather than the real—toward perfection rather than either reality or pleasure. Because it has no basis in reality, its strength is determined by the rigidity of the parents and by the environmental values it has internalized. Furthermore, it is composed of two subsystems, the *ego-ideal* and the *conscience*. In essence, these are two sides of the same moral coin. The ego-ideal includes those internalized values which are considered good, and which when adhered to are rewarded by a feeling of pride and a lessening of tension. The ego-ideal strives for perfection instead of reality testing. The conscience is composed of those internalized values which are considered "bad" and which bring about a feeling of guilt or inferiority. The superego, like the id, does not distinguish between the subjective and the objective; the mere thought of something considered bad will invoke guilt feelings.

These three systems—the ego, the superego, and the id—are in constant conflict with each other, vying for psychic energy and control of the personality. They are like three warring tribes each with its own goals and each seeking to conquer the other. The id strives for immediate satisfaction, the superego judges whether or not immediate satisfaction is socially "acceptable," and the ego tries to locate the appropriate need-reducing object in the environment. The greatest conflict is that between the id and superego. It is responsible for much of the "mental illness" that occurs in later life. This conflict chiefly centers around the sexual desires of the id and the inculcated cultural mores and prohibitions of the superego.

The id, ego, and superego expend psychic energy. Freud used two terms, *cathexis* and *anticathexis,* to describe this expenditure. "Cathexis" refers to the directing of energy toward an object. It is an urging force, and a cathected object is any desired object toward which energy is directed or invested (as food or sex object). "Anticathexis" refers to the directing of energy against any object or against the urging forces. It is a checking force. Thus, an anticathected object is any undesired object which is repelled by expended energy, such as anxiety-provoking events or thoughts. Cathexis and anticathexis may be directed toward both the external and internal environments. Often they oppose one another or vie for the same object and a psychic conflict occurs.

Freud's most salient contribution to motivational theories was his differentiation between *conscious* and *unconscious* processes. Consciousness is defined as that which is in the immediate focus of attention, all the elements (such as images or thoughts) of which the individual is immediately aware. The unconscious is all that which is not in consciousness. It is convenient to consider it as a continuum of entities possessing different degrees of anticathexis. Within this continuum two levels are recognized—the *preconscious,* which contains entities easily brought into consciousness, and the *unconscious,* which contains entities not readily brought into consciousness. The extent to which something is anticathected determines its position on the continuum and the ease with which it will be brought back into consciousness. There are only three means by which an entity can be brought back into consciousness: (1) a stronger cathexis, (2) a weaker anticathexis, and (3) a removal of energy for other purposes. Symbolic activity occurs when a thought rises very rapidly toward consciousness. Only when it nears the threshold of consciousness does the ego displace enough energy to anticathect it; nevertheless, this anti-cathexis is not totally efficient and the thought often achieves indirect symbolic expression. It should be noted that the term *unconscious* is not necessarily synonymous with the term *id*. The terms *conscious* and *unconscious* merely refer to qualities of mental phenomena irrespective of the process involved.

THE DEFENSE MECHANISMS

The great importance of unconscious thoughts is that they exert a profound influence on behavior. They are unconscious motivators of behavior. For example, the processes used to alleviate anxiety by disguising reality are found there. These are commonly referred to as defense mechanisms and have four general characteristics: (1) they are irrational ways of dealing with anxiety because they distort, hide, or deny reality and so hinder normal (meaning "socially desirable") psychological development; (2) they tie up psychic energy which could be more efficiently used; (3) their overuse reduces the individual's flexibility and adaptability; and (4) their failure to function results in the ego's becoming overwhelmed by anxiety.

The more important of the defense mechanisms may be briefly described. *Identification* is the incorporation of the qualities of an external object into one's own thought system. Most typically, identification involves relating to oneself the desirable character-istics of socially acceptable objects or persons. In general, its function is the discharge of painful tension through mastery of the individual's frustrations, anxieties, and inadequacies (as when the sports enthusiast identifies himself with the football hero).

Displacement and *sublimation* are essentially the same process of shunting or rechanneling energy from one pathway to another. In displacement the long-range goals remain constant and only the immediate activity changes; the means are altered to achieve a persistent end. For example, the student who gets a poor grade in class is liable to displace his emotional reactions upon his roommate. In sublimation, which is generally associated with the sex drive, the long-range goal is changed and an alternative goal is substituted. It is commonly used to explain creativity in cases where the long-range goal may be changed from overt sexual display to some type of artistic release.

Repression occurs when a memory, idea, or perception is taken out of consciousness by an anticathexis. It abolishes anxiety by *denying* the existence of an external or internal threat. The closer the anticathected object comes to consciousness, the more anxiety is experienced and consequently the more energy is required to anticathect it.

Projection involves attributing a cause to an external condition in order to relieve anxiety associated with the individual's own motives. Its most important characteristic is that the subject of the feeling is altered. Instead of "I hate him," it surreptitiously becomes "he hates me."

Rationalization is defined as the attempt to find a justifiable excuse in the external world for doing something that is frowned upon by one's superego. It also refers to the substitution of a socially approved motive for a socially disapproved one.

Reaction formation refers to manifested thoughts or feelings which are just the opposite of that which the person really feels. A classic example is the overzealous reformer whose behavior may be motivated by an unconscious and repressed desire to perform the very activity he is protesting, such as drinking alcohol.

Regression refers to a person's retreat to an earlier, less efficient type of behavior. A person who has no effective way of coping with a stress situation may regress to an earlier form of behavior associated with security. The behavior is effective in coping with anxiety; it is ineffective in coping with the situation. An example is found in the man who has a fit of temper and acts as if he is a little child having a temper tantrum.

Fixation is said to occur when an individual fails to progress beyond a particular developmental level in order to prevent a drive state from causing anxiety. Fixation may result from the individual's actually experiencing the anxiety-producing condition and regressing to a level where he is free from this anxiety, or it may occur because the individual only perceives the situation as anxiety-producing but never actually experiences it.

PSYCHOSEXUAL DEVELOPMENT

Freud also believed that psychic energy produced differential motivational effects during an individual's life. Perhaps the most celebrated illustration of this is found in his treatment of personality development and its relation to the movement of sexual energy through the erogenous zones of the body. These zones are any regions of the body where tension becomes localized and where it is subsequently removed by the manipulation of that region. Freud emphasized three primary regions: oral, anal, and genital. These were held to be of the utmost importance because they are the *first* sources of sexual irritation and satisfaction.

The *oral period* occurs in the first two years of an individual's life, and involves the oral zone, the lips and oral cavity. Not only does the baby achieve need reduction from nursing, but manipulation and tactile stimulation of these areas produce erotic (sexual) pleasure. During this period prototypes develop in respect to the various oral functions. A *prototype* is an original mode of adjustment to a painful or disturbing body state. Although a person develops beyond this stage, he seldom loses the preoccupations which he has built up. The prototype may remain, and only the amount of energy invested in it decreases; a pipe may replace the teething toy and cigarettes may replace thumb sucking. One of the hallmarks of Freudian theory is that the habits and prototypes established in early life almost completely determine the individual's personality structure and the manner in which the person adjusts to the conflicts of life.

The *anal period* is predominant in the third and fourth years of childhood and includes the anus and the adjacent areas. The elimination and the retention of feces represent the two modes of anal functioning, and the influence of the toilet trainer determines the anal prototype. If toilet training is strict, the child may retaliate by soiling himself. He may also develop a propensity for messiness and/or carelessness. The anal phase is generally considered artificial because toilet training is a product of the culture, and many psychoanalysts believe that the period would disappear if children were allowed to train themselves.

The *phallic* period (often called the period of masturbation) is prevalent between the ages of four and seven. During these years the sex drive increases in strength and its instinctual object becomes more distinct and specific. It is during this period that the much publicized *Oedipus complex* occurs. It is characterized by hate for the parent of the same sex and love for the parent of the opposite sex.

The *latency* period occurs between the ages of seven and fourteen, and is characterized by an apparent lack of sexual motivation and disdain for the members of the opposite sex. Freud did not believe that the sex drive actually changes. He attributed the superficial lack of sexual interest to the fact that the phallic period and Oedipus situation required the child to choose a new love object. This choice is augmented by cultural pressures forcing the child to participate in social interactions. The child thus cathects someone of his own age and sex.

The sex drive again is manifested during puberty. Here it cannot be satisfied by any of the earlier means. This stage is called the *genital* period and is the final developmental stage; it continues throughout adulthood. The instinctual object is now reproduction. Prior to this period love was narcissistic, but now it is directed toward an external object—a person of the opposite sex. However, the child or adult does not entirely relinquish his previous goals but merely invests less energy in them. Therefore, sexual intercourse does not entirely satisfy the sex drive, because these other lesser goals, such as those found in the oral and anal periods, are not adequately fulfilled.

PSYCHOANALYTIC METHODOLOGY

The vast majority of Freud's data stemmed from the use of three major techniques. The first of these was *hypnosis,* which he became acquainted with while working with Charcot on hysterical reactions. Through this method, Freud first discovered the unconscious motivators of behavior and the importance of sex. Although Freud used this method extensively in his earlier years, he slowly became aware of two serious limitations: the inability to place all of his patients under a hypnotic trance, and the temporary effectiveness of hypnosis even when successfully administered.

The use of hypnosis led to the method of *catharsis,* in which the patient, fully awake and conscious, was permitted to free associate (talk about whatever came into his mind) and talk out his problem. This method was discovered by accident (Breuer and Freud, 1895; tr. 1937) in the famous case of "Anna O." (Bertha Pappenheim). Bertha was a girl with multiple symptoms: a double personality, disturbances in visual and auditory modalities, paralysis of three limbs, inability to consume food, and a nervous cough. After Breuer had talked to her about one of her symptoms, he suspected that this talk resulted in the subsequent elimination of the particular symptom. He tried this method with other symptoms and similar results occurred. Later, Breuer and Freud separated, but Freud retained this method and used it to great advantage.

Finally, Freud came to rely upon the *interpretation of dreams.* This method, coupled with his own self-analysis, was probably his most productive source of information. He believed there are two parts to any dream, the *manifest* and the *latent* content. The manifest content represents the obvious and apparent meaning of the dream—what the dream represents to the uncritical eye. Lurking behind this facade is the latent meaning, filled with the symbolic representation of repressed desires. It is here, through the interpretation of symbols, that the unconscious can be tapped of its hidden meaning.

Freud combined these three techniques in his case studies. Although he published only six case studies, undoubtedly his theory was grounded on a vast number of unpublished studies. In all likelihood those that he published were intended primarily as illustrations of his major theoretical concepts. At least a glance at these studies would indicate this: "The Rat Man," "Wolf Man," and "Little Hans" are good examples (see Hall and Lindzey, 1957, pp. 61–62).

JUNGIAN ANALYTIC PSYCHOLOGY

Although Carl Jung (1875–1961) was at one time Freud's closest disciple, he eventually revolted and developed his own brand of psychoanalysis—*analytic psychology.* The split occurred over Jung's lack of agreement concerning Freud's pansexualism (that is, his great stress on sex in all its various manifestations) and over Freud's skepticism concerning Jung's mystical and religious feelings. Although Jung believed that sex was important he did not consider it omnipotent. He used the term *libido* to represent psychic energy in general without restriction to the special sexual overtones accruing to it in Freudian terminology. Like Freud, Jung believed that psychic energy was derived from physical energy. Moreover, this energy expresses itself in the over-all development of the personality and at various periods of development the energy is utilized in different ways. That is, the libido expresses itself in the manner most appropriate to the organism at a given moment (eating, elimination, or other). This view is not dissimilar from Freud's, with the important exception that although Freud recognized the different possible functions of the libido, he believed that the sexual aspect far outweighed its other functions and so practically eliminated them from his theory.

Jung was far more optimistic about life than Freud. Freud viewed human life as being controlled or propelled from situation to situation by the interplay and interrelations among the various motivational instincts and drives. Moreover, the permanent effects of unfortunate early childhood experiences upon personality necessitated a rather gloomy picture of life, with little hope for changing one's pattern of behavior. Jung developed a more optimistic view by tempering the causal interpretation of Freud with teleological (purposive) factors. Not only is behavior "pushed" by drives through the vissicitudes of life, it is also "pulled" by future goals. This purposive element allows man to be guided by his aspirations and desires as well as by his past history. An individual's adjustment to life may be interpreted not only by knowing where he has been (past history) but also by knowing where he is going (purpose). The most important of these purposes is self-actualization—the blending of all the different aspects of one's personality into a completely meaningful and relatively stable unit. Freud had no such purpose, and in his view stability was seldom, if ever, permitted by the interaction among the psychic motivators.

Not only did Jung project into the future; he also retrogressed into the past and looked to experiences which occurred in the evolution of the human species, experiences never witnessed by a person in his own lifetime. Man brings into the world both a biological and a psychological heritage from the past. Jung may be viewed as a "psychic evolutionist." The psychic past is transmitted from generation to generation through the *collective unconscious*. The *personal unconscious*, along with this collective or transpersonal unconscious, forms the bipartite division of unconsciousness. In the personal unconscious, motivational determinants are readily accessible to the conscious mind (*ego*, in Jungian terminology). The latter is similar to Freud's preconscious. However, the collective unconscious was a radical departure from Freud's unconscious. The collective unconscious contains the racial and ancestral heritages which form the basis for the personality. In Jung's words "the form of the world into which he is born is already inborn in him as a virtual image" (1953 collection, p. 188). The structural components containing these racial agents have been referred to in various ways by Jung; the most common of these are *primordial images* or *archetypes*. Archetypes motivate behavior but are always below the level of conscious awareness. They can be evaluated only through an analysis of the history of mankind, with its myths, religions, beliefs, emotions, and the like, and by relating these to the personality of modern-day man through his overt actions as well as by probing his unconscious thoughts through dreams, free associations, and symbolic interpretations. Archetypes function as separate but interacting systems and can be modified by experience.

Four of the archetypes are sufficiently evolved to merit special consideration: *persona, shadow, animus* or *anima*, and *self*. The persona is an individual's public image, while the shadow represents the animal instinct inherited by man. The anima represents the female psychological characteristics present in the male; the animus relates to the male characteristics found in the female. Finally, the self is the center of the personality, which operates in the interest of unity and promotes equilibrium among the systems. Thus, the self is motivated toward *self-actualization* or wholeness.

Jung's most cited concept is his classification of behavior orientation into two types: *introversion* and *extroversion*. In the former, a majority of a person's motivation is focused upon the subjective world, while in the latter it is oriented toward the external world. Jung believed that each person could be characterized by one of these two orientations. However, it is now generally believed that all individuals have some of both components and the one which is exhibited depends upon the particular environmental situation which is present as well as the person's underlying typological predisposition.

JUNGIAN METHODOLOGY

Jung's primary source of data was the same as Freud's and the rest of the psychoanalysts'—the case study. However, Jung incorporated an innovation in dream analysis. Instead of concentrating on a single dream, Jung analyzed a series of dreams. He believed that this procedure lent greater continuity, systemization, and internal consistency to dream analysis. Moreover, the symbolic nature of the dream must be explained to the patient, for unlike Freud, Jung did not believe the patient had the capacity to completely understand the symbolism.

Another Jungian method, the conscious counterpart to dream analysis, was the use of active imagination. The patient is required to concentrate on an imaginary object and describe what changes occur over a period of time. Unconscious motivators manifest themselves in a manner similar to the dream manifestation but in a more vivid form, since they occur in a waking state. Also, descriptive recall, the lack of which is a problem in dream analysis, is a valuable aspect of active imagination because the changes are related as soon as they are imagined; there is no time lag between their occurrence and their description. Active imagination is one of the earliest examples of the projective techniques, currently exemplified in the TAT and the Rorschach (ink-blot) test, where the patient is presented with an ambiguous set of stimuli and asked to invent and relate a story of what he sees. The essential difference between Jung's method and the later projective techniques is the instigation of a set of objective stimuli coupled with quantifiable response indices.

Jung's experimental technique of word association is perhaps his most lasting contribution to experimental psychology. Although the invention of the technique is usually credited to Galton, Jung was the first to see its relevance for personality evaluation. The test consists of reading a list of words to the person tested, who replies with the first word he can think of. The degree of emotionality associated with the stimulus is reflected by the duration of time it takes the subject to respond. The longer the response time, the greater the person's emotional involvement. Intensity measures such as pulse rate, heart rate, and respiration also indicate the extent to which a word reveals emotional involvement. Jung felt that by combining the duration and intensity measures an adequate appraisal of the person's verbal response could be ascertained. He used these methods as a diagnostic technique to achieve a quick impression of the patient's repressions. Furthermore, he believed the motivation underlying the repression was as important, if not more important, than the repression itself.

ADLERIAN INDIVIDUAL PSYCHOLOGY

Alfred Adler (1870–1937) holds the distinction of being the first psychoanalyst to stress the importance of social factors in the development of personality. While Freud stressed instincts and Jung archetypes, Adler posited that all individuals natively possess a social orientation to life. Each individual is born with a natural motivation toward socialization—man is social rather than sexual by nature. However, this capacity, like any other capacity, can be modified by social experiences and by environment, thus accounting for the great diversity in personalities. Furthermore, a person's particular adjustment to life determines his sexual characteristics, rather than sexual characteristics determining his way of life. Although both Freud and Jung had mentioned society and its influence on behavior, it occupied a rather obscure and theoretically unimportant position in their systems. The inordinate amount of attention devoted to the unconscious by Freud and Jung was bypassed by Adler. He did not entirely reject unconscious processes, but he relegated them to a minor position in his theory.

An attraction of Adler's theory is found in its relatively few and simple constructs. Man is born with a single innate propensity or goal—a *"will to power"* or striving toward superiority. From this simple source, all other motivators are derived. Because of this approach, Adlerian psychology is often classified as a single-factor theory, as opposed to the Freudian dual-factor theory (life and death instincts) and the Jungian multifactor theory (archetypes).

Adler's theory, like Jung's, is founded on teleological or purposive principles. Whereas Jung was very general in his exposition concerning the future, Adler was quite specific in discussing the monolithic structure of superiority—a person strives for superiority over himself and over others. There is no single way to achieve this perfection of life, but there are many alternative routes to the fulfillment of the goal. The way man traverses life's paths is called the individual's *style of life,* which is the banner of the Adlerian school of *individual psychology.* The name "individual psychology" is derived from the belief that each person has his own unique individualistic life style. It originates in infancy and the pattern developed during this period continues to motivate and direct the individual's behavior throughout life. Essentially, a person's style of life is developed to overcome an infantile inferiority feeling resulting from the parents' domination of the child's infantile world. The child strives to lessen or escape his inferiority feelings by growing up and trying to become an equal to his parents or even achieve a dominant status. It is this striving which produces the guideline for adolescent development.

Also important is the structure of the home, particularly the order of sibling birth. Adler believed the personality developed, in part, as a function of family position, of being first, second, or third born. The child experiences specific but diverse social influences as the family unit increases in size. The second child cannot possibly have the same general experiences as the first, since there is an inherent differential factor of family size. First-born children are seen as tending to be hostile and potentially social deviants; second or middle children as ambitious and slightly better equipped to adjust to society; and third or youngest children as spoiled and potentially neurotic. Thus, the middle child has the best chance of successful adjustment to future life, with the prognosis for the first and last less optimistic.

As the child matures psychologically he enters into more competition, again producing feelings of inferiority, which increase impetus toward the goal of superiority. The inferiority may be either real or imagined, and in normal proportions is not an indicator of an arrested personality development. In fact, Adler believed that inferiority is a universal and natural trait and that it serves as a motivator or developmental catalyst.

The integrator of Adler's system is the *creative self*. It is the source of all behavior and molds man's personality out of experiences and endowed capacities. It is *not* a passive field upon which other forces joust and do battle, but is itself a dynamic and active organizer—the mason of the personality, using the bricks of heredity and experience to construct its personality edifice. Although this creative self is a necessary part of Adler's system he is vague concerning its locus and origin. The concept appears *as if* Adler needed an integrative principle, called it "the creative self," and was unconcerned with details other than it served its necessary function.

ADLERIAN METHODOLOGY

Adler's data came almost entirely from case studies and self-analysis. The methods used focus upon assessing the individual's style of life through an analysis of the clinical interview. The clinical session differed from Freud's in that Adler consciously tried to demonstrate where discrepancies and inconsistencies existed and where his patients were wrong, instead of letting them discover these facts by themselves. Thus he assumed an active rather than passive role in therapy. He was not strongly concerned with the analysis of dreams as the transmitters of unconscious motives. Dreams were seen as useful only in projecting the individual's life style into the future in terms of the dream's relation to present expectations and future goals. The therapist's role was to analyze and reconstruct the individual's style of life, to substitute realistic goals for unrealistic ones, and to make the client a well-rounded, secure, and well-integrated person able to cope with the realities of life.

HORNEY'S NEO-ANALYSIS

The psychology of Karen Horney (1885–1952) is an excellent example of Neo-Freudian or ego psychology. This branch of personality theory has retained the basic Freudian methods and principles of unconscious conflict, while advancing the important but hitherto largely neglected variable of the social and cultural foundations of personality. Determinism is not rejected in entirety, only Freud's particular brand with its irrevocable biological elements; and the influence of early childhood is viewed from its social context. Although the idea of the personality as a complex of innate drives bandying the individual to and fro is repudiated, the Neo-Freudians recognize that biological factors are influential and attempt to view them in a proper perspective. That is, they do not emphasize cultural elements to the exclusion of everything else.

Horney's theory centers around the concepts of *basic anxiety*, *strategies* or *neurotic trends,* and *needs.* Basic anxiety results from social interactions which disturb a child's security; it is a feeling of being isolated in a potentially hostile world. Basic anxiety, however, is not a necessary consequence of childhood and does not occur in a proper home environment.

When basic anxiety does occur a child may adopt one of several strategies or neurotic trends to alleviate his feeling of isolation. He may become hostile, aggressive, submissive, or competitive, depending upon which approach is most effective for him.

Closely related to these strategies is the development of specific needs which arise from basic anxiety. These needs can be placed into three categories, determined by the general behavioral patterns which they motivate: (1) moving *against* people (need for power) ; (2) moving *toward* people (need for love) ; and (3) moving *away from* people (need for isolation) . These basic approaches to life are not necessarily mutually exclusive. In fact, the well-adjusted person will use whatever approach best reduces his present needs. On the other hand, the neurotic person focuses his entire motivation on a single method and this orientation dominates his entire personality and produces seemingly unresolvable conflicts. Conflict is defined only in terms of the present social situations and the demands it places on the person. Neurosis is defined in relation to the ability of a person efficiently to cope with his culture.

Horney's basic concepts of anxiety and strategy bear a striking resemblance to Adler's principles of inferiority feelings and style of life. There are, however, two important differences: (1) Adler assumed an innate social drive while Horney did not; and (2) Adler incorporated in his will to power a teleology which is almost totally absent in Horney's theory. However, as did Adler, Horney gave a great deal of attention to the home situation and the child's reaction to it. Moreover, Adler and Horney did not view maladjustment as an inevitable consequence of early life, as Freud and other biological determinists believed.

CRITICISMS OF PSYCHOANALYSIS

Most of the criticisms of psychoanalysis center around the method employed by the analysts in developing and evaluating their theories. Their chief source of data is the case study or clinical interview; but the number of patients seen by even an active therapist within a single lifetime is relatively small. This criticism, in itself, is not telling, but associated with it is the conspicuous lack of experimental control. As described above (Chapter 1), the principle of control involves the systematic assessment of one or more of a small number of variables while other presumably relevant factors are held constant. This method, the keystone of all scientific inquiry, is essential for disentangling the myriad of relevant and irrelevant influences upon behavior. The major reason for this lack of control stems from the fact that the primary purpose of the clinician is *not* to verify a theory but to help his patient. Because of this role the therapist seldom becomes sufficiently detached from his work to obtain the objectivity required for scientific investigation. Furthermore, as has been indicated, one of the most important variables is the personality of the therapist. The therapist accordingly, as well as the factors incorporated in the theory, may be an influencing factor in treatment outcomes.

Thus, there seems to be no way in the *clinical setting* to

separate the effects of the therapist from the effects of the theory. However, preliminary experimental techniques have been developed and to some extent used. For example, a straightforward test could be employed to determine which of two techniques or theories is the more effective. This test would involve a number of different therapists equally well versed in the two theories. Each therapist would use each approach in treating the same number of patients having similar background and etiology. It would then be possible to determine which technique is the more effective and whether there are differences in the effectiveness of the therapists.

Many clinicians typically accept the patient's verbal description as valid and infer from it the relevant variables of the past and, for that matter, of the present. The reliability of this procedure is very questionable, since without verification there is no way of ascertaining the degree of distortion that may have occurred. Furthermore, there is a tendency to interpret the verbalizations of the patient so that they fit the theoretically generated expectancies of the therapist. Thus in fact, distortion may occur at both ends. The patient's verbal production should be evaluated along with other information. In treatment it is very important to know whether the patient's verbalizations are accurate or distorted. If they are distorted, it is important to know why, since this explanation provides additional and often insightful information about the patient. It is therefore encouraging to find among some clinicians a trend toward the realization of the importance of validating the patient's verbal report. Another difficulty centers around the relationship between the therapist and patient. Since the two necessarily communicate in confidence, consequently the information exchanged between them is not made public. Thus, the data cannot be evaluated by the rest of the scientific community, which may have an orientation different from that of the original clinician.

There is no concrete evidence even that therapy itself is beneficial, irrespective of the question of theory confirmation or disconfirmation. Although undoubtedly therapy confers some benefits to the patient, very few studies have been performed in which a group has been included to control for the possibility that merely

the passage of time or some other variable, such as paying attention to the patient, is the dominant influence rather than the
therapeutic session in itself. Even after the therapeutic session is
completed, a definitive answer cannot be achieved unless the
patient is observed over a considerable period of time in order to
detect remissions and thereby determine the remission rate for
groups of patients. Longitudinal studies dealing with the development of the individual are direly needed. By this method
investigators could achieve some information concerning the validity of the principles underlying psychoanalytic theory.

The most often cited criticism against psychoanalytic theory is
its lack of conceptual specificity. It is impossible, at the present
time, to translate the essential parts of Freudian conceptualizations into scientifically adequate—that is, empirically identifiable—terminology. We have used these terms—*id, libido,* and the
others—as much as possible in their Freudian meaning. Asking
critical questions about these conceptualizations ("where" and
"how" does the id "transform" psychical energy?) is easy, and has
been done frequently by many critics.

The cardinal criterion for a scientific theory is its empirical
testability. That is, the theory must be capable of disconfirmation
as well as confirmation and the concepts must be of sufficient
clarity to predict in advance of the results what the outcome
should be. A theory, in the scientific sense, must be predictive.
Apart from its conceptual inadequacies, psychoanalysis has been
accused of being so ambiguous that it cannot be disproved. This
criticism is not without justification. However, Freud viewed
psychoanalysis not as a science of *prediction* but as a discipline
interested in explaining events after they had occurred—a *post-
dictive* endeavor. This criticism is therefore not as immediately
devastating as it appears—it does not relegate a theory to obscu-
rity. But, it does point the way in which the theory *must* develop
if it is ever to be accepted within the realm of scientific knowledge.

The above criticism has often been countered by the comment
that experimentalists are not ingenious enough to discover ways
of testing psychoanalytic theory. Although this argument may
contain an element of truth, it still does not obviate the fact that

for anything to be tested it must be stated in testable terms. Around 1940, a few attempts were made to test experimentally some of the psychoanalytic concepts (investigators include: Lippitt, 1940; N. E. Miller, 1939, 1941; P. S. Sears, 1941; Sears and Sears, 1940). However, most of these concepts have been taken out of context and many of the experiments have been done with infrahuman subjects, thus casting doubt on the generality of the research.

In a review of the psychoanalytic literature, Hall and Lindzey (1957) have noted the following trends: (1) the elaboration of the ego as a more or less autonomous system of personality, (2) a greater emphasis upon noninstinctual determinants of personality, (3) observational studies of babies and children, (4) the experimental testing of psychoanalytic propositions, and (5) an increasing rapprochement of psychoanalysis and psychology.

Since psychoanalytic theory does not, by its very nature, lend itself to experimental verification, the future may realize R. R. Sears' (1944) hope that the experimentalists will glean from psychoanalysis primary insights and hunches, and then set themselves the task of developing a systematic personality theory based on behavioral and experimental data rather than on solely clinical sources. This is an endeavor that we strongly endorse. In Chapter 3 we will discuss such an attempt—the Miller and Dollard (1941) amalgamation of Freudian concepts with learning principles.

INSTINCT PSYCHOLOGIES

Although a number of definitions of instinctive behavior have been used at one time or another, one which is typical of modern usage is as follows: Instincts are unlearned, highly stereotyped sequences of responses which result from a particular complex of stimuli. Their important characteristics are four: First, the behavior is not learned; rather, complex patterns of behavior such as nest building are completed in a particular, fixed fashion in the absence of practice or previous experience. Second, the basic behavior patterns of the instinctive act are the same for all members of a species. Third, particular stimuli must be identifiable as the elicitors of the instinctive pattern. Fourth, instinctive behavior tends to occur in a chained set of responses which have a certain utility in the species (as mating or maternal behavior).

Instincts become less prominent in organisms high on the phylogenetic scale, but are important motivators of the more primitive organisms. There is a definite positive correlation between the level of complexity of a species and the extent to which its behavior is modifiable. Once an instinctive act such as nest building has started, it is very difficult for the organism to interrupt that activity even if continuing it endangers life. The animal appears to be "driven" to complete the task.

The study of instincts has had an important place in motivation theory. At the turn of the twentieth century, "instincts" became a popular explanatory concept in the field of psychology and were even applied extensively, in theory and speculation, to human behavior. This trend reached a peak during the third decade of the century. The psychologist who was chiefly responsible for this development was the Englishman, William McDougall (1912, 1923).

A more recent trend in psychology, particularly in Europe and England, is the ethological study of behavior—that is, the study of behavior in its natural environment. This has produced a substantially different orientation toward instinctive behavior from that proposed by McDougall. Representative of the ethological approach are the European biologists Konrad Lorenz and Nikolas Tinbergen. Lorenz, the ethologist who first gained prominence in the resurgence of this movement, performed important early research on imprinting in birds. He has also written a number of popular yet scientifically sound books (one is *King Solomon's Ring*, 1956). Tinbergen has proposed a theory of behavior based on the concept of the instinct, and has also done some particularly interesting experimental work with the mating and fighting instincts of the three-spined stickleback fish.

MCDOUGALL'S INSTINCT THEORY

The system of William McDougall (1871–1938) places emphasis upon the instinctual and purposive aspects of human nature. McDougall and Freud developed their respective theories independently at about the same time. McDougall states that all behavior is purposively and teleologically directed toward the achievement of the goal of self-preservation. Innate propensities are the forces guiding behavior. A *propensity* is an inherited tendency which motivates all thought and action and provides the raw material for the development of human personalities. McDougall subdivides innate propensities into two classes: (1) *specific tendencies* or *instincts,* and (2) *nonspecific tendencies* or *capacities.* Instincts correspond to rigid, stereotyped behavior, whereas nonspecific tendencies are experientially pliable.

Each instinct has four constituent parts: (1) perceptual, (2) cognitive, (3) emotional, and (4) behavioral. The sequence of events preceding a behavioral act is as follows: Stimuli impinge upon and are perceived by the organism. This perception activates the instinctive tendency to which cognitive (intellectual) and conative (emotional) elements are related. The cognitive elements are those which actually direct the overt behavior toward goal attainment, for "every instance of instinctive behavior involves a knowing of some thing or object and a striving towards or away from that object." (McDougall, 1908, p. 26) The emotional elements (fear, anger, and the like) are the most rigid and unmodifiable aspect of the instinct. The final aspect of the sequence is the overt goal-striving behavior itself.

In McDougall's book, *Outline of Psychology* (1923), fourteen instincts and their corresponding emotions were listed. Furthermore, McDougall stated that this list was only tentative and that when more instincts were discovered they should be added. This position accelerated the trend in psychology toward classifying all kinds of behavior into instinctive categories. McDougall conceded that instincts can be modified and that few remain in their pure form above the infrahuman level, and further that the specific emotional relationship is evident only when a pure instinct is present. Originally the emotion of fear may perhaps be elicited by a single event (say, a loud noise), producing the characteristic response of withdrawal. However, in later life, the eliciting stimuli are numerically increased, and although the emotional or motivating nucleus remains essentially unaltered, its manner of expression is varied. Since the major changes come in the cognitive and behavioral aspects it is extremely difficult in adult humans to analyze behavior and isolate the different instincts with their distinctive emotional core.

Both instincts and nonspecific tendencies coalesce into an orderly system of *sentiments*, such as love, hope, patriotism. These complexes are structured slowly as the result of many diverse experiences. Also, since pure instincts are rarely, if ever, found in adult humans, the sentiments are the more enduring and permanent features of the personality. In sentiments, because of the great number and diversity of the tendencies comprising them, there are no specific emotional counterparts. Finally, sentiments combine into an integrated system called the *character*. The character is what is commonly referred to as the dominant or salient aspect of one's personality (for example, strong willed, fun loving).

McDougall was not a determinist. Freedom for him was the distinguishing mark of the mind. Furthermore, he was very much concerned with the problem of the interaction between mind and body. His research methods were a mixture of mentalistic introspection and behavioral observation directed toward ascertaining the different types of instincts present in humans. Behavior was not studied for its own sake, but was believed to express the functioning of the mind.

Although McDougall's views cannot be said to have any substantial direct following in contemporary psychology, they have nevertheless had an appreciable effect historically, and are approximated at least in certain of the more phenomenologically oriented contemporary personality theories.

ETHOLOGICAL THEORY

Recently the ethological approach to instincts has occupied the interest of many psychologists. As a method of studying animals in their natural environment, ethology relies heavily, but not exclusively, on observational techniques. Although, as was mentioned above, the pioneer in this area was the German biologist Lorenz, Tinbergen has provided the clearest account of ethological method and theory in his book, *A Study of Instinct* (1951).

An instinct is defined by Tinbergen as a nervous mechanism,

hierarchically arranged, which responds with coordinated movements to external and internal stimuli, releasing and directing
impulses. It should be noted that the term *instinct* is not defined
in relation to its purpose, as McDougall had defined it, but rather
as a neurological entity. Furthermore, Tinbergen maintains that
instincts are composed of several specific, innate behavior correlates. For example, the reproductive instinct in the stickleback is
composed of the drives of nest building, fighting, mating, and
care of offspring.

Drive, as used by the ethologists, usually refers to the motivating aspects of behavior. Each of these drives is implemented by
any one of a number of specific activities. Thus, fighting may be
accomplished by biting, threatening, chasing, or other behavior,
and nest building by digging, gluing, testing of material, and
related activities. Although the specific behavior depends upon
the activation of the general instinct, the exact manner of behavior is determined by very specific stimuli. The reproductive instinct may be produced by the lengthening of the day, rise in
temperature, and so on; while the type of fighting behavior is
related to a specific stimulus, such as the intrusion of an invader.
It is in this context that Tinbergen introduces his concept of a
neurological coordinating center. Each separate act has its own
particular neurological center in which energy specific to a definite response accumulates. The greater the accumulation of energy the less intensive are the triggering stimuli required to
release the activity. In other words, the stimulus threshold is
lowered. Thus at certain times of the year (autumn and winter)
no mating responses can be produced regardless of the stimulus
intensity, while in the spring a minimum amount of stimulation
will effectively elicit a response. The concept of a specific neural
center, Tinbergen believes, provides a thread of commonality
between different instincts. Purposiveness of instincts is one of
their important features, but if the investigator concentrates
solely on this aspect they all seem different with little relationship between them. If he includes such a locus as a physiological
center, the instincts may be better subsumed under the single
rubric of neural mechanism and the laws governing them may be
more easily ascertained.

Every energy source must have some mechanism necessary to release it. The releasers are, as in most psychological theories, different stimuli. These may be either external or internal. Tinbergen mentions that the internal stimuli which both qualitatively and quantitatively motivate the animal are hormones, internal sensory stimuli, and automatic neural impulses produced by the central nervous system. He refers to the effective external stimuli as *sign stimuli* and has devoted a great deal of effort to determine which of the environmental stimuli are encompassed under this heading. In fact, these studies and their results provide the empirical foundations for his theory. The courting behavior of the male stickleback is in response to at least two sign stimuli—the female posture and the swollen female abdomen. The fighting behavior between male sticklebacks is elicited by color sign stimuli—the intense red throat and belly. Sign stimuli are tested by dummy experiments—experiments which use different models of the animal, each lacking the usual characteristics except the one being tested.

Tinbergen holds, furthermore, that each act (set of muscular contractions) is related to a single stimulus. This view leads to the following problem: Either the stimuli themselves must have innate triggering properties, or the animal must have some means of discriminating effective from ineffective stimuli. The latter hypothesis apparently appeared the more plausible and Tinbergen posited an *innate releasing mechanism (IRM)*. For each center there is an IRM, which is most simply viewed as a selective stimulus filter allowing passage of only those particular stimuli which elicit or release behavior.

The elicited behavior is divided into two separate but related categories: *consummatory acts* and *appetitive behavior*. A consummatory act is the final product of the instinct, that which satisfies the animal and decreases its motivation to pursue the act further. This is the stereotyped aspect of the instinct (for instance, mating behavior). These movements are controlled by centers of a lower type and are rarely activated by external stimuli alone. They usually require internal stimuli from a higher or superordinated center, one which controls the lower centers. Activation of the center, in addition to transmitting impulses to the lower centers, results in appetitive behavior. This is characterized by either (1) an increase in readiness to respond or (2) in some type of exploratory behavior characterized by its randomness. Thus, once the mating drive is activated, searching behavior ensues until an appropriate stimulus is located to release the consummatory behavior. The consummatory behavior itself may be relatively simple; its most complex form is a chain of reactions each of which is controlled by a physiological center and its accompanying IRM. Appetitive behavior is purposive activity composed of many different types of behavior, and is activated by all the centers above those guiding the consummatory act.

In summary, the activation of the neurological centers, chiefly by internal stimulation, constitutes the motivational aspect of this theory. The motivation first impels the animal to engage in appetitive behavior, controlled by higher centers. The appetitive behavior brings him into contact with specific external stimuli. These activate the IRMs whereby consummatory behavior is initiated under the control of lower centers. Once the consummatory activity terminates, the goal is achieved, the motivation decreases, and the animal returns to a state of relative quiescence.

CRITICISMS OF INSTINCT THEORIES

Dunlap's (1919) article, "Are there any instincts," signaled the beginning of the decline of instinctive explanations of behavioral phenomenon. L. L. Bernard (1924) pointed out the lack of agreement between different authorities on the exact number of instincts, and cited several examples of how many of the "instincts" varied from culture to culture. This fact clearly violated the criterion of instinctual universality and indicated that instincts might have important acquired components rather than merely innate characteristics. As the evidence against instincts mounted, the pendulum swung in the other direction with an overemphasis on the acquired aspects of behavior. Kuo (1930), an extreme environmentalist, showed that by manipulating early environment, kittens could be made to "fear," "love," or kill rats. He also demonstrated (1932a, 1932b, 1932c, 1932d, 1932e) the relationship between embryonic development and behavior in the chicken. He replaced part of the shell with a transparent window to study more than 3,000 chick embryos and was thus able to observe the course of embryonic development. His early reports are classics of their kind and should be consulted directly.

Experiments performed to determine whether behavior is learned or innate are typically classified as *isolation experiments*. In these studies the control subjects are raised or tested without permitting them to interchange experience with others of the species. Hoarding experiments in rats provide a good example of this type of experiment and the possible errors that may result. Rats raised in isolation from each other may be tested to see whether or not they hoard. If the results indicated that they do, the conclusion is that hoarding is a natural or instinctive process. However, as Lehrman has pointed out (1953), an animal isolated from members of its species is not necessarily isolated from the effects of events which may control the development of any particular behavioral pattern. The real question is, "From what is the animal isolated?" In the experiment just mentioned, where the possibility for all acquired behavior was eliminated by intraspecies isolation, innate hoarding behavior was assumed because of the acceptance of an implicit hypothesis. That is, acquired behavior was assumed to result only from the imitation of the behavior of others. The fallacy of such an assumption is suggested by a series of studies (Marx, 1951, 1957; Marx and Brownstein, 1957) which point to the importance of the consumption of the food in the development of hoarding behavior. In one study, for example, when animals raised in similar environments were prevented from consuming food by having it removed from their mouths when they returned to the home cage, they failed to hoard under later test conditions whereas animals which were allowed to consume their food later showed hoarding behavior. Thus, the original "instinctual" conclusion, based on a single type of isolation experiment, needs to be qualified. The exact role of experience still needs to be fully explicated. This is but one illustration of the dangers of failing to isolate the important variables. If the instinctual interpretation had been accepted instead of questioned, no further research would have been accomplished.

The shift of emphasis from instinct theories of motivation and the decline in their popularity stem from two main factors. The first concerns the circular nature of "instinct"—it merely substitutes one mystery for another. A case in point is the migration of birds. Typically this phenomenon is described as an instinct. However, if one asks the question, "What produces the migratory behavior?" the answer is that it is the result of instinctive powers, or "birds fly because of the instinct to fly." Thus nothing is really explained, and only a verbal reclassification (so-called "word magic") is accomplished. The behavior is considered as the manifestation of a particular neural mechanism which was inferred, in the first place, from an observation of the behavior. The process has become a "thing." The second reason for the decline of instinct theory is that, as suggested above, if instincts are accepted as explanatory concepts, then further behavioral research on the phenomenon is halted. If the behavior is classified as an instinct, it does not generate any light on either the origin or the development of the behavior; instead of promoting knowledge it obscures it under the cloak of ignorance.

The current trend has been (1) to analyze the underlying processes of activities commonly called "instinctive," (2) to substitute the term "species-specific behavior" for the term "instinct," and (3) to regard the term "instinct," whenever it is used, as merely a descriptive term devoid of any explanatory powers. Several authors (among them Beach, 1955; Lehrman, 1953; Verplanck, 1955) have advocated abolishing attempts at dividing behavior into the two categories of learned and unlearned. They argue that the characteristics of learned behavior are not delineated sufficiently to permit such a dichotomy. Furthermore, any attempted definition of a class of behavior as the absence of some characteristics (instinct, for instance, as behavior in the absence of learning) is an extremely tenuous position, as well as one which is difficult to test experimentally. The currently most accepted approach is to study the origins, characteristics, and development of a behavior until enough data are accumulated to permit its classification; but also, and more importantly, to determine the influential variables for each particular behavior problem, regardless of their classification.

Suggested Readings

Freud, S. [1917.] *A general introduction to psychoanalysis*. Translated by
J. Riviere. Garden City, N.Y.: Doubleday, 1943.

Hilgard, E. R., L. S. Kubie, and E. Pumpian-Mindlin. 1952. *Psychoanalysis as science*. Stanford, Calif.: Stanford University Press.

Jones, E. 1953, 1955, 1957. *The life and work of Sigmund Freud*. New
York: Basic Books. Vol. 1, 1953; Vol. 2, 1955; Vol. 3, 1957.

Lorenz, K. Z. 1956. *King Solomon's ring*. London: Methuen and Co.

Munroe, Ruth L. 1955. *Schools of psychoanalytic thought*. New York:
Dryden Press.

Tinbergen, N. 1951. *The study of instinct*. Oxford: Clarendon Press.

Chapter 3

CLASSICAL THEORIES OF MOTIVATION: COGNITIVE AND STIMULUS-RESPONSE INTERPRETATIONS

Here we continue our treatment of the major, historically significant accounts of motivation. Cognitive or field theory and stimulus-response (S-R) learning theory are discussed. Each of these is experimentally oriented, in contrast to the more rationalistic and naturalistic approaches treated in Chapter 2.

COGNITIVE OR FIELD THEORY

The term *field theory* was originally introduced as an analogy to the field forces used in the physical sciences. In physics, a field is a direct inference from the movements of the parts within a given space, and is given a specific mathematical formulation from which future movement may be quantitatively predicted. In psychology, the term *field* is most often used to denote nothing more than a psychophysical environment with its antecedent-consequent relations. The term is also employed to indicate that a theorist is interested in analyzing the entire situation rather than concentrating on particular aspects of it. Thus, a field theorist is one who concentrates on the "dynamics" as well as the structural facets of behavior, analyzes the total situation, includ-

61

ing its objective and subjective aspects as well as its physical and psychological characteristics, and may use a mathematical representation of the field. However, despite their intentions to be inclusive, field theorists devote particular attention to the perceptual and cognitive aspects of the field. These two aspects provide them with their major basis for explanation of behavior.

The most influential and important field theorist was Kurt Lewin (1890–1947). His theory (1935, 1936) attempted to represent the various multicausal factors of behavior, such as the objective environment, the person and his goals, forces, needs, drives, tensions, and actions, within a single integrated conceptual schema. Central to his schema are the motivational concepts of *need* and *tension*.

The psychology of E. C. Tolman (1886–1959) is a further example of the cognitive approach and is an excellent example of how a mentalistic term (purpose) may be used in an objective manner.

Finally, Douglas Lawrence (b. 1918) and Leon Festinger (b. 1919), even though they are not field theorists in the strictest sense of the word, are included because of their reliance on cognitive and perceptual explanations. Moreover, their work represents one of the most recent attempts at motivational theorizing.

LEWINIAN FIELD THEORY

The major structural concept of Lewin's theory is that of the *life space* (Fig. 1). The life space is a representation of the subjective relationship between the person and his psychological environment. It consists of two major parts: the *person* (P) and his psychological *environment* (E). The person is surrounded by the psychological environment, which is divided into different regions by boundaries that change from moment to moment as new psychological variables come into the field. The E is not to be viewed as the physical environment (which lies outside of E) but as the area containing all of the potential psychological factors or conditions which at a given moment can influence behavior. These factors (such as past experiences, ongoing events or future goals) may or may not be present in the immediate physical environment. The regions within E represent the factors and the boundaries portray the relationships between the regions. The perceived relationship of the person to his environment guides the individual's actions. The person is also divided into different areas corresponding to motor processes (behavior), perceptual processes, and inner-personal processes or areas (memory, emotion, and the like). In general, the life space is supposed to represent all of the variables which can influence behavior—the total psychological field.

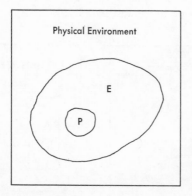

FIGURE 1. LEWINIAN LIFE SPACE.
(Life Space = Person + Psychological Environment)

The different regions of the life space are characterized by three dimensions: (1) proximity (nearness-remoteness), (2) permeability, or ease of movement between the regions (firmness-weakness), and (3) responsiveness to impinging events (fluidity-rigidity). The first two of these are the most frequently employed in behavioral analyses.

In the example of Figure 2, left panel, the person (P) is in region A of the environment. The life space includes all that within the larger circle. That which is outside of the life space is the physical world which may or may not influence behavior, depending upon how it influences the psychological environment. If P desires to leave region A he must go into either B or G initially, but B will be much easier to enter since, as the light demarcation of the barrier indicates, it has a more permeable boundary and is therefore not a difficult barrier to pass. However, if the person wishes to move to area D, he must choose between going through G, which is the shorter but more difficult route, or through both B and C, which will be less difficult but longer.

This type of schema is based upon a non-Euclidean geometry of space called *topology*. In topology, the size and shape of the regions are not important. Only their relative positions and the existence of the boundaries are important. For example, the diagram in the right panel of Figure 2 has exactly the same meaning as the one in the left panel.

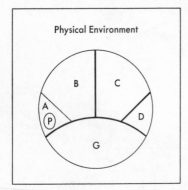 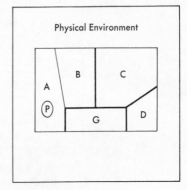

FIGURE 2. BARRIERS IN THE LEWINIAN LIFE SPACE.

Beside these structural components, Lewin incorporated several directional features: forces, valences, and vectors. These are represented in a *hodological* space, which is a geometry of paths or vectors devised by Lewin specifically for this purpose. A *vector* (———→) is a mathematical representation of the properties of force, direction, and point of application. The length of the line represents the force, the shaft its direction, and the arrowhead the point of its application. The vectors are a property of the environment and not of the person. They impinge upon the person and direct his behavior. *Valence* refers to the attraction (positive valence) or repulsion (negative valence) of an object. This property is imparted to the vector—that is, the valence of an object determines the direction and force of the vector in relation to the person. For example, a positive valence results in a vector which directs the individual toward the object, while a negative valence has the opposite influence. The force of the vector is determined by the needs and tensions of the individual.

The central motivational constructs of Lewin are *energy, need,* and *tension.* Since Lewin was concerned only with psychological space, the relation between psychological and physical energy did not interest him. Man's goal is to be in equilibrium, a state of balance and harmony between the different regions of the life space. Whenever this state is disrupted, the major cause of disruption being the arousal of a need, psychological energy is expended in an attempt to return the person to this condition. Lewin made no attempt to list all the possible needs but he enumerated some of them and classified them as either physiological (for instance, hunger, thirst) or psychological (desire, intention). These latter needs he termed "quasi-needs." Quasi-needs are those arising from a specific intention, such as the preference to eat at one restaurant rather than another, or from a desire to perform a particular task, such as finishing a job, recalling a name, or mailing a letter. Both needs and quasi-needs are capable of producing tension—the emotional psychological state within the inner-personal region which corresponds to the need or quasi-need. Needs impart meaning to objects by giving them a momentary valence. Thus the valence of an object indicates the degree and kind of motivational state existing within the person. If the object will reduce tension, the person will be highly motivated to achieve it, and the goal has a high positive valence. If, on the other hand, an object will increase tension, the person will be highly motivated to avoid it, and the valence is negative. Characteristic of tension is its propensity to discharge energy in some type of action or *locomotion,* thus returning the organism to a state of equilibrium. Tension may be discharged or reduced by one of the following processes: (1) achieving the original goal, (2) reaching substitute goals, and (3) imaginary fulfillment.

The locomotion involved in tension reduction is not physical movement. It is defined by Lewin as the traversing of a path through different psychological regions in the life space. Thus, thinking about leaving class or being lost in a daydream or walking down the street are equally authentic locomotions. Locomotion and its direction are determined by all of the various components previously discussed. The chain of occurrences generally proceeds in a manner similar to the following: A perception within the person arouses a need, which in turn confers a psychological valence on an object in the psychological environment and also causes tension within the person. The valence (not the need) then creates a force or vector toward the goal, and locomotion is initiated. Upon reaching the goal the need and the tension are reduced, the force is diminished, and the person returns to a state of equilibrium. One unique aspect of the motivational concept of need and tension is its relation to behavior or motor functions. Usually in other theories a need is directly related to the motor action, but Lewin links need to the environment through valences. Certain properties of the environment determine the type of behavior that will occur. Therefore, all locomotor activity is a direct function of the environment and is an indirect effect created by needs and valences.

The most widely known application of Lewin's field theory is found in the area of conflict, where it has been applied in an attempt to conceptualize the different types of conflict situations. The results of such an analysis suggest the three following types of conflict: approach-approach, approach-avoidance, and avoidance-avoidance. *Approach-approach* conflict occurs when the person desires two goals, each of which has a positive valence, but is permitted to attain only one (a person sees two types of food at the store but can afford to buy only one). *Approach-avoidance* conflict is present when a single object has *both* a positive and negative valence (one desires the monetary rewards of a job but dislikes the work involved). *Avoidance-avoidance* conflict is characterized by two goals, each possessing a negative valence, with the person forced to choose one of them (a man must choose between cleaning the garage and washing the car).

The most prominent series of motivational experiments that were derived directly from Lewin's theory relate to his concept of the tension system. Two of the best known of these, mentioned in

Chapter 1, will be described. These experiments are based on the premise that once tension is present, certain psychological processes will operate until this tension is discharged; the undissipated tension continues to energize the psychological processes.

Zeigarnik (1927) hypothesized that one of these processes would be memory, and that tension could be induced by interrupting an ongoing goal-oriented activity. She tested this notion by giving several different series of tasks, some of which she permitted the subjects to complete and others of which were interrupted and not completed. After each experimental session, the subjects were asked to enumerate the tasks on which they had worked. The results showed a significantly greater recall of interrupted tasks than completed tasks. This phenomenon became known as the Zeigarnik effect.

Another one of Lewin's students, Ovsiankina (1928), used a similar procedure. Instead of presenting a recall test she allowed the subjects to return to the experimental room where they were permitted to resume any activity which they had experienced on the preceding periods. More subjects returned to the uncompleted tasks than to the completed ones, apparently in an attempt to reduce the residual tension not dissipated during the preceding sessions.

TOLMANIAN PURPOSIVE BEHAVIOR

Tolman called himself a purposive behaviorist, thereby indicating his leaning toward a psychology which simultaneously included objective methods of research and the concept of purpose. Purpose is objectively defined as the approach toward or away from a goal. Tolman emphasized the molar (that is, larger and more meaningful) components of behavior rather than the underlying movements of the glands and muscles. His system consisted of independent variables such as hunger, intervening variables such as cognition and perception, and dependent variables such as speed of response. Hull also used this general format, which we will meet again in the following section of this chapter.

In Tolman's theory the major independent variables motivating behavior are different drives, including both the appetitive (food, water) and the aversive (pugnacity, fear). Beside these first-order drives, there are also innate second-order drives (curiosity, imitation), and learned third-order drives or quasi-needs (for money, attention). Tolman also emphasized different capacities and temperamental variables. These are easily remembered since their first letters combine to spell HATE (heredity, age, training, and endocrine conditions). These factors were primarily used to explain individual differences which exist among organisms.

Tolman's major intervening variables are behavioral space, cognitions, and belief-value matrices. The *behavioral space* is similar to Lewin's life space. It contains the totality of the psychological environment with its different goals (objects as perceived or as they are expected to be perceived), the resultant field forces, and positive and negative valences. These provide the essential motivational core for his theory. Tolman (1959) states that the animal does not run the maze to lower his hungriness or his curiosity; rather, it is the positive and negative goals which the animal wants or does not want. Thus the locomotion, either physical or psychological, is at least partly the result of the valences and forces in his environment. The major *cognitions* include sign-gestalt-expectations and cognitive maps. *Sign-gestalt-expectations* are the beliefs that the world and its corresponding objects and signs are organized in an orderly manner, which can be best understood when a given situation is viewed in its totality. *Cognitive maps* represent the different possible paths to a goal. The *belief-value matrix* is a hierarchical group of means-end expectations, a "set" or predisposition to respond in a particular manner to environmental objects.

This system in general bears a striking resemblance to Lewin's, with its emphasis upon the total situation, behavioral space, and perceptual and cognitive components. Yet it differs in its emphasis on the HATE variables and in its implementation by animal research.

Tolman and his associates (Elliott, 1929; Blodgett, 1929; Tolman and Honzik, 1930; Herb, 1940) performed an especially fruitful series of motivational experiments assessing the effects of reward on behavior. These became known as latent-learning experiments. The interpretation of their results stimulated the important distinction between learning and performance. The assumption underlying this research was that learning is basically a function of cognition, or of perceiving "what leads to what," and that the appropriate motivational conditions must be present before any behavior occurs as a result of such learning. Learning is assumed to be a basically cognitive process which must be inferred from behavior. Without the proper motivation, however, the subject does not have any reason to demonstrate that learning has occurred.

The typical latent-learning experiment consisted of training two groups of hungry rats in a maze. Control subjects received a reward (food) each time they reached the end of the maze (the goal box), while experimental subjects did not receive any reward. After several days of such training the performance of the control group was clearly superior to that of the experimental group. Then the experimental subjects were rewarded and within a very small number of trials their performance equaled that of the control group. The sudden shift in performance of the experimental group was explained as the result of increased motivation and not as a sudden increment in learning. That is, it was argued that learning had taken place on the nonrewarded trials but was not demonstrated in the absence of an appropriate motivator (food).

COGNITIVE-DISSONANCE THEORY

One of the most recent attempts to deal with the motivational aspects of behavior is the cognitive-dissonance theory of Festinger (1957, 1961). Originally this theory was developed only with respect to human behavior but it was broadened to include infrahuman behavior by Lawrence and Festinger (1962).

The fact that a certain amount of information about an environment is obtained through a person's perception of the environment provides the basic principle underlying the cognitive-dissonance approach. Such information is referred to as a *cognition*. Cognitions never exist in a vacuum but always occur in relation to some other cognitions. The result of interpreting a set of cognitions is some type of behavior. Furthermore, behavioral consequences yield additional cognitions, which are then compared with the information which led to the behavior. This step in turn influences subsequent behavior. It is this feedback relation between postbehavioral cognitions and prebehavioral cognitions and their impact on future behavior that bears the major theoretical burden in the Festinger schema.

Normally, it would be expected that a person seeks that which is pleasurable and avoids that which is not pleasurable. However, what about those situations where the person has to endure pain or embarrassment in order to obtain his goal? Or where the reward is clearly less than had previously been given? Questions such as these, stemming from situations in which behavior does not seem to fit with the common-sense view, are of considerable interest and largely comprise the subject matter for cognitive-dissonance theorists.

The central presumption of the cognitive-dissonance theory is that all of the different relationships among cognitions can be classified as either consonant or dissonant. A *consonant* relationship exists when there is correspondence between the cognitions concerning one's actions and the consequences of that action; a *dissonant* relationship exists when a lack of correspondence between the cognitions occurs. For example, if a student expects a course to be a "snap" and upon taking the course finds his expectation correct, a consonant relation exists and there is little trouble in explaining why the student remains enrolled in the course. However, suppose that this same student, after enrolling in the course, finds his expectation incorrect and the course very difficult. A dissonant relationship exists and if the student remains enrolled in the course there would seem to be some difficulty in explaining the reason, on a common-sense basis, since his expectations have not been fulfilled and presumably the experience is an unpleasant one.

Cognitive-dissonance theory examines this kind of situation more closely. According to it, dissonance produces a state of tension which the individual tries to remove or reduce, and consequently is motivational in nature. But there are only two ways by which the dissonance can be removed: (1) the individual can change his behavior (the student could withdraw from the course), or (2) the individual (student) can change his cognition. According to Lawrence and Festinger (1962) "the individual sets about discovering values or rewards in the situation that satisfy some motivation he may have other than the motivation that led him to take the action in the first place." Perhaps the student unexpectedly finds the subject matter valuable and interesting or discovers that he is attracted to the girl in the adjacent seat. These discovered values are generally referred to as *added attractions* and are used to explain much of the behavior which exists in the face of a dissonant relation.

The magnitude of a cognitive dissonance is determined by the relative importance of the variables that enter into it. These may be prebehavioral cognitions (information, expectation) related to postbehavioral cognitions (consequent activity). The most important variables in determining the magnitude of dissonance are the amount of effort involved in the task and the quantity of the reward. Finally, in cases where more than one dissonant relationship is involved the total dissonance is the sum of all the contributing dissonances.

An experiment by Aronson and Mills (1959) affords a good example of the procedure used in cognitive-dissonance research. The hypothesis was that persons who undergo severe initiation in order to join a group would like the group more than persons who do not receive such a severe initiation. Women college students who volunteered to take part in a discussion group were assigned randomly to three experimental conditions: One group received a severe initiation; these students had to read very embarrassing material aloud to the experimenter before they could join the discussion group. A second group had to read mildly embarrassing material for the initiation. The control group had no initiation.

Upon completion of the initiation all subjects listened individually to a recording of a discussion which they were told was an actual meeting of the group they had just joined. This recording contained thirty minutes of rather meaningless material. Afterward the subjects were asked to fill out a questionnaire evaluating the discussion and the participants. Subjects who received a severe initiation rated the discussion group as significantly more valuable than the other two groups.

Aronson and Mills interpreted the experiment in the following manner. "Negative cognitions about the discussion which they formed from listening to it were dissonant with the cognition that they had undergone a painful experience to gain membership in this group. The presence of dissonance leads to pressures to reduce it. Subjects in this condition could reduce their dissonance either by denying the severity of the initiation or by distorting their cognitions concerning the group discussion in a positive direction. The initiation of the subjects in the severe condition was apparently too painful for them to deny—hence, they reduced their dissonance by overestimating the attractiveness of the group." (Aronson and Mills, 1959, p. 180)

CRITICISMS OF FIELD THEORY

The major general criticism that has been leveled against field theory concerns the vagueness of its empirical referents. This is not so much a stricture against the use of cognitive or "mentalistic" terms as a criticism of their lack of operational specificity. Questions which are frequently asked of the field theorist are, "How are the concepts of life space, tension, added attractions, and the like empirically defined?" "How does one meaningfully relate these terms to experimentally testable situations?" (See Estes, 1954.)

A second and related criticism is the general lack of specification of the relationship between the hypothesized "cognitions" of an organism and its actions. Field theorists, with their strong perceptual and cognitive orientation, have tended to ignore the motor or response aspects of behavior. Guthrie (1935, p. 172) aptly commented that Tolman leaves the rat "buried in thought," indicating that although Tolman may have generated an adequate set of concepts to account for the cognitive side of behavior, he failed to specify how this mental activity was translated into observable behavior.

A third criticism is that the theories are not sufficiently precise to admit of their being confirmed or disconfirmed by experimental test. For example, "added attractions" are extensively employed as an explanatory concept. Yet the term is so broad and so vaguely related to the other constructs of the theory that it may be interpreted to explain anything and everything—which is tantamount to saying that it explains nothing. This criticism is not unique to field theory for it is safe to state that all behavioral theories to some degree suffer from such inadequacy. However, field theory and psychoanalysis are those most frequently cited as violating the criterion of specificity of relationship in theoretical concepts.

For all its methodological shortcomings, field theory (like psychoanalysis) has been an important force in motivational theory, functioning as an irritant to other theories, especially S-R theory, as well as being a contributor in its own right. Its major contribution has been as a stimulus to experimentation on problems of perception and cognition which have been largely ignored by other approaches. Any criticism must be tempered by recognition of the positive contributions of field theory to the science of behavior as well as by the fact of its contemporary significance in both research and theory building.

STIMULUS-RESPONSE (S-R) LEARNING THEORY

The S-R theorists discussed in the following section are often classified as learning theorists, or more generally as behavior theorists, but motivation is of cardinal importance in their theories. They differ from the cognitive theorists in that they are mainly concerned with the connection between different stimuli and responses. They are typified by a concern for functional relationships and by correspondingly little attention to intraorganismic integrating principles. While they make no specific denial of important functions within the organism (in fact, constructs such as "response-produced stimulation" are used frequently), the S-R theorists focus their attention upon more readily quantified and observable extraorganismic events and tend to ignore information-processing or cognitive functions. Cognitive theorists are less concerned about the stimulus-response relationships and focus their attention on the perceived aspects of the situation and on how the relevant cognitions influence behavior.

Clark L. Hull (1884–1952) is considered the founder of the modern S-R school. His book, *Principles of Behavior* (1943) was a landmark in this movement. Hull's system aimed at explaining all mammalian behavior. Kenneth W. Spence, John Dollard, and Neal E. Miller are the S-R theorists who have been the most active in perpetuating the Hullian tone while modifying the original Hull formulations, mainly in the direction of greater specificity.

Hull's system is patterned after the mathematicodeductive models of mathematics and physics. His theory is based on specific hypotheses, or postulates, which are empirically grounded and logically connected so that theorems may be deduced from them. These theorems are then directly tested in an experimental setting. If the data support the theorems the postulates are retained; if the data do not support them the postulates are either rejected or modified. In Hull's final work, *A Behavior System* (1952), he lists 17 primary postulates, 17 corollaries, and 133 deduced theorems.

Within this framework Hull, like Tolman, considered three kinds of variables: (1) inputs, or stimuli, (2) organismic or intervening variables, and (3) outputs, or responses. Figure 3 represents the main core of Hullian theory. Each of the major variables relates to an assumed intervening variable within the organism. Thus, *incentive reinforcement* (K) is a function of the amount and/or delay of reward, *drive* (D) is a function of deprivation, and *habit strength* ($_sH_R$ or H) is a function of the number of reinforced trials. These first-order intervening variables combine in a particular manner to form second-order intervening variables, such as *reaction potential* ($_sE_R$), and *total inhibitory potential* ($_sI_R$). Finally, these coalesce into a third-order variable called the *net reaction potential* ($_s\bar{E}_R$). It is expressed, in behavior, in one of four different response measures: latency, amplitude, number of extinction (nonreinforced) trials, and probability of response. This presentation is oversimplified; variables not essential to the general understanding of the system are omitted.

A concrete example may help to clarify matters. Two groups of 23-hour-hungry rats are trained to run down a straight runway. Each day there are 10 trials. At the end of the runway one group receives 5 pellets of food (high reward), while the other group

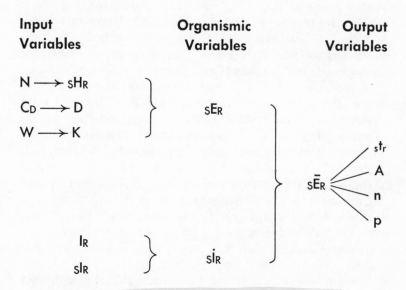

FIGURE 3. SCHEMA OF HULLIAN BEHAVIOR THEORY.

N = number of trials
C_D = deprivation condition
W = amount of reward
sH_R = habit strength
D = drive
K = incentive reinforcement
I_R = reactive inhibition

sI_R = conditioned inhibition
$s\dot{I}_R$ = total inhibitory potential
$s\bar{E}_R$ = net reaction potential
$_s t_r$ = latency
A = amplitude of response
n = number of extinction trials
p = probability of response

receives 1 pellet of food (low reward). After 10 days both groups
are extinguished. That is, all subjects receive no food at the end
of the runway and are given trials until they fail to run (within,
say, 180 seconds) for three consecutive trials. Let us assume that
the running speeds of the high-reward group are faster and that
those subjects take more trials to extinguish (stop running) than
the low-reward subjects. Hull would explain these results in the
following manner: Both groups would have the same habit
strength (sH_R) and drive (D) since the number of rewarded
trials and deprivation conditions were the same. The major
difference would be in incentive reinforcement (K), which
would be greater for the high-reward group than for the low-

reward group because of the reinforcement differential of 5 to 1. These three factors would then combine into the reaction potential $(_sE_R)$: $_sE_R = f(_sH_R \times D \times K)$. $_sE_R$ after combining with inhibitory factors would be reflected in one of the response measures, in this case latency (or speed) and number of extinction trials. Within the system Hull used several motivational concepts. *Drive* (D) is the most important of these. Not only do primary drives initiate behavior but they also indirectly form the basis for learning. Drive may be characterized by two functions. The first of these is that it sets up the basic condition for learning. Hull believed that a drive must be reduced by reward if learning is to occur. Second, drive activates $_sH_R$, producing $_sE_R$; hence, without drive there would be no response. Drive is also instrumental in directing behavior, since its stimulus components become associated as cues with responses. These may then function as discriminative stimuli which help the organism to locate the drive-reducing reinforcers in the environment.

The incentive-reinforcement component (K) also multiplies $_sH_R$ and is related to the important motivational variables of delay of reinforcement and magnitude of reinforcement. The shorter the delay and the greater the magnitude of reinforcement the greater is the motivation.

The final important motivational construct is the *inhibitory potential*. This acts as a deterrent or negative motivator and subtracts from $_sE_R$. It is the result of two other inhibitory factors, reactive inhibition (I_R) and conditioned inhibition $(_sI_R)$. Reactive inhibition occurs with every action and is analogous to fatigue. It discourages further activity, is a temporary condition, and has the properties of an aversive drive. Whatever is associated with its reduction (usually rest) becomes conditioned to its stimulus components. This rest or nonactivity thus acquires a permanent, negative habit strength and is called conditioned inhibition. $_sI_R$ is the total negative reaction potential resulting from the summation of $_sI_R$ and I_R. When its strength approaches that of $_sE_R$, the referent behavior decreases and eventually ceases.

According to this view, extinction is related to the amount of effort involved: the greater the effort, the greater $_sI_R$ is and the faster extinction occurs. In reviewing the relevant literature,

Kimble (1961) reports that several experiments have confirmed this prediction. For example, Capehart, Viney, and Hulicka (1958) trained three groups of rats to barpress for food with different amounts of pressure required (5, 40, 70 grams). The results indicated a direct relationship between the weight of the bars and the speed of extinction: the 70-gram group extinguished first, the 40-gram group second, and the 5-gram group last. Thus, effort appeared to work against or inhibit the performance on a test.

SPENCE'S MODIFICATION OF HULLIAN THEORY

Kenneth W. Spence (1907–1967) is the theorist who was the most active in modifying Hull's original theory in relation to new data. Although Spence (1956, 1960) made a number of changes in the theory, only the three most important will be discussed.

The first change was to make $_sH_R$ a function of the number of trials instead of the number of reinforced trials. This change is crucial since it eliminates the dependence of learning on the presence of reward and drive reduction. Consequently, Spence has not been in the difficult position of trying to defend a drive-reduction view of learning when many data had accumulated against this view.

Spence's biggest change was the fuller incorporation of the motivational construct K, now called *incentive motivation*. In Spencian theory, K and D are the motivational constructs responsible for performance. Although Hull, in his latest work, *A Behavioral System* (1952), dealt with K and its underlying properties, Spence has done much to develop this concept systematically.

The third of these changes is that K is viewed as an additive rather than a multiplicative element in determining $_sE_R$. In Spence's theory, $_sE_R = H (D + K)$, whereas in Hull's system $_sE_R = H \times D \times K$. This is an important change since it accounts for the fact that the referent behavior occurs in the absence of either D or K. In Spence's theory *both* D and K must be zero before $_sE_R$ becomes zero, while in Hull's theory $_sE_R$ becomes zero if either D *or* K is zero.

The best way to explain incentive motivation (K) is to observe a rat in a runway. The eating response is referred to as the goal response, or R_G; its implicit form, which can occur without the presence of the goal object, is called an anticipatory fractional goal response, or r_g. Both of these responses become conditioned to the surrounding goal stimuli in whose presence they occur. Moreover, through the principle of stimulus generalization similar stimuli further from the goal acquire the power to elicit the r_g. That is, stimuli similar in time and space have similar response-eliciting properties in a continuum from the most proximal to the most distal stimuli. Eventually, because of stimulus generalization, the stimuli in the start box can produce an r_g. Every r_g produces an internal proprioceptive stimulus, called the s_g, which in turn becomes conditioned to other responses, in most cases the locomotion or running response of the animal. The running response in turn brings the animal into contact with new alley stimuli, which produce new r_g-s_g combinations. These, along with the alley stimuli, are conditioned to the running response. The K construct represents the motivational properties of the r_g-s_g mechanism, whose motivational strength is determined by the magnitude of the incentive, the quality of the incentive, and the delay of reinforcement.

Spence thus differs from Hull in that reinforcement is no longer assumed to affect the associative factor of habit, but only the motivational factor of K. In other words, reinforcement is crucial to performance but not to learning. The relative importance of the motivational factors of D and K can be assessed in two ways. If changes in both are equal, then mathematically speaking D and K are equally powerful since they both multiply H. However, if one looks toward explanatory power rather than mathematical power, K is by far the more important of the two. For example, H is assumed to be a gradually increasing function of reinforcement, yet in many experiments it has been demonstrated that sudden shifts in behavior occur with changes in incentive. This association, according to Spence, is the consequence of the incentive's relation to K. Also, Spence needs some concept to account for the initiation and direction of behavior after a task is learned. Again K is employed. In essence, r_g-s_g is to S-R theories what expectation is to the cognitive theorists.

THE MILLER AND DOLLARD THEORY

Neal E. Miller and John Dollard have synthesized Hullian theory and Freudian principles to produce an influential personality theory. Their theory (Miller and Dollard, 1941; Dollard and Miller, 1950) is actually an attempt to retain the psychoanalytic phenomena as subject matter and reduce the psychoanalytic terminology to S-R terms which lend themselves more readily to empirical confirmation. Miller's (1959) experimental program investigating conflict is an outstanding example of how specific predictions may be deduced and experimentally tested from a theoretical superstructure.

The major assumption underlying the Dollard-Miller theory is that an individual's personality is largely a product of learning. Moreover, neuroses and other personality disorders are also the result of learning and they can be treated through the application of learning theory. In other words, that which is learned can be unlearned. Therapy, they believe, provides the conditions by which neurotic behavior may be unlearned and nonneurotic habits instituted in its place.

The individual at birth is endowed with reflexes and drives; it is from these innate responses that the personality develops. The innate responses are hierarchically arranged in respect to their probability of occurrence. Dollard and Miller believe that the "random" behavior frequently displayed by infants is not truly random but reflects the probabilistic functioning of the innate responses in that some responses are more likely to occur than others. Drives are the powerful stimuli (hunger, shock, fear) which impel the organism to respond until the stimulation is reduced. They activate behavior but do not initially direct the activity; direction is later achieved through learning. As the child develops, Dollard and Miller account for the presence of new drives and motives, the elimination of some responses and the addition of others, and the extension of original responses to new situations by the application of such Hullian principles as habit strength, inhibition, and the like. However, these principles are also used to explain aggression, hostility, anxiety, guilt, and the like. Here the Freudian-Hullian amalgamation is most evident, for nowhere in Hull's work can one find any reference to personality-oriented terminology such as "guilt" and "neurosis."

In Miller and Dollard's theory, learning, and hence personality, is characterized by four elements: drive, cue, response, and reward. Put somewhat more loosely, the organism must (1) want something, (2) notice something, (3) do something, and (4) get something. *Drive* initiates behavior. *Cues* are stimuli of different intensity which guide the *responses* and determine when and where the response will be made. The type of response chosen is a function of the hierarchy of learned and/or innate responses. *Reward* or reinforcement cements or strengthens the associative bond between the cue and the response by the reduction of the drive stimuli.

Motivation is chiefly a function of drives. The existence of acquired or learned drives in addition to the primary or unlearned ones complicates the evaluation of drive effects. The secondary drive of fear is the prime example used by Dollard and Miller to illustrate the importance of secondary drives and how learning processes can often explain "irrational" actions. If an observer were to walk into an empty white room and see a person trembling, terrified, and pounding the wall, and if he were unable to discern any apparent reason for the person's behavior, he would probably classify it as irrational and somewhat mysterious. However, the term "irrational" is often a substitute for lack of knowledge on the part of the observer; in this case, it may simply indicate a lack of appreciation of the individual's presituational experiences.

A concrete example of how fear becomes an acquired drive is provided by Miller (1948). Rats who were shocked in a white box escaped into an adjacent black box when a door was opened by the experimenter. When the shock was discontinued the rats still left the white compartment. Now the experimenter no longer opened the door and the aimals learned to turn a wheel which opened the door. Later, when the wheel would not open the door the animals, without further shock, learned to press a bar which opened the door. The white box, through its association with the shock, produced the same fearful state as did the shock. Moreover, escaping from the white box reduced the fear, and this drive reduction in turn reinforced the association between the fear and subsequent barpressing. Thus, fear is not necessarily an innate drive but in some instances it becomes attached to previously neutral cues and achieves the motivational properties of a drive, much in the same manner as may have happened with the hypothetical disturbed person in the room. A secondary drive may be viewed as both a response (for instance, the fear response itself) and as a cue for other behavior (for instance, barpressing). The strength of the secondary drive is a function of the intensity of the primary drive, the number of occurrences, and the effectiveness (drive-reducing properties) of the reward. Moreover, like any other response it can be extinguished.

One of the most extensive applications of this theory, as witnessed by a series of experiments by Miller (1959), has been in the area of conflict. The systematic investigation of conflict was undertaken because of the similarity between behavior in the experimental setting and in a variety of other situations. It was assumed that the laws underlying conflict would be applicable to the understanding of the etiology and treatment of human conflict.

The basic experimental design was to place the animal in a situation where it was exposed to both aversive (shock) and appetitive (food) stimulation. The animal was placed in a harness which recorded its speed, approach behavior, and avoidance behavior, as well as the strength of pull toward or away from the goal. For example, hungry harnessed rats would be placed in a straight runway which had food at one end. On some trials the subjects were shocked and on others they were allowed to eat without aversive stimulation. Thus, a conflict was produced between the desire to obtain food and fear of being shocked. Following are the basic postulates relating to this situation from which specific predictions were later deduced:

1. The tendency to approach a goal is stronger the nearer the subject is to it; the relation between these variables is called the gradient of approach.

2. The tendency to avoid a feared stimulus is stronger the

nearer the subject is to it; the relation between these variables is called the gradient of avoidance.

3. The strength of avoidance increases more rapidly with nearness to the goal than does that of approach. That is, the gradient of avoidance is *steeper* than that of approach.

4. The strength of tendencies to approach or avoid varies directly with the strength of the drive upon which they are based. Increments in drive raise the *height* of the gradient.

5. When two incompatible responses are in conflict, the stronger will occur.

Figures 4 and 5 illustrate how predictions can be deduced from these postulates. From Figure 4 it was derived that an approach response would occur from distance Z to distance Y and that an avoidance response would occur from distance Y to distance X. That is, the approach tendency is stronger far from the goal, while the avoidance gradient is stronger near the goal. At the intersection of these two gradients (distance Y) the effects associated with each would be neutralized and the animal would

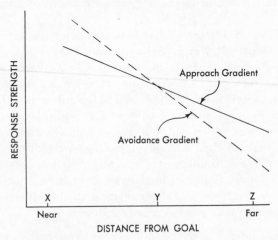

FIGURE 4. THEORETICAL RELATIONSHIP BETWEEN APPROACH AND AVOIDANCE GRADIENTS. (Adapted from Neal E. Miller, "Experimental Studies of Conflict," in *Personality and the Behavior Disorders,* edited by J. McV. Hunt. Copyright 1944 The Ronald Press Company, New York.)

stop. Therefore, it was predicted that in a runway where the subjects have had experience with both the positive and negative stimuli they should start to approach the goal and, part way there, they should stop.

Figure 5 represents the relationship between the approach (A and A′) and avoidance (B and B′) gradients when one is held constant and the other is changed, or when both are changed. From Figure 5 it was predicted that (1) when the approach gradient is kept constant (A), an increase in the strength of the avoidance gradient (B to B′) would result in the subjects stopping further from the goal than under the original avoidance level (B); and (2) when the avoidance gradient is kept constant (B) an increase in the strength of the approach gradient (A to A′) would result in the subject's stopping closer to the goal than under the original approach level (A). Furthermore, if both gradients increase, the subject would stop further from the goal than under the original gradients. The predictions from both of the figures have been experimentally supported.

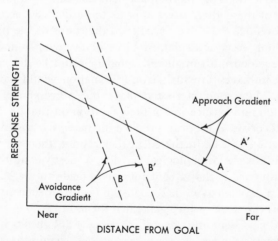

FIGURE 5. THEORETICAL RELATIONSHIP BETWEEN INCREASED APPROACH AND AVOIDANCE GRADIENTS. (Adapted from Neal E. Miller, "Experimental Studies of Conflict," in *Personality and the Behavior Disorders,* edited by J. McV. Hunt. Copyright 1944 The Ronald Press Company, New York.)

CRITICISMS OF S-R THEORY

The most telling criticism of Hull's work is that he failed to produce the logically tight system that he set out to achieve. Critical examination readily reveals that the constructs possess only a superficial logical connection. Perhaps the most devastating single critique was by Koch (1954), who logically and systematically analyzed the Hullian position and pointed out its methodological deficiencies.

A second major criticism concerns the S-R theorists' attempt to explain all behavior as the result of a few primary drives. Harlow (1953) and Hebb (1955) among others have all argued that many activities are unrelated to primary drives or to their derivatives, secondary drives. Furthermore, behavior is too complex to be classified in a scheme consisting of half a dozen or more drives. Bindra (1959) states that response to these criticisms can take one of two forms: (1) the number of primary or unlearned drives can be increased, or (2) an explicit demonstration of how secondary drives operate in complex behavior can be undertaken. The first of these alternatives appears to be the least acceptable. It would reduce the drive doctrine to the status of the instincts. That is, for every unexplained piece of behavior a new drive would be added until finally all behavior could be described by reference to drives, but little true explanation would have been achieved. The second alternative places the full responsibility for clarification and explication of their position on the shoulders of the S-R theorists. If they can produce the necessary evidence then their position will be furthered; if they cannot, their theory will tend to fall by the psychological wayside. A most valuable feature of this approach is that a contribution is made to the empirical content of psychology even though the results of such study fail to support the theory which generated them.

A third persistent and general criticism of S-R theory is that it totally ignores the very factors—perceptions, cognitions, and the like—which are central to other theoretical efforts, such as field theory and much personality theory. How important this disregard of phenomenological matters is remains to be seen; it is much too early in the development of psychological science to dispose of any approach which holds promise of making a substantial contribution to our understanding of behavior.

Suggested Readings

Festinger, L. 1957. *A theory of cognitive dissonance.* Evanston, Ill.: Row, Peterson and Co.

Hilgard, E. R., and G. Bower. 1966. *Theories of learning,* 3rd ed. New York: Appleton-Century-Crofts.

Hill, W. F. 1963. *Learning: A survey of psychological interpretations.* San Francisco: Chandler Publishing Co.

Koch, S., ed. 1959. *Psychology: A study of science,* vol. 2. New York: McGraw-Hill Book Co.

Skinner, B. F. 1959. *Cumulative record.* New York: Appleton-Century-Crofts.

Spence, K. W. 1960. *Behavior theory and learning.* Englewood Cliffs, N.J.: Prentice-Hall.

Tolman, E. C. 1951. *Collected papers in psychology.* Berkeley: University of California Press.

Chapter 4

MOTIVATION AND PERSONALITY

Motivation holds a central position within the field of personality for at least three reasons. First, an understanding of the dynamics of motivation is imperative for the evaluation of an individual's behavior, much of which represents at best a small proportion of the range of potential responses. In other words, behavior is selective. Which behavior occurs is often a joint product of one's motives and one's personality characteristics. Second, motivational determinants are not only powerful factors in the normal development of personality but also have important therapeutic implications for the treating of personality and character disorders. Third, whenever any type of personality test is administered the subject's level of motivation profoundly influences the results. Within the past two decades significant findings have been made which show not only that the optimal level of motivation differs among subjects, but also that a maximum level of motivation is not necessarily the most efficient one. That is, it was previously believed that poor performance was the result of a deficit in motivation, but it has been demonstrated recently that equally detrimental effects may result from *either* too much *or* too little motivation.

The first section of this chapter is devoted to some of the methods of testing and evaluating personality and its underlying motivational determinants. The second section contains experimental findings in current areas of investigation, such as anxiety and experimental neurosis. Finally, some of the more recent attempts to cure behavior disorders will be discussed. In recent years, stimulated by Szasz's (1961) book, *The Myth of Mental*

Illness, many psychologists have vigorously objected to the term "mental illness" and there has been an increasing trend toward the substitution of the term "behavioral disorder." This change reflects the empirical and experimental approach toward the study of personality and related disorders which is becoming more prominent within the field of psychology. We will not attempt to classify the different types of neurosis and psychosis or to differentiate among the different types of personalities or personality theories except in those cases where doing so is helpful in understanding the experimental data. Rather, we are more interested in examining different measures and experimental approaches irrespective of their relevance to different theories.

The relationship between many personality variables and the various ordering motivational constructs and principles is generally rather devious. Hence in the present chapter the reader will be required to fill this relationship in for himself to a greater extent than in the other chapters. It will be helpful if he keeps in mind the fact that, from the present point of view at least, any significant behavior and its underlying personality characteristics may be considered as having corresponding motivational correlates, whether or not they are overtly apparent or clearly conceived.

METHODS OF TESTING PERSONALITY

Personality has been defined in various ways, each emphasizing a different aspect. Some theorists emphasize the biosocial aspects, others the biophysical, and so on. Broadly speaking, it may be stated that one's theoretical position largely determines the definition used. In view of this fact we will follow Hall and Lindzey's (1957) suggestion that no universal definition of personality can be generated and in the present chapter personality will be viewed operationally in terms of the empirical measures employed by different tests.

The variety of personality tests can be divided into four separate but related classes: self-report inventories, projective tests, interest inventories, and situational tests. In describing these, however, we remind the reader of the two general concepts— validity and reliability—which are essential ingredients of any good test and are discussed in Chapter 1.

SELF-REPORT INVENTORIES

Self-report inventories are in essence self-rating scales which contain a series of questions designed to evaluate both an individual's overt behavior and his feelings about himself in relation to his environment. The questions are so constructed that they can usually be answered *yes, no,* or *maybe* by an appropriate mark on the accompanying score sheet. In contrast to self-rating essay questions, this procedure has the practical advantage of rapid scoring (often done by machines) and relatively easy development of validity scales. Certain disadvantages, however, are present, such as the limited range of possible answers. This limitation severely restricts the range of differential responses to a question. That is, a subject may interpret a question as relating to one type of situation and therefore respond in one manner, but will respond differently if he perceives it in relation to another environmental setting; and the self-report inventories, like all "objective" tests, provide no means for expressing such different interpretations.

The most widely used of the self-rating personality inventories is the Minnesota Multiphasic Personality Inventory (MMPI). The test consists of 550 statements (such as, "I am worried about sex matters") which can be answered *yes, no,* or *cannot say.* Since the original purpose of the MMPI was to provide a single test to evaluate the various behavioral disorders, the questions were selected and grouped on the basis of several different clinical categories (among others, schizophrenia, hypomania, depressive psychosis, paranoia). The questions were then validated by correlating the predicted categories derived from the test with diagnoses from hospital staffs. Recently, the clinical categories upon which the test was based have been largely rejected by clinical psychologists as inadequate. In keeping with this trend the authors of the MMPI have replaced the names of the original categories with different numbers ranging from 1 to 9 (the number 2, for example, represents those questions which supposedly differentiated depressives from normal people). Although changing the labels from psychiatric categories to numbers does not change the original rationale underlying the construction of the test, it does lend itself to a more empirical or quantifiable determination of types of personalities. This is achieved by the use of profiles.

A profile is simply a bar graph that presents a person's scores on different sections of the test. By comparing the subject's profile patterns with those of different people having somewhat the same behavior, an investigator can characterize the composite factors of his personality. Some would maintain that these profiles *are* the personality. Many others, however, would reject such a notion since they view personality as something personal and dynamic. All, however, must recognize that the very amorphous nature of such definitions precludes any rigorous scientific investigation. However, if personality is defined, at least partially, in terms of test scores, two important advances are seen: (1) precise language is used, thus alleviating the problem of communication; that is, when one investigator refers to such and such a type of profile, others can look at the profile and understand what he is talking about; and (2) this approach is a starting point for more careful and analytic work into the factors comprising each characteristic. Although this idea of personality is introduced in conjunction with the MMPI, it is not necessarily limited to this particular test. It will be readily admitted that this inventory-profile approach is not a panacea, but it does represent at least a starting point for better experimental work in the area of personality.

The MMPI contains several unique scales which greatly strengthen its usefulness and serve as safeguards against misunderstanding, deliberate falsification, and carelessness on the part of the client. Some of these scales are the "question score," "lie score," and "validity score"; a high score on any of the three measures indicates that the test results are suspect. The "question score" represents the number of questions which the person places in the *cannot say* category. The "lie score" is based upon 15 questions which, if answered truthfully, place the subject in an unfavorable light. For example, "I do not like everyone I know" applies to all people and, realistically, should be answered *Yes* by everyone. However, people trying to create a favorable impression will often answer such questions as this in the negative. The "validity score" is computed on the basis of 64 items which 90 per cent of normal people answer in a consistent manner and any significant deviation from consistency in these provides an indication of lack of validity of other answers. The lack of validity usually indicates that the subject was careless or haphazard in his approach to the test. An additional "K" score measures the subject's defensiveness and his tendency to give socially desirable responses.

We shall see in a later section how certain MMPI questions have been combined by Taylor into the Manifest Anxiety Scale (MAS) and how the MAS has been employed to investigate the effects of anxiety on performance.

PROJECTIVE TESTS

The major difference between self-report inventories and projective tests is the degree of structure in the test. The inventories consist of a structured set of presumably unambiguous questions while the projective tests rely upon an extremely unstructured and purposefully ambiguous set of stimuli such as inkblots, incomplete sentences, photographs, or the like. The rationale behind such a procedure is that the ambiguous situations promote a climate which encourages the individual to project his own feelings into the situation, revealing to trained personnel deep-seated motivations. Thus the term *projective technique* is derived from the Freudian concept of *projection*—an unconscious process in which a person attributes his own thoughts and emotions to the environment or attributes his own desires and needs to other people. Projective techniques enable the tester to obtain information about the subject which he would presumably be unable to achieve by other techniques for two reasons: (1) the structured situations characteristic of other tests may *not* be germane to important aspects of the subject's motivations, and (2) the projective tests are designed to tap the deep-seated motivational reservoirs of which the subject is not consciously aware or which he is reluctant to reveal.

The two best-known projective tests are the Rorschach (inkblot) Test and the Thematic Apperception Test (TAT). Herman Rorschach, a Swiss psychiatrist, developed the inkblot tests from 1911 to 1921 as a method for clinical diagnosis. (See illustration following p. 96.) In its present form it consists of 10 cards, each containing a symmetrical inkblot. The cards are presented to the subject one at a time with the question "What does it look like?" or "What could this be?" No time limits are imposed and the answers are recorded verbatim. In addition, several other factors are noted: (1) the time between the subject's first seeing the card and his first response, (2) the time between responses, (3) the total time for all responses, and (4) the position in which subject holds the cards. After all 10 cards have been shown, they are reshown a second time with the examiner asking specific questions in an attempt to clarify the previous accounts. The answers are scored on the basis of four categories: (1) *location*—the areas which the subject perceived as important; (2) *determinants*—perceived shading, color, motion, form, or the like; (3) *content;* and (4) *popularity-originality*—the degree of conformity of the answers, obtained by comparison with those given by other subjects. The interpretation of these categories is largely subjective but there are certain guidelines. For example: if motion is indicated in the response, it is taken as evidence of a high degree of association; color is interpreted as the chief index of a person's impulsiveness and emotional relations; and shading responses are supposed to relate to affectional needs such as anxiety, depression, and inadequacies.

Needless to say, establishing validity and reliability for this kind of test is extremely difficult. In addition to the more standard methods of establishing reliability (parallel series, split-half, and test-retest), two other methods have been used. The first of these is referred to as "interjudge reliability." Several different specialists independently interpret the protocols (records), then compare their results. Studies such as these produce fairly consistent results but are seldom used because of the time and effort involved. A particular criticism of this method is that the degree of consistency may well depend upon the similarity of theoretical approach between the different judges rather than on unbiased interpretations. Another method is to compare Rorschach-test responses with those on other conceptual and perceptual tasks. This is a relatively new method and there appears to be some perceptual and conceptual consistency between the different tasks.

Freedman (1962, p. 632) mentions seven methods used in validating the Rorschach:

1. Known groups are compared.

2. Rorschach diagnoses are compared with diagnoses by psychotherapists and clinical interviews.

3. Rorschach findings are compared with consistent observations of behavior over an adequate period of time.

4. Rorschach interpretations are matched with clinical case reports.

5. Rorschach protocols obtained before and after therapy are compared, with reference to changes in behavior.

6. Single Rorschach variables, or combinations of a few, are related to observed aspects of behavior.

7. Experimental validation is used: (a) influencing the subjects, (b) varying the stimuli, (c) measuring physiological reactions.

Special attention should be given to the method of experimental validation. The subjects may be influenced in a variety of ways (hypnosis, drugs, surgery), with Rorschach tests administered before and afterward; their responses may then be compared to see if the treatment has produced any differential results. Another method is to vary the stimulus dimension of the card. Experiments along these lines have seriously questioned the value of the color responses. Finally, the relationships between autonomic physiological activity and Rorschach responses have been studied in an attempt to answer such questions as "What effects does stress have on Rorschach responses?" The data reveal some correspondence between the responses and the autonomic activity, thus supporting the contention that the Rorschach responses largely reflect unconscious or involuntary motives.

The Thematic Apperception Test (TAT), originated by Morgan and Murray (1935) at Harvard, was developed under the directions of Murray (1943, 1953). The test itself is more structured than the Rorschach in that it contains 30 pictures rather than inkblots. However, these pictures are sufficiently ambiguous to permit a great variety of different possible responses. The subject is told that the TAT is a test of imagination and he is instructed to make up stories about the pictures including the past, present, and future. The data are usually interpreted in two categories: (1) environmental forces, and (2) personal or internal forces. The methods of establishing reliability and validity are comparable to those used with the Rorschach.

Besides the greater degree of structure, the TAT differs from the Rorschach in one other major way. The Rorschach is designed to determine the organization or structure of the personality, whereas the TAT is designed to evaluate the content of the personality (needs, conflicts, drives, fantasies, and the like). However, this is not a rigid dichotomy and often both tests are used to evaluate the above factors.

One of the most interesting applications of the TAT—and an unusually direct utilization of a projective test in a strictly motivational problem—has been recently described by McClelland (1965). A total of 140 management personnel or teachers in the United States, Mexico, and Japan were put through a two-week course designed to increase their achievement motivation. Some dramatic results are cited by McClelland. Even the "failures" are held to be enlightening; for example, one man decided very early in the course that he was fitted neither for the course nor for his management position, in which he had been inadequate. Accordingly, he quit both the course and his position to become a chicken farmer, a decision respected by McClelland "as a good example of honest self-evaluation" (p. 327).

ATTITUDE TESTING

Several different techniques, are used to measure attitudes and interests (for example, opinion polls, attitude scales, market research, and vocational-interest tests). Measurement of interest is important since interests determine much motivated human behavior, such as the selection of jobs, schools, political candidates, and marriage partners. Two tests, the Strong Vocational Interest Blank and the Kuder Preference Record, will be reviewed as representative of this group of tests.

The Strong test was developed by obtaining from successful people employed in different occupations (criterion groups) their specific interests, in terms of their ratings of various activities and their other preferences, and then compiling these interests or items into a test. In taking this test, the subject states his degree of preference for various items as either *like, indifferent,* or *dislike.* The subject's responses are then compared to the responses of each of the criterion groups and the results are presented in profile form. It should be noted that the test measures interest and *not* ability, so that the results refer only to what the person *says* he likes to do and not necessarily to what he is best qualified to do. If the person is qualified, which can be determined on the basis of aptitude tests, the results of the interest tests may be valuable in suggesting occupations, since it has been found that people successful in a particular occupation have a commonality of preferences which distinguishes them from other occupation groups.

The Kuder test has three types of preference inventories: Vocational, Occupational, and Personal. The Vocational form provides interest scores divided into 10 general areas (such as outdoor, artistic, musical, clerical) while the Occupational form is scored for a specific occupation, such as physician, minister, architect. Of special interest is the Personal inventory, which is designed to assay five different preferences which are characteristic of different groups of jobs: (1) direction of others (lawyers, policemen), (2) conceptualization (professors, authors), (3) unchanging situations (toolmakers, high-school teachers), (4) activity in a group (insurance salesmen), and (5) avoiding conflict (professors, physicians). The chief difference between the Kuder and the Strong tests is that the former was largely designed to show interest in broad vocational areas, whereas the latter considers interests characteristic of specific occupations.

SITUATIONAL TESTS

Situational tests are those which place the individual in a simulated life situation where his behavior is then observed and evaluated. The main advantage of such a procedure is independence of the assumption of a high correlation between verbalizations and behavior which marks the tests heretofore described. The observed behavior of the individual in a given situation is evaluated rather than the behavior which a person states that he might perform under certain conditions. That is, on the earlier-mentioned tests the person's answers reflect what he predicts he would do under certain conditions, while in situational tests the person actually does perform the task.

Probably the most cited of the behavior tests is a project initiated during World War II by the Office of Strategic Services (OSS) in an attempt to evaluate and select personnel for military intelligence. Ten variables were considered essential in such an evaluation of the candidates: motivation, intelligence, initiative, emotional stability, leadership, social relations, security, propaganda skills, observation ability, and physical ability. In an attempt to assess these characteristics, a series of simulated conditions were devised (such as crossing a brook, a stress interview, improvisations, and construction). The construction test is an excellent sample of a typical stress situational test. On the surface, the test appeared to be a test of ability to direct two fellow soldiers in building a simple wooden frame. Unknown to the candidate, the two "helpers" were actually members of the testing staff; one was passive and sluggish while the other was aggressive and critical. The candidate was then observed as to how he reacted to the situation in terms of frustration tolerance, emotional stability, and leadership.

The results of this battery of tests were evaluated by four different groups: (1) overseas staff, (2) theater-command staff, (3) reassignment-area staff, and (4) returnees. In general, the results showed only moderate validity and reliability.

Another type of situational test is psychodrama, in which the individual is required to play an unrehearsed role in a specific situation. The "play" involves a director (therapist), a principal role, and minor actors. The rationale underlying psychodrama is that by acting out or participating in lifelike situations a person gains emotional release and demonstrates the motivation underlying his behavior, providing the therapist with information which may not be readily attainable in any other way. The therapist then uses this information and attempts to direct the client in acting out his troubles in other psychodramas. It should be noted that this test serves the dual functions of ascertaining the subject's underlying motivational structure and being a vehicle for therapy.

SELECTED RESEARCH PROBLEMS

This section is concerned with a review of a small number of research areas which have been experimentally attacked over a relatively extended period of time. Although the examples discussed can by no means be considered as thoroughly resolved issues, they nonetheless do serve to illustrate what can be done, in the way of experimental and theoretical development, on the complex problems of personality and motivation.

LEVEL OF ASPIRATION

The concept of *level of aspiration* was first introduced by Dembo (1931). Formally, it has been defined as: "the level of future performance in a familiar task which an individual, knowing his level of past performance in that task, explicitly undertakes to reach" (Frank, 1935). Informally, "level of aspiration" means the prediction of future goals from knowledge obtained through attempting to reach a similar goal in the past. It refers to a person's desires or expectations concerning his behavior. In general, a person's level of aspiration is a compromise between the desire to better himself (or to do better on the next trial, or to beat the other person) and an estimation of his own capabilities based on past experiences. More specifically, a person's level of aspiration may be affected by any number of factors, such as the importance of the goal he is trying to achieve, the calibre of the people competing against him, his past history of success and failure, and so on.

The experimental paradigm used to investigate level of aspiration is straightforward, and requires the barest minimum of equipment. Some type of task is employed (perhaps an ordinary dartboard) that enables the subject to obtain knowledge of his results. On the basis of his results he tells the experimenter what he expects to get on the next trial. This estimate is called the subject's level of aspiration. After performing the second trial, he reevaluates his goals, verbalizes his revised level of aspiration, and so on. Diagrammatically, this sequence is shown in Figure 7.

Four main points are distinguished in a typical sequence of events in a level-of-aspiration situation: last performance, setting the level of aspiration for the next performance, new performance, and the psychological reaction to the new performance. The difference between the last performance and the level of the new goal is called the *goal discrepancy;* the difference between the aspired goal and the achieved level of the new performance is called *attainment discrepancy.*

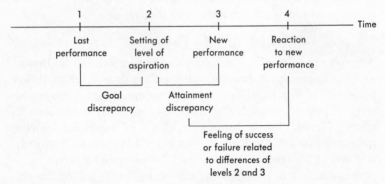

FIGURE 7. TYPICAL TIME SEQUENCE IN LEVEL-OF-ASPIRATION STUDIES. (Reprinted from Kurt Lewin, Tamara Dembo, Leon Festinger, and Pauline Snedden Sears, "Level of Aspiration," in *Personality and the Behavior Disorders,* edited by J. McV. Hunt. Copyright 1944 The Ronald Press Company, New York.)

The goal discrepancy is positive if the level of aspiration is higher than the previous goal attainment and negative if it is lower. The attainment discrepancy is positive if the goal achieved is higher than the level of aspiration and negative if the achieved goal is lower. Consider, for example, the task of throwing darts; assume that the first score is 6. If the subject states his level of aspiration to be 7 on the next trial he is said to have a positive goal discrepancy; if he sets his level at 5 he has a negative goal discrepancy. Then, if on the succeeding trial his score is 9, the resulting positive attainment discrepancy interacts with the goal discrepancy to determine the next level of aspiration.

PERSONALITY FACTORS

Gardner (1940) attempted to obtain some general picture of what personality factors influence a person's level of aspiration. He divided his subjects into two groups; one group contained those with the highest positive total goal-discrepancy scores, the other those with the highest negative scores. Gardner then analyzed the subjects in each category in respect to possible differentiating characteristics. He found that subjects in the high positive group ranked highest in a desire for intellectual achievement and dissatisfaction with their present status. The high negative group ranked lowest on realistic outlook, motivation, and sense of security, and highest on fear of failure.

Pauline Sears (1941) performed a similar experiment, including a third group with moderate or low positive scores. In general, these results substantiated Gardner's findings for the two similar groups. In addition, Sears demonstrated that a *low* positive group was characterized by high self-confidence, was realistic in outlook, and tended to experience a relatively high degree of success in whatever was attempted.

SUCCESS AND FAILURE

Two types of studies relate level of aspiration to success and failure. The first type is devoted to the effects of success and failure within the experimental session. Steisel and Cohen (1951) and Ausubel and Schiff (1955) have found that intrasession failure to achieve a stated expectation significantly decreases subsequent levels of aspiration. Other studies have substantiated this finding and it may be generally concluded that the stronger the degree of success within an experimental session the higher will be the subject's level of aspiration, whereas the greater the failure the lower will be the subject's level of aspiration.

A second aspect of the success-failure dimension is the extent to which a person comes into the experimental situation with a past history of habitual success or failure. Jucknat (1937) investigated this problem by dividing 500 school children into three groups (good, medium, and poor) according to their performance on school assignments. Mazes arranged in ascending order of difficulty and rated from 1 to 10 were presented to these students and they were asked to pick one which they believed they could master. The good students set their initial aspiration level between 7 and 10, while the medium students' level was in the middle range between 5 and 6. However, the poor students set their initial level either extremely high (7–10) or extremely low (1–4). The expected results were obtained with the good and average students, but poor students' scores were unpredictable, indicating the presence of some influence other than past performance on school work.

It seems quite reasonable that the performance of the poor students in the Jucknat study may be accounted for on the basis of an unrealistic attitude. Data reported by Festinger (1942) support this hypothesis. They indicate that the greatest variability in level of aspiration occurs for subjects who have an unrealistic attitude.

DIFFERENTIAL RESPONSE TO TASK

An analytic investigation by Gould (1939) of the responses to the question, "What will you do next time?" also indirectly supports the hypothesis that variations in the subject's response to the key question play a significant role in level-of-aspiration experiments. Gould was able to distinguish three different groups on the basis of how they responded to the question: (1) those whose stated level of aspiration approximated what they really expected to achieve, (2) those who set their level artificially high and did not really expect to achieve it, and (3) those whose level represented goals which they tried to exceed. Thus, the possibility exists that the extremely high aspiration levels for some of the poor students in the Jucknat study resulted from the subject's responding to the question in the manner of category (2).

Few studies, if any, have been designed to investigate the important relationship between the quality of students and the way they tend to interpret level-of-aspiration questions. However, Frank (1936) found that the questions, "What do you think you will do?" and "What do you intend to do?", which are often assumed to be equivalent, produced differences in performance;

the former produced a greater likelihood of the subject's performance approximating the stated level. Studies of this nature are important since it is typically assumed that the instructions are unambiguously interpreted and that similar questions produce the same types of interpretations. However, a given stated level of aspiration does not necessarily represent the same thing for different subjects. This probable variation is a confounding factor not controlled in most studies and presents definite problems when one attempts to generalize from one study to another. That is, contradictory evidence could be an artifact resulting from different interpretations of the instructions—one experiment might be overloaded with subjects who interpreted the question in one manner, and the other might contain a high incidence of subjects who interpreted it in another manner. Thus, the unitary motivation which most level-of-aspiration studies are assumed to be measuring may be in reality different types of motivation stemming from different responses to the instructions.

SOCIAL FACTORS

Level of aspiration may be influenced profoundly by certain social factors. Typically, the lower the level of discrepancy scores, the higher the subject's socioeconomic standing. The discrepancy scores are considered to be an indication of stress (Gould, 1941). Members of the lower socioeconomic classes are assumed to be more susceptible to stress.

Pertinent evidence is provided by studies in which different groups of subjects compete against a reference group which may be higher, equal, or lower in respect to some ability or status. The classical study in this area was done by Chapman and Volkman (1939). Four groups of students were asked to estimate their level of performance on a multiple-choice examination of literary ability. Before taking the test each group was informed of the highest possible score and also the score obtained by chance. Then each experimental group was told the scores which another group had supposedly achieved (literary critics, students, WPA workers). One control group received no reference scores. Thus the only difference between experimental groups was the comparison group paired with it; the comparison group scores were all the same. The subjects were then asked to state their level of aspiration. The results showed the groups which had the literary critics as their comparison group had the highest scores, followed by those that had the student comparison group and the WPA reference group. Thus, it may be concluded that internal variables are not alone in influencing level of aspiration but that external factors may also exert considerable influence. That is, the greater the status of the comparison or reference group the higher the induced level of aspiration. These results were verified by Gould (1941) and by Festinger (1942).

The implications of level-of-aspiration studies are readily seen in relation to developmental psychology. Most children tend to expect they will do better on each trial when learning a new task. Since it has been shown that success tends to raise the level of aspiration and failure to lower it, the task should be so constructed that each time the child obtains success the next trial is a little more difficult. In this way, the child's level of motivation can be maintained over repeated trials, and the child does not become bored because the task is too easy or discouraged because the task is too difficult. The task must be constructed so that it is within the child's mental and physiological limits. In the words of McCandless (1961, p. 413), "Keep each child reaching but see to it that he has some hope of grasping what he reaches for."

One additional point should be made. McCandless (1961) also points out that there seems to be little predictive ability from one type of level-of-aspiration study to another. This finding is really not surprising, he adds, since we have previously seen the vast importance of past behavior and its effect on level of aspiration. Thus a person's ability in one type of situation is liable to be much different from that in another type, with corresponding differences in his level of aspiration.

FRUSTRATION AND AGGRESSION

Most authorities agree that aggression in one form or another is an important consequence of frustration. "Frustration" is used here to refer to the blocking of goal-directed behavior. A large number of studies have investigated this motivationally important variable. Our treatment of the role of aggression follows that of Berkowitz in his recent book, *Aggression, a Social Psychological Analysis* (1962).

DEGREE OF FRUSTRATION

McClelland and Apicella (1945) subjected persons to different degrees of insulting comments while they were performing a card-sorting task in which failure was produced on certain trials. They found a positive relation between the degree of insult and aggressive reaction of the subjects as measured by their verbal responses. A classic study by Hovland and Sears (1940) further suggests that the greater the interference with ongoing activity the greater the degree of resultant frustration. They assumed that in the South the degree of economic failure (lowness of cotton prices) represented the strength of interference to security. They used the number of Negro lynchings as a measure of the aggression. When curves were plotted for cotton prices during 1882–1930 and for the number of lynchings during the same period, it became evident that as cotton prices fell, lynchings increased. It should be understood that the trends of these two sets of events do not necessarily present a cause-and-effect relationship. Nevertheless, the correlation clearly suggests that the greater the threat to security (blocking of a goal) the stronger the aggressive response.

Several studies have been concerned with the effects on aggression of the number of previous frustrating or interfering events. It was originally hypothesized by Dollard and his colleagues (1939) that aggression increased with repeated frustrations. However, more recent evidence has shown this view to be an oversimplification. For example, Berkowitz (1962) mentions that the aggressive response may be altered by the occurrence of other responses, such as anticipation of the frustrating event. Through anticipation individuals can learn other actions or undertake other goals which either alleviate or decrease the aggressive response. Thus, the number of alternatives perceived by or available to the subject is an important variable in determining the degree of aggression. More generally, in any frustrating situation the kind and number of response alternatives available to an organism are most important determinants of resulting behavior. Several studies adequately illustrate this point. Otis and McCandless (1955) found, with children, that the more frequent the frustration the greater the aggression, while McClelland and Apicella (1945), using a similar task, failed to find such a relationship. The disparity between these two sets of data can be explained by focusing attention on the degree to which alternative responses were present. The children in the former study were younger and may not have yet learned a sufficient number of appropriate nonaggressive responses.

SOCIAL AND VERBAL FACTORS

Other deterrents of aggressive behavior involve personal interactions. A powerful deterrent for "undesirable" behavior is verbal chastisement. Using this form of punishment, Chasdi and Lawrence (1955) reproached an experimental group of children for aggressive behavior while children in the control group were not reproached. The data revealed a relative decrease in the frequency of aggressive behavior for the experimental group. Apparently, aggression had been inhibited to avoid anticipated verbal punishment.

Not only does verbal punishment itself inhibit behavior but the source of verbal punishment, which is usually associated with some type of status, also is important. Cohen (1955) found that college girls stated that they would exhibit less overt aggression toward a high-authority figure (such as a professor) than to a person with less status. Similar reports with children have been reported by Graham and colleagues (1951). Thibaut and Riecken (1955) subjected Air Force reservists to hostility-arousing orders from officers believed to have different ranks. An analysis of the comments given in a subsequent interview revealed an inverse correlation between aggression and rank. The differences do not mean that there was an absence of aggression directed toward the "higher" officers, but merely that it was not overtly expressed. To paraphrase Berkowitz (1962) : verbal chastisement produces hostility; but other situational factors, such as the presence of high-status people, may evoke tendencies incompatible with aggression and if strong enough these incompatible responses can inhibit the hostile behavior.

Praise can promote, encourage, and reinforce aggressiveness. This is most evident in a social setting where certain types of mores are inculcated and a particular kind of behavior is expected. Pelz (1958) has suggested that when a group supports a given aggressive act, inhibition previously established which prevented such an act can be readily shed. Stotland (1959) found that people working with each other had stronger overt responses than those working alone. Apparently the chance to talk over problems increased their confidence in their opinions and actions, producing an increment in hostile behavior. The facilitative effect of social permissiveness was demonstrated also by White and Lippitt (1960). Three types of leadership ("authoritarian," "laissez-faire," and "democratic") were evaluated in respect to the behavior of boys. Boys under an authoritarian leader often became submissive to the leaders with little display of aggression. These same boys, when placed in the more permissive laissez-faire or democratic environments, frequently displayed a marked increase in hostile behavior. Undoubtedly, much of the behavior was the result of the contrast between the two situations. The important aspect is that the later situation was structured so as to reinforce or even encourage such a display.

The manifestation of hostility or aggression is not in itself "good" or "bad" from a social point of view. Whether or not social expression of hostility is desirable depends largely upon the prevailing set of social values. Consideration should also be given to whether or not expressions of hostility affect personality development. Not only do overt verbal punishment and praise channel aggression, but also more subtle forms of punishment and praise have equally powerful effects. The most obvious of these are religious beliefs, such as those held by the Quakers that aggression of any type is morally wrong.

Another influence is the way in which an individual judges the aggression-arousing situation. Inhibition of hostile reactions may occur where individuals perceive the frustration as justified and frequently for such a situation any hostility on their part may be regarded as unreasonable. It has been demonstrated that overt aggression is weaker if the subjects feel that the instigator cannot help himself (E. E. Jones, and colleagues, 1959). In this study two groups of students were exposed to derogatory remarks by persons believed to be either emotionally maladjusted or well adjusted. Hostile responses were found to be less frequently directed to the "maladjusted" person than to the "normal" person, presumably because the subjects felt that the former was relatively helpless. Moreover, if a person feels that aggression is morally wrong he often experiences anxiety as a result of his own aggressive tendencies. That is, the presence of aggression produces a certain degree of anxiety which may, depending upon the strength of the anxiety, inhibit or prevent overt expression of aggressive feelings. Clark (1955), using the TAT, recorded sexual and aggressive responses of a group of college men who had been shown pictures of nude women and a group which were not shown the pictures. Surprisingly, the latter group had *more* sexual and aggressive responses than did the former. Clark explains these results by hypothesizing that anxiety occurred in the sexually aroused subjects which inhibited their normal sexual responses to the TAT cards. He later demonstrated that this anxiety would be reduced in a permissive situation (say, a beer party) and once this anxiety was reduced a significant increase in the number of sexual themes occurred. Thus, when the situation is such that social disapproval is removed, the anxiety associated with the anticipated disapproval dissipates and the normal response tendencies are reinstated.

DISPLACEMENT OF AGGRESSION

In general, aggression may be said to be manifested either directly or indirectly. Aggression directed against the instigator is fairly common and does not need to be discussed. However, indirect aggression against objects and people not principally involved in producing the original aggression is not so self-evident. One form of indirect aggression is self-aggression. This seems to occur when all other avenues for aggressive responses are blocked and the subject turns his aggressive tendencies inward toward himself. The typical and most extreme example of this type of indirect aggression is suicide. Other less extreme forms can be seen in various types of guilt reactions.

Another form of indirect aggression is displacement, where the aggression is directed to another object. Several studies dealing with this and related problems have found that when direct expression of aggression is blocked, there is an increase in the amount of indirect aggression (Bandura and Walters, 1959; Thibaut and Coules, 1952).

The most cited studies in the area of indirect aggression are those concerning scapegoating. Scapegoating is a form of displacement in which the aggression is directed toward an innocent bystander. Three important aspects define scapegoating: frustration results in aggressive behavior, attempts to aggress against the source of the frustration are thwarted, and indirect aggression is then displaced upon some other person in a nonretaliatory position. A number of experiments illustrate this point. The previously described classic Hovland and Sears (1940) study is a good example of scapegoating. Bettelheim and Janowitz (1950) found that hostility toward Jews and Negroes was highly correlated with social position of the subjects, with hostility decreasing as the social status increased. This point is supported in a study by Pettigrew and Cramer (1959). Their results indicated that the less prosperous Southern communities vote for racist political figures more often than do the more prosperous areas. Cowen, Londes, and Schaet (1959) found that college students became more unfriendly to Negroes following frustration. However, other studies (Stagner and Congdon, 1955; White and Lippitt, 1960) have failed to produce differences in the expected direction, thus casting some doubt upon the generality of the scapegoat concept.

This lack of consistent results may stem, at least in part, from the use of different types of personalities or from other individual differences which produce different reactions to frustrations, and, consequently produce different patterns of behavior. It is also possible that particular objects in the environment are more likely candidates for displaced aggression and that their availability may influence the degree of displacement manifested in a particular experiment. Allport (1954, pp. 350–351) has listed some important qualifications of the scapegoat theory: (1) aggression is not always the dominant response to frustration, (2) aggression is not always displaced onto some innocent victim, and (3) the safest available object is not always the recipient of the displaced aggression. In any case it should be quite apparent that this important research problem was originally vastly over-simplified and is in need of more definitive experimental investigation.

ANXIETY

The concept of "anxiety" has received a great variety of theoretical treatments. The one with which we shall deal was originated by Janet Taylor in an attempt to investigate certain implications of research finding between learning, drive, and performance; Taylor's theory was chosen primarily because of the vast amount of experimental work it has generated. She (1956) views anxiety as a motivator or drive in which increments and decrements are assumed to increase or decrease performance. In developing a test to measure anxiety, she first asked some clinical psychologists to select 50 test items from the MMPI which they felt would differentiate between high and low anxiety. She then combined these with 175 other buffer items into a scale called the Manifest Anxiety Scale (MAS). Then on the basis of scores from the MAS she began investigating different aspects of anxiety.

Before reviewing this literature, we want to emphasize two points which Taylor made in her (1956) review article. First, there was no attempt to claim that the differences between high and low MAS scores are attributable only to "drive." She readily admits that other contributory factors may be present, but for her purpose of relating drive to performance she was not interested in these. Second, originally, no attempt was made to validate the test against clinical judgments, nor was it designed to serve as a diagnostic tool.

THEORETICAL ORIENTATION

A brief review of the Hullian theoretical position from which Taylor and the Iowa group worked should be given. In its simplest aspect, the theory states that performance is a multiplicative function of a learned habit and drive level. When a single habit is present, the greater the drive (anxiety in this case) the greater the performance. However, the human organism possesses a large number of habits arranged hierarchically with respect to their probability of occurrence, and in the typical task only one of these is correct. Therefore, in a given situation several different responses may be competing against each other, so that if an incorrect one is stronger a high level of drive produces inferior rather than superior performance. Stated in another way, "as the strengths of the correct tendencies increase relative to the incorrect, high-drive groups should become less inferior and eventually superior in performance to the low-drive groups." (Taylor, 1956, p. 305) Taylor further states that in order to relate the results of an experiment to the Hullian theory one must know the competing response tendencies independently of the effects of drive.

TASK COMPLEXITY

In classical conditioning, only one response is typically measured. It therefore provides an appropriate situation in which to test the effects of drive on performance. Several studies (Spence and Farber, 1953; Spence, Farber, and Taylor, 1954; Spence and Taylor, 1953; Taylor, 1951) have found that subjects with high MAS scores perform at a higher level than subjects with low MAS scores. Most of these experiments used only extreme scores. When middle-range scores are included, the results frequently do not demonstrate the same difference. For example, Bitterman and Holtzman (1952) divided a group of college students into two groups on the basis of MAS scores—the upper 50 per cent and the lower 50 per cent. No statistically significant findings were present although there was a slight trend in the expected direction. Furthermore, Taylor states that "middle-anxiety subjects tend to show a performance level closer to the low-scoring than high-scoring groups."

Maze learning with human subjects provides an excellent task for the study of drive and how it affects performance when several habits are simultaneously acquired. Taylor and Spence (1952), using a verbal maze where the stimuli are verbally presented and the subject must learn a particular sequence, and Farber and Spence (1953), using a stylus maze where a blindfolded subject must follow a path with a stylus through a series of blind alleys in order to reach a goal box, provide examples of the effects of anxiety on complex performance. In these studies it was found that the more anxious subjects made more errors (entered more "blind" alleys) and took more trials to learn the maze than low-anxiety subjects. The latter study also found that there was a tendency for anxious subjects to make more errors as the difficulty of the task increased.

I. G. Sarason (1960), in a more recent review article on anxiety, found that most of the studies dealing with the problem of task complexity demonstrated that as task complexity increases, high-anxiety subjects progressively perform at a lower level. This finding is consistent with the Yerkes-Dodson (1908) Law—the more complex the task the lower the optimal drive level; the simpler the task the higher the optimal drive level. However, Sarason also points out that several other studies have failed to show this relationship, and he indicates that the critical variable in studies varying the degree of task complexity may be the degree of stress involved. That is, it is possible that the complexity of the task affects anxiety indirectly by increasing stress, and in tasks where the stress factor is minimized the above relationship does not obtain. It is apparent that further research is needed to differentiate between the degree of difficulty and degree of stress involved in complex tasks before any definitive statement can be made concerning the relationship between task complexity and performance as related to the MAS.

SITUATIONAL VERSUS CHRONIC ANXIETY

The level of anxiety may be affected by situational factors. This fact leads to an interesting set of questions such as: "Do the MAS scores reflect different levels of chronic anxiety?" or "Do they reflect the degree of emotionality in response to an anxiety-evoking situation?" It is extremely difficult to isolate chronic anxiety which occurs in most situations from a predisposition to be anxious in a given situation. The reason for this difficulty is that the method of measuring anxiety may itself be anxiety-producing; most of the test scores are obtained from college students and there is ample evidence that any type of test is likely to produce anxiety. Consequently, most studies have concentrated on determining whether or not different situational variables affect anxiety level.

An experiment by Spence, Farber, and Taylor (1954) illustrates the types of procedure used to investigate this effect of situational variables. Three groups of subjects were classically conditioned under one of the following conditions: (1) occasional electrical shock, (2) threat of electrical shock, and (3) neutral. The results indicated superior conditioning for the first two conditions. When the data were further analyzed on the basis of high and low MAS scores, the high-anxiety subjects who were shocked or threatened with shock performed at a much higher level than the low-anxiety subjects who received the same experimental treatments. This study strongly suggests that negative stimulation (here shock) differentially affects anxiety and that high MAS scores indicate a strong disposition to be anxiety-prone.

In her (1956) review article, Taylor has summarized the research on this problem. When noxious stimulation is used, the performance of subjects usually is affected in the same direction as with high MAS scores, and the extent of the difference between anxious and nonanxious subjects either remains constant or increases in magnitude. Yet, when psychological stress is induced by verbal statements such as "Your score is low" or "This is an extremely important but difficult task," there seems to be little agreement between studies. However, four years later the literature on this problem was greater, and the earlier lack of agreement disappeared with the advance of more data. This is indicated by I. G. Sarason's (1960, p. 411) conclusion that "The performance of high anxious subjects is detrimentally affected by verbally administered highly motivating communications."

EXPERIMENTAL MODIFICATION OF BEHAVIOR

Modification of behavior, and thereby of "personality," is the ultimate objective of many who are interested in the more practical and applied areas of psychology. The remainder of this chapter is devoted to a discussion of two of the more active types of this kind of endeavor. The discussions concern certain aspects of the major problems of neurosis and psychosis, each of which may be recognized as having central motivational components. The approach is essentially historical, with certain of the currently more significant movements (such as, behavior therapy) treated at the end of the section.

EXPERIMENTAL NEUROSIS

The term *experimental neurosis* generally refers to an abnormal emotional condition or reaction which is both generalized and persistent. Much work has been done with different species of animals in which experimental manipulation of certain variables produces extensive emotional impairment. The results of these studies provide merely a cue and should be generalized to the human level only with extreme caution. However, studies of this nature are valuable in throwing light on possible causes of the complex nature of human personality disorders and are in themselves interesting demonstrations of the manipulation of motivating variables.

RESEARCH BY PAVLOV

Pavlov (1906; 1927 tr.) is credited with identifying the concept of experimental neurosis and his experiments with dogs are considered classic examples. In one of these experiments, a discrimination problem, a response to a circle was rewarded but a response to an ellipse was not rewarded. After the dog achieved a satisfactory degree of performance, the ellipse was gradually changed to approximate a circle. Eventually, the dog's discrimination failed to improve and his behavior showed some obvious signs of emotional disturbances such as barking, howling, and tearing at the harness which positioned him in front of the apparatus. Furthermore, subsequent retests on the earlier and easier discriminations showed a lower level of performance than had been previously established.

RESEARCH BY LIDDELL

Liddell pioneered this kind of research in America at Cornell University, where he and his associates worked largely with sheep. The typical procedure used was as follows: An unconditioned stimulus (electrical shock) was applied to the foreleg of the sheep, resulting in a quick muscular flexion. A conditioned stimulus (light) was then paired with the shock. The conditioned stimulus came to elicit the leg flexion. In addition, various physiological measures were recorded, such as respiration and heart rate. These studies showed that, as the experiment continued, the animals resisted entering the laboratory; once inside, they remained calm until the experimenter left the room, signaling the beginning of a particular experimental test session. Immediately the sheep showed fidgety movements of the foreleg. This same behavior was noted in the interval between the stimuli. In addition, "Sheep in which an experimental neurosis has been developed reveal, upon examination, a cardiac disorder which is characterized by a rapid and irregular pulse and by extreme sensitivity of the heart's action to conditioned and other stimulation." (Anderson, Parmenter, and Liddell, 1939, p. 100) Other indices of experimental neurosis were hyperirritability, restlessness, postural changes, elimination, and a tendency to remain isolated from the rest of the animals. In accordance with Pavlov, these investigators subsequently found that the most efficient procedure for inducing abnormal behavior involved a discrimination between positive and negative stimuli.

In another series of experiments by the Cornell group (Liddell, 1951, 1954, 1955; Patton, 1951; Tanner and Inhelder, 1956), offspring of one mother were used in different situations in an attempt to control for possible genetic differences. Two experimental findings are worth special mention. First, kid goats isolated from their mothers in the testing room developed experimental neurosis quicker than did kid goats paired with their mothers during testing. In fact, the impairment was so severe in one of the subjects in the isolated group that it died after refuseing to suck milk from its mother. Second, the experimental (isolated) goats were retested two years later and were found much less resistant to development of neurotic symptoms than the control (social) goats. Evidence of the experimental neurosis could still be found by merely placing the subjects in the restraining harness and presenting the previously used stimuli.

Liddell explains these behavior disorders as the result of stress emanating from the conditioning procedure. This stress causes a state of vigilance or intense expectation which eventually leads to neurotic behavior which is increased by monotony (unvarying repeated pattern of stimulation), isolation, and overstimulation. Lundin (1961, p. 342–343) points out two significant variables in these studies relating the development of neurosis: (1) "a considerable degree of restraint is necessary so that when an animal is placed in an experimental situation any possibilities of escape or avoidance are eliminated, and (2) a situation is presented which the animal cannot master so that achievement of positive, or escape from negative, reinforcement is impossible. By placing an animal in a situation in which he is forced beyond his discriminative capacity, for example, a degree of conflict is induced."

RESEARCH BY MASSERMAN

Another procedure, used by Masserman and his associates, differs from Liddell's and Pavlov's in that it involves instrumental rather than classical conditioning (see Chapter 6). In keeping with Masserman's psychoanalytic bias, his results were cast in a qualitative rather than quantitative form, and he does not have the least hesitancy in anthropomorphically attributing to animals concepts and terms usually reserved for describing and explaining human behavior. Despite these shortcomings, his studies are ingenious and deserve attention.

Masserman's (1943) basic procedure was to place a hungry cat or dog in a small compartment with a food box at one end and train it to lift the top of the box in order to obtain food. On some of the trials an aversive blast of air (physically harmless) was blown across the top of the box onto the subject's head as soon as it began eating. Sometimes the air blast was paired with shock; sometimes it was presented alone. Such a procedure was assumed to induce a conflict between avoiding a fear-producing stimulus (air) and satisfying the subject's hunger. Three different types of reactions occurred as a result of these experimental manipulations. Masserman classified these as (1) regressive and defensive, (2) anxious, and (3) phobic. Regressive responses were those which bore a striking resemblance to behavior displayed by kittens, such as excessive licking and kittenish vocalization; one animal exhibited the rather unusual behavior of sticking its head in the food box whenever the conditioned stimulus was presented but would never eat even though it was deprived of food for days prior to the experimental session. Anxiety reactions were characterized by trembling, hair standing on end, dilated pupils, shallow irregular breathing, and increased blood pressure. The phobic response (a strong or irrational fear of the particular object usually characterized by avoidance of the object) was a total avoidance of the box to the point of starvation.

When Masserman subjected the cats merely to an air blast without training them to lift the food-box top, few emotional reactions developed. Apparently one of the critical variables is the association of the noxious stimulus with goal-oriented behavior such as feeding. Masserman interpreted these emotional disturbances as resulting from motivational conflicts instigated by his experimental manipulation. He then investigated different possible "therapeutic" methods designed to reduce the conflict and resulting abnormal behavior. Periods of rest and placing the experimental subjects with a naive subject did not alleviate the symptoms. However, Masserman and Yum (1946) did find that if alcohol was given before the introduction of the noxious stimulus, abnormal behavior failed to develop. Also, Wikler and Masserman (1943) found that injections of morphine dissipated the abnormal behavior. In general, it may be said that some type of sedative drug was the most effective therapeutic agent for relieving the neurotic behavior.

LEARNING AND THERAPY

From the first realization that mental illness could be alleviated, various therapeutic methods have been employed, the most publicized being psychoanalysis. Recently, however, psychologists have shown rising interest in a more empirically based understanding of the principles involved in therapy and behavior modification. Essentially, this position maintains that the therapist attempts to alleviate behavior disorders by systematic utilization of learning principles. Bandura (1961, p. 143) points out that the fundamental assumption of psychotherapy is "that human behavior is modifiable through psychological procedures." He further states that a more meaningful question is, "Can human behavior be modified through psychological means and if so what are the learning mechanisms that mediate behavior changes?" The present section is addressed to this question.

Miller and Dollard (1941) and Dollard and Miller (1950) have repeatedly emphasized the role that extinction procedures play in abolishing undesirable behavior. Since extinction is defined as responding in the absence of reinforcement, the critical factor in applying this technique is for the therapist to locate the reinforcing events. In many cases, the reinforcement seems to be some type of fear-reduction or anxiety-reduction associated with a given act. For example, a situation that the patient experiences or anticipates arouses fear or anxiety; the patient reduces this by the undesirable behavior; and the reduction reinforces the undesirable behavior. The task of the therapist then is to structure the situation in such a manner as to eliminate the occurrence of the original anxiety whose subsequent reduction is reinforcing. This may be achieved through the therapist's permissiveness. Many therapists seldom, if ever, criticize the patient, irrespective of what the patient says or does, and in this manner gradually weaken the guilt or anxiety associated with behavior. Eventually, the occurrence of anxiety is eliminated entirely.

Elimination of anxiety does not need to be confined solely to the clinical setting, as was aptly demonstrated by Herzberg (1941) in his treatments of a patient who for some reason became very anxious whenever she walked in the street by herself. Herzberg suggested, on the basis of other information he obtained, that the patient should walk alone in the park—a much less anxiety-producing situation. After the anxiety reaction had become extinguished in this context, she was instructed to walk on infrequently traveled streets until her anxiety to this kind of situation was extinguished. Finally, after several such graduated steps, she was able to leave the house and walk wherever she desired without any hesitation or avoidance behavior.

Extinction is not always an economically feasible or practical procedure. Some experimental findings indicate that extinction is more readily achieved with massed rather than with spaced sessions. In traditional therapy, the patient and therapist meet at most five or six times a week (spaced sessions), and the interval between sessions provides ample opportunity for events occurring in the patient's everyday environment to reinstate the anxiety. Intensive treatment (massed sessions) is not a frequent practice because of the burden it puts on the patient's finances and on the therapist's time. Even with massed extinction, Williams (1955) demonstrated the influence of environmental factors in reinstating the response. After a child's temper tantrums about going to bed at night had been extinguished through the parents' ignoring them, the child's aunt paid attention to the tantrums and greatly increased their frequency. However, subsequent extinction sessions again decreased the rate.

COUNTERCONDITIONING

Counterconditioning, which involves conditioning two *incompatible* responses to the same stimulus, is another method commonly employed to eliminate undesirable behavior. Frequently, this involves conditioning an incompatible reaction to a stimulus cue which has in the past elicited anxiety or fear reactions. The classic study in this area was reported by M. C. Jones (1924). Her patient was a boy who had a generalized fear and consequent avoidance of furry objects—animals, cotton, hair, and the like. Jones was able to remove these symptoms by establishing a positive reaction of eating in the presence of a rabbit. At first the boy ate while the rabbit was some distance away, and on subsequent trials the rabbit was moved closer to the boy until finally the boy ate with the rabbit sitting on his lap.

Counterconditioning has been successfully applied in other types of clinical settings. For example, Mowrer and Mowrer (1938) devised a technique based on the counterconditioning paradigm to eliminate bed wetting (enuresis) in children. The bed pad usually placed under enuretic children to protect the mattress was wired so that as soon as micturition occurred a loud buzzer sounded and awoke the child. Prior to this process, bladder tension was a natural cue for immediately urinating; but through association with the buzzer the tension became a cue for waking up and controlling urination—going to the toilet. Eventually, the buzzer was eliminated and the bladder tension became the only conditioned stimulus for control; the child was then able to sleep normally for long uninterrupted periods. Mowrer and Mowrer, in their original study, reported total success with 30 children. Davidson and Douglass (1950) have supported their results in a study in which 15 out of 20 chronically enuretic children were cured by this method and the other 5 greatly improved.

Alcoholism and drug addiction have also been treated by applying the counterconditioning technique. However, the problem here is a slightly different one. In most of the other applications the behavior to be inhibited was associated with the occurrence of some negative emotional state (such as fear) and was abolished by substituting some positive act—one which produced pleasure or lack of fear. In alcoholism and drug addiction, however, the process must be reversed. That is, the act to be inhibited is presumably associated with a pleasurable state for which a negative act or feeling must be substituted. Nauseant drugs are typically employed to achieve this. Bandura (1961, p. 145) reports that "usually 9–10 treatments in which the sight, smell, and taste of alcohol is associated with the onset of nausea is sufficient to produce abstinence. Of 1,000 or more cases on whom adequate follow-up data are reported, approximately 60 per cent of the patients have been totally abstinent following treatment."

Lindesmith (1947), working with morphine addicts, has shown how counterconditioning may occur in a natural environment, and furthermore, how this may be useful in treating drug addiction. Originally, puncturing the skin with a needle is a pain-producing cue; but with continued morphine injections, the hypodermic needle becomes a pleasure-producing cue. Lindesmith demonstrated how this pleasurable aspect may be useful in counteracting withdrawal symptoms commonly occurring in addicts. For example, one of the patients had become so conditioned to the entry of the needle as signaling pleasure that he reacted to injections of a neutral solution (saline) *as if* it were morphine. This conditioned reaction to some degree alleviated the patient's dependency upon morphine. Rubenstein (1931) also has reported successful results using a similar procedure. These studies illustrate the importance of psychological processes accompanying physiological ones and question whether drug addiction is totally a physiological process.

REINFORCEMENT

The methods of extinction and counterconditioning are chiefly employed where the therapist desires to eliminate a segment of behavior. However, they are seldom effective in establishing a new behavior not present in the client's response repertoire; to achieve this, some type of reward is employed. It should be noted that the other methods implicitly assume a reinforcement mechanism. However, it is our purpose here to demonstrate how deliberate manipulation of reward may be used to produce behavior changes in mental patients. In dealing with mildly maladjusted patients, the reward involved in the therapist's comments and attitude is fairly obvious and we will not belabor this aspect. We turn to the treatment of the psychotic individuals who are in little contact with reality and whose prognosis for improvement is generally extremely poor.

Peters and Jenkins (1954) increased the hunger drive in chronic psychotic patients by administering insulin. This routine was continued for three months, during which time the patients were assigned several tasks with fudge as the reward. Gradually the tasks changed from those involving strictly motor skills to those involving verbal-reasoning problems and the reward was shifted from primary reward to social rewards. The subjects showed a significant improvement in the social relationships in the hospital as compared with a control group.

A most intensive series of experiments with psychotic patients was started by Skinner, Solomon, and Lindsley (1954) and more fully implemented by Lindsley (1956). Lindsley's procedure was to place subjects in a soundproofed room equipped with experimental manipulanda, such as a plunger or lever found in a candy machine. The patients were instructed to pull the lever to obtain reward. Using this method with patients who had been institutionalized for a considerable duration, Lindsley made some interesting discoveries. The severity of mental disturbances correlated highly with irregular and low rates of responding. Each patient had his own characteristic pattern of responding, with definite cyclic sequences occurring over periods of days or months. Patients' records were analyzed with respect to their rate and irregularity of response in order to provide an estimate of degree of deterioration. This measure, when compared with the hospital staff's diagnosis of severity of illness, showed a high positive correlation. Mednick and Lindsley (1958) have suggested that the less severe patients (higher and more regular response rate) are more sensitive to social reinforcement and possess the ability to interact successfully with their environment to obtain reward.

The full impact of these findings may be seen as threefold: (1) diagnosis, (2) selection of treatment, and (3) personnel. First, if it can be reliably established that operant-response patterns are valid indicators of the degree of behavior disorder, they can serve as a much-needed clinical test for chronic patients. One merit is that an initial lack of verbal communication or a subsequent breakdown in verbal communication between the patient and the therapist would not be detrimental in this operant-evaluation technique, whereas it would be so in the more classical methods. (2) Moreover, the operant method may have direct implication for the choice of therapy type to be used (extinction, positive reinforcement, or other), for the kind and amount of reinforcement to be used (M & M candies, social approval, or other), as well as for the specific type of behavior to be manipulated or changed. The operant method is thus in direct contrast to traditional clinical tests such as the Rorschach, which supposedly reveal the personality of the patient but have very little direct implication for treatment. (3) Further, and more speculatively, if Mednick and Lindsley are correct in their interpretation, then examining the response records would help in selecting subjects with the best chances of benefiting from therapy. This guidance would be extremely beneficial, considering the lack of adequate numbers of hospital personnel, for it would enable those available to direct their time and effort in the most efficient manner by concentrating therapy on the best prospects. Still further, the kind of work involved can very easily be performed by trained nonprofessional personnel, thus enormously increasing the amount of work that can be accomplished.

The reinforcement paradigm has also been used in counseling situations where the patients are not so badly incapacitated by their problems. Usually these clients have some specific problems relating perhaps to marriage, to education, or to occupation rather than some incapacitating defect. Here the counselor's job is to promote better adjustment within a limited part of their environment.

Although the counselor's goal is usually to change behavior characteristics other than merely verbal behavior, occasionally he is called upon to manipulate verbal behavior by substituting socially appropriate phrases for socially inappropriate ones. Irrespective of what type of behavior is being modified, the major tool the counselor and clinician rely upon is the interview. For these reasons studies concerned with verbal conditioning are pertinent.

Verbal conditioning is just what it says it is—conditioning verbal behavior by reinforcing different portions of the subject's speech. For example, Greenspoon (1954) in a classic study found an increment in plural responses when each response was followed by "mmm-hmm" (positive reinforcement) and a decrease followed by "huh-uh" (negative reinforcement).

Directly applicable to the counseling situation are the following more recent examples: Binder, McConnell, and Sjoholm (1957) found that the frequency of hostile words in sentences was increased by the word "good"; Salzinger and Pisoni (1957a, 1957b) were able to reinforce affective (emotional) responses by a similar technique. Moreover, Hildum and Brown (1956) found "good" to reinforce positive attitudes and Nuthmann (1957) demonstrated that "good" increased "acceptance of self" responses. Other examples may be found in Krasner's (1958) review article.

In all of these studies there are common characteristics: (1) the subjects are not instructed to learn; (2) the stimulus situation is structured so as to require the emission of verbal behavior—the subjects are instructed to behave verbally and/or are placed in a stimulus situation that requires verbal behavior; and (3) the reinforcing stimuli are independent of any particular deprivation state. Some of the stimuli that have been effective as reinforcers are "good," "mmm-hmm," "un-hum," "huh-uh," "right," "yeah," "I see that's correct," and so on.

In summary, it should be noted that these examples involve only a few of the principles of learning that underlie therapy. One other point deserves mentioning. The above analysis of therapy is from a learning bias, and the principles explained are not necessarily deliberately applied by the therapist. Rather, they represent one kind of interpretation of the methods that he does use. In fact, Bandura (1961, p. 154) states, "In reviewing the literature on psychotherapy, it becomes clearly evident that learning theory and general psychology have exerted a remarkably minor influence on the practice of psychotherapy, and, . . . most of the recent serious attempts to apply learning principles to clinical practice have been made by European psychotherapists." He gives two reasons for this lack of integration between the two areas. First, learning principles imply deliberate manipulation of behavior, which the psychoanalysts among others view as antihumanitarian; they believe that the chief method should be such that it enables the patient to understand himself. This objection seems rather strange when one realizes that manipulating behavior is precisely what the psychoanalyst is paid to do. Second, and probably more important, the psychoanalytic background is steeped in the study of unconscious processes, inner conflicts, and the like, and many analysts are reluctant to accept the newer behavioristic principles. They believe that the use of such principles is "symptom treating" and does not get at the deep-seated emotional problems. Yet the data presented here strongly indicate that emotional disorders can be successfully treated without adverse effects by applying learning principles. In fact, the notion of symptom substitution seems to have remarkably little empirical substantiation (see Ullman and Krasner, 1965).

BEHAVIOR THERAPY

The most active current movement, mainly but by no means exclusively involving work by operant conditioners, is a deliberate attempt to "treat the symptoms"—that is, to focus on the behaviors themselves. This approach has several important consequences. First, modern behavior therapy begins its treatment procedure with concepts of learning and develops therapeutic programs with them *before the fact,* whereas earlier learning therapies (such as that of Dollard and Miller, 1950), began with an already existing therapy and tried to explain it in learning terms. Consequently current behavior therapists ask what behaviors need to be increased or decreased, what contingencies are maintaining the behaviors, and what reinforcement may be used to alter the behavior. Another implication of the current movement is that there is no distinction in the process of development of adaptive and maladaptive behaviors, the development of both being explained by learning-theory concepts. The conceptions of underlying illness or intrapsychic conflict are firmly rejected. Another critical difference between current behavior therapists and traditional learning therapists is a strong trend to do research and use its results as well as to use theory.

The contemporary form of behavior modification initiated by Wolpe (1958) has become an important and rapidly growing type of clinical effort. The best sampling of new research and theoretical material was brought together in Krasner and Ullman (1965) and Ullman and Krasner (1965). These workers cite experiments which deal with speech deficiency, stuttering, verbal fluency, and the reinstatement of verbal behavior as well as demonstrations of behavior modification by direct reinforcement or with the aid of hypnosis and modeling procedures. They also include studies of attitude change, group behavior, drugs, physiological correlates of social stimuli, classical conditioning, sensory deprivation, and other problems. Some of the more interesting studies are those which deal with the development of "token economy systems" in which entire wards with large numbers of people are treated according to a reinforcement approach.

Since behavior therapy is marked by a primary emphasis on modification of the subject's behavior as such, there is generally a concomitant and explicit disregard of the manipulation of any presumed internal factors such as motivations and personality variables. The recent and growing success of the behavior therapists, and of those researchers concerned with what is more generally called behavior modification, certainly raises some questions concerning the role of motivational factors. These questions can be resolved, in general, by two major types of considerations.

First, with regard to the use of operant conditioning and reinforcement techniques, we may regard the reinforcement function as manipulating, primarily, motivation rather than learning (see also Chapter 6 for a further discussion). It is to be noted that this conclusion is not one that would normally be drawn from statements of the behavior therapists themselves, because they do not often speak in terms of motivation. But, semantics apart, it should be apparent that what we and others typically consider to be motivation is centrally involved.

Second, the behavior disorders with which the behavior therapists have had their greatest success are those in which specific symptoms tend to be predominant (for example, enuresis, phobia). These conditions obviously lend themselves most readily to behavioral changes. But more generalized or chronic disorders in which specific behaviors are less apparent are also those in which more generalized motivational conditions are more important. The extent to which behavioral therapy, or some related techniques, is successful with this type of disorder remains to be seen.

Suggested Readings

Allport, G. W. 1961. *Pattern and growth in personality*. New York: Holt, Rinehart and Winston.

Bandura, A., and R. H. Walters. 1963. *Social learning and personality development*. New York: Holt, Rinehart and Winston.

Berkowitz, L. 1962. *Aggression, a social psychological analysis*. New York: McGraw-Hill Book Co.

Dollard, J., and N. E. Miller. 1950. *Personality and psychotherapy: An analysis in terms of learning, thinking and culture*. New York: McGraw-Hill Book Co.

Hall, C. S., and G. Lindzey. 1957. *Theories of personality*. New York: John Wiley and Sons.

Lindzey, G., and C. S. Hall, eds. 1965. *Theories of personality: Primary sources and research*. New York: John Wiley and Sons.

Ullman, L. P., and L. Krasner. 1965. *Case studies in behavior modification*. New York: Holt, Rinehart and Winston.

Chapter 5

PHYSIOLOGICAL BASES OF MOTIVATION

For many years behavioral scientists were prone to ignore or overlook the neurophysiological bases of behavioral phenomena. This attitude resulted from the relatively speculative nature of most neurophysiological theory as well as from the avowed intention of many researchers to hold strictly to a behavioral level of investigation and interpretation. The flavor of this attitude is well captured by the popular expression "black box," referring to the nervous system and related afferent-effector systems as a more or less closed affair whose penetration was not to be attempted. Another way of describing this long period in the not-too-remote history of psychology is to term it the era of the "empty organism."

Within the past decade, however, these negative attitudes toward physiological matters on the part of numerous psychologists have been markedly softened if not entirely eliminated. This radical change in attitude has been due in large part to a number of remarkable improvements in methodology in neurophysiology and physiological psychology, producing what the popular press is likely to refer to as "breakthroughs." Certain of these have very obvious implications for an understanding of motivation and are therefore treated in this chapter.

The plan of this chapter is to present, first, a short review of the basic information concerning the mammalian nervous system, as preliminary to the material that follows. Four major sections are then presented. The reticular activating system (RAS),

125

treated in the first of these sections, appears to be directly responsible for the maintenance of general alertness and for mediation of the selective attention that is so important in behavioral processes. The second section deals with what is perhaps the most interesting of the new experimental techniques, intracranial self-stimulation (ICS). In this technique, the organism is allowed to stimulate its own brain with a weak electrical current. The results obtained from this technique demonstrate that certain brain areas, collectively referred to as the limbic system, appear to mediate reinforcing functions, as is outlined below. The chapter concludes with treatments of two of the most fundamental mammalian motivational systems—hunger-thirst and sex. Each of these systems is basically physiological in nature, depending upon hormonal as well as neural factors, but each also has important behavioral (learned) overtones.

SUMMARY OF MAMMALIAN PHYSIOLOGY

NEUROANATOMICAL STRUCTURES

The following thumbnail sketch of anatomical structures and their physiological functions provides a review of the basic material needed for the present chapter. For a more detailed account the reader may consult any standard physiology text.

There are three general aspects to any behavioral act—stimulus, neural transmission, and response. The stimulus impinges upon a receptor organ (eye, ear, or other) and elicits a neural impulse that travels to a part of the spinal cord (which controls many types of reflexive or automatic behavior) or of the brain. This upward movement is accomplished through ascending or sensory pathways which are either specific (terminate in a particular structure) or diffuse (project to a variety of different structures). The impulses associated with these pathways are called afferent or sensory impulses. After the afferent impulse reaches its destination in the nervous system, it activates other nerve fibers, which then transmit downward impulses called effector or motor impulses through the descending or motor tract.

These impulses eventually excite (stimulate) an effector (muscle or gland). It should be noted that in its course of travel the impulse connects with many other nerves. These interconnections permit feedback among different nerves, facilitating some impulses and inhibiting others.

The brain is connected to the spinal cord and is divided into three major parts: hindbrain, midbrain, and forebrain. The *hindbrain* is really an extension of the spinal cord and is composed of the medulla (the vital center, as it is often called), which controls breathing, blood pressure, and heartbeat, and the cerebellum, which controls motor coordination. The *midbrain* is essentially a bridge connecting the hindbrain and the forebrain. It is the *forebrain* with which we are chiefly concerned. It is composed of the thalamus, the hypothalamus, and the cerebral cortex (plus some other lesser structures not essential for the present discussion).

Most of the fibers going to the higher parts of the brain must pass through the thalamus. The thalamus is accordingly considered to be the relay center of the brain. It contains specialized nuclei (clusters of neural fibers) which join the lower centers, including the spinal cord, with the higher centers. The hypothalamic nuclei are divided into two different planes: anterior-posterior and medial-lateral. These are general terms and are used to refer respectively to the front-back dimension and the center-periphery dimension of an organ. Thus, the posterior-lateral nuclei are those at the back and outside edge of the hypothalamus. The major functions of the hypothalamus include regulation of temperature and of water and food intake as well as integration of afferent and efferent impulses. The cerebral cortex is the layer of neural tissue lying closest to the top of the head. It mediates the higher intellectual capacities. In proportion to the rest of the nervous system it is the largest part, for it comprises more than one-half of the total weight of the nervous system, being far more developed in man than in the lower animals. Its superior size and function are to a large degree the features which distinguish man from the lower species. Consequently, it has received a great amount of experimental investigation.

In addition to the above areas and functions, two other rather diffuse subsystems within the nervous system are of special importance—the reticular system and the limbic system. These will be discussed in greater detail under their specific headings later in this chapter.

NEUROPHYSIOLOGICAL METHODS

The first experimental method for studying neurological pathways is to transect a nerve at a chosen point. This produces neural degeneration characterized by identifiable changes in the cellular composition of the nerve. Without the benefit of these distinctive changes, it would often be an insurmountable task to trace the path of a nerve through the complex matrix of its microscopic neural connections. This method is extremely useful in collaborating functional relationships by supplying the necessary anatomical connections. For example, if fibers have been transected in one part of the reticular formation and cells in another part of the nervous system exhibit degeneration, it is fairly certain that the cut nerve connected these two points.

One of the most common methods of determining neural functions is to remove (extirpate), destroy (ablate or lesion), or isolate (transect) some part of the brain and observe the consequences either in behavior or through one of the other methods to be mentioned. The assumption underlying this type of technique is that if a given structure mediates a particular response, the removal of the structure will result in the absence of the response. However, there is the inherent danger that some unintended part will be inadvertently destroyed and that the results may then reflect some other physiological artifact. In order to minimize this possibility, the animals are sacrificed at the end of the experiment and both the location and the extent of the destroyed area are determined histologically. This procedure of histological verification is generally followed in all methods which use any type of electrode implantation, such as are discussed in the following section. The difference between ablation and lesion is really one of degree, with the former generally referring to the destruction of large areas. Recently, the word *lesion* has become associated with the method of destruction by high electrical voltage.

A neural function may also be ascertained by measuring changes in the electrical potential of the cortex by means of the electroencephalograph (EEG). This technique has two aspects—stimulation and recording. The stimulus may be applied either peripherally (as by a blinking light) or centrally (as by implanted electrodes transmitting shock).

In some cases drugs may be used as an alternative to the electrical stimulation. In either case the stimulus produces changes in the electrical potential of the brain, known as "brain waves," which are picked up by electrodes located on either the skull or cortex. The impulses are transmitted to and magnified by an amplifier and recorded by pens on a moving sheet of paper. Essentially brain waves are nothing more than electrocortical rhythms possessing a certain amplitude and frequency. The waves are named for their frequency characteristic. Although there are several different waves, the alpha wave, which occurs at a frequency of 10 to 12 cycles per second (cps), is typically considered as the major EEG index of an awake and relaxed subject. This wave is used as a base from which activation and somnolence are evaluated. That is, when the individual is asleep, the frequency decreases to 4 or 5 cps with a corresponding decrease in amplitude, and when certain parts of the brain's reticular activating system are stimulated, the resulting arousal effect is reflected in the EEG record of a low-amplitude, desynchronized fast wave characteristic of the alert state. On the other hand, when an activating area is ablated, the EEG response returns to a slow wave.

THE RETICULAR ACTIVATING SYSTEM (RAS)

The vast importance which psychologists attribute to the reticular formation and its related properties is captured in a statement by French (1957) : "Investigators have discovered that this bit of nerve tissue, no bigger than your little finger, is a far more important structure than anyone has dreamed. It underlies our awareness of the world, our ability to think, to learn and to act.

Without it an individual is reduced to a helpless, senseless, para-
lyzed blob of protoplasm."

MOTIVATIONAL FUNCTIONS

Motivation as defined in Chapter 1 contains two components: an
associative component (habit) and an activation or energizing
component. It is this latter function which many psychologists
believe is directly a function of the reticular formation. Stimulation of the RAS produces the behavior of an alert, awake, and
highly motivated subject; conversely, when part of the RAS is
removed, the resulting behavior is of a sleepy and lowly motivated subject. Moreover, excitation of the RAS leads to several
other phenomena which are clearly related to motivation: it can
influence the receptivity of the cortex for incoming information,
actually modify the incoming afferent impulses prior to their
arrival at the cortex, activate habits or associations "stored" in
the cortex, inhibit or facilitate learned or reflexive responses, and
determine discrimination and selective attention. In short, it is
the activation component of motivation.

Anatomists have known about the general structural aspects of
the reticular formation for quite some time. However, its functional, physiological properties were largely obscured until Moruzzi and Magoun (1949) discovered that electrical stimulation
of the reticular formation produces cortical activity resembling
the behavioral condition of alert wakefulness. Since that time,
the reticular formation, now commonly known as the reticular
activating system (RAS), has been one of the most popular of all
the psychophysiological bandwagons.

NEUROANATOMICAL RELATIONS

The reticular formation is a diffuse system of neural fibers which
project from the base of the brain to the cerebral cortex. Nerve
fibers from other organs feed into it at different points. Such an
anatomical arrangement is important since it provides a feedback
system whereby the RAS and the specific organs, the muscles, and
the other parts of the brain can reciprocally influence one another. Futhermore, the RAS may be dichotomized both anatom-
ically and functionally into two distinct but related systems—the

brain-stem reticular formation (lower portion) and the *thalamic* reticular formation (upper portion). The specific parts of the brain which are included in each of these two systems are relatively unimportant, for our purposes; but it is important to remember that there are two systems since occasionally differences between them will be mentioned.

Another important distinction must be made between the RAS fibers and the specific sensory pathways projecting to the cortex. The former is a rather diffuse system capable of being activated by any of the sense modalities, but the classical afferent neural paths are stimulus-specific. That is, each modality possesses a specific pathway composed of numerous neurons and nerve fibers which can be triggered only by energy sources relating to that modality. Thus, an auditory stimulus cannot elicit an impulse in the optic nerve, and, likewise, a visual stimulus is unable to produce auditory transmission.

EXPERIMENTAL RESULTS

EXCITATION

As was mentioned earlier, the first study which clearly demonstrated the activating or arousal properties now commonly attributed to the RAS was performed by Moruzzi and Magoun (1949). They directly stimulated a cat by means of electrodes implanted in the lower portion of the reticular formation. They found that the direct electrical stimulation produced a desynchronized brain wave of low intensity, which is characteristic of an awake and motivated subject. Subsequent studies, summarized by Samuels (1959), have shown a positive relationship between intensity of stimulation and level of activation: at low voltages a sleeping animal opens its eyes; at higher voltages animals engage in behavior reflecting fear, agitation, and escape. There does not appear to be a specific area of cortical activation but rather a general response projected over most of the cortex. It is *as if* the RAS "sprayed" the entire cortex, thereby activating the total cortex instead of specific localities. Samuels (1959, p. 5) has stated that at a gross level of analysis "it would seem perfectly appropriate to equate the arousal function of the brain stem reticular formation with a generalized drive state, since this system does possess the anatomical and physiological attributes (i.e., control of the level of activation of the organism by virtue of its sensitivity to extero-ceptive, interoceptive, hormonal and cortical stimuli) which would enable it to fulfill the behavioral requirements of a drive concept."

INHIBITION

If stimulation produces an alert and aroused subject, lesioning of the RAS should result in the opposite behavioral pattern of an unaroused and inattentive subject—in brief, a response pattern characterized by a low degree of motivation. A dramatic demon-stration of the latter relationship was first reported by Bremer (1935). He showed that the removal of certain reticular areas resulted in a comatose, behaviorally unarousable animal. Other studies have continued this line of experimentation. For exam-ple, Lindsley and his colleagues (1950) investigated the effects of destroying sections of a cat's specific sensory pathways without disturbing the lower RAS. After the cat had recovered from the operation, the behavioral observations and the EEG records were those of an alert and awake animal which could stand and move about. On the other hand, lesions in the lower RAS, when the specific pathways were intact, changed the normal EEG record of low-amplitude fast waves to the high amplitude and slow fre-quency typical of normal sleep. Behavioral observations verified the EEG record. Only by intense stimulation (loud buzzer) could the animal be aroused. Even so, arousal consisted of noth-ing more than the cat raising its head and opening its eyes. When the stimulus was withdrawn, the behavior ceased. Several other investigators (French and Magoun, 1952; French, Verzeano, and Magoun, 1952; French, Amerongen, and Magoun, 1952) inflicted relatively large lesions, with the specific paths left intact, and were unable to elicit any behavioral arousal even with extremely strong peripheral stimulation.

These findings are particularly interesting. They clearly dem-onstrate that even when the specific impulses reach the cortex, they are not sufficient to maintain alerted or aroused behavior if the RAS has been partially destroyed. Thus, it would appear that although the sensory impulses provide the *content* of conscious

awareness, they cannot by themselves directly produce wakefulness—activating impulses from the RAS are necessary to supplement the sensory information and translate it into meaningful
and adaptive behavior.

DIFFERENTIAL RESPONSIVITY

It has been shown that certain sense modalities have a greater
potential for activating the RAS than others (Bernhaut, Gellhorn, and Rasmussen, 1953). Nociceptive (pain) stimuli have
the greatest potential, followed by proprioceptive (internal muscle feedback), auditory, and visual, in that order. This result is
consistent with and may explain the finding that under certain
conditions learning is easier to achieve with auditory stimuli
than with visual ones (Chow, Dement, and John, 1957; Morrell
and Jasper, 1956). Modalities which have the greatest innate
capacity to elicit activation may be the most efficient in the
learning situation. Whether this increased efficiency results from
a greater ease of forming associations between stimulus and response units, or from greater attention to the stimuli, has not
been determined. More than likely, both components are interrelated.

Not only is the RAS differentially activated by different modalities, but the RAS also has a facilitative effect on the reception of
these specific impulses (Li and Jasper, 1953). Thus, if the RAS is
stimulated prior to the arrival of specific sensory impulses, the
stimuli (say, color) which produced the impulse will be perceived more readily. In other words, the cortex is "alerted" for
the arrival of a particular type of stimulus. It is *as if* the cortical
area's threshold for incoming messages has been lowered. This
observation has a striking implication for the frequently asked
question, "Why does a mother hear a child's cry at night when
the father does not?" It is possible that certain experiences of the
mother establish cortical traces which are activated by the RAS so
as to lower the effective threshold for such stimulation. For
example, suppose that a child has shown signs of discomfort all
day and that the mother, because she has been with the child, is
aware of this fact. Then at night the child's crying produces RAS
activation in the mother, which in turn lowers the auditory

threshold, and the mother awakens. Exactly how the trace is left, its specific locus, or how the threshold is actually lowered are not at the present time understood. But at least an opening wedge has been thrust into the welter of brain-behavior relationships that have until recently defied all attempts at understanding.

REDUCED STIMULATION

The fact that the RAS "prepares" the cortex for the arrival of specific impulses may be relevant to studies of "isolation" or "stimulus deprivation." The typical procedure used in these studies is to place the subject in a room or chamber which is designed to eliminate, as much as possible, all sensory stimuli such as noise, light, and the like. The results of such a procedure have led to the conclusion that a certain minimal level of stimulation is necessary for the maintenance of normal psychophysiological processes. If the input is below this minimal level, as occurs in many of these experiments, the subject reports certain hallucinatory experiences. For example, phenomena such as bright lights are experienced in the absence of their appropriate external stimuli. It may be that the nonspecific impulses prepare the cortex for specific sensory impulses presumed to follow. At a low level of stimulus input, the RAS activation may slowly build up an electrical potential which when not dissipated by the expected input produces spontaneous neural firing and thus hallucinations. Although no data have been reported bearing directly upon this conjecture, Mundy-Castle (1953) and Heron, Doane, and Scott (1956) have produced evidence strongly suggesting a functional relationship between hallucinations and low level of input of reticular impulses.

EMOTIONALITY

The reticular activating system also has relevance to certain emotional effects. The literature is replete with examples of intensely motivated individuals failing to learn a task or performing it poorly, and court records contain innumerable examples of the inability of witnesses to remember certain traumatic events. Several sources of information point to the RAS as one major controlling mechanism for these emotional losses of efficiency.

Adrenaline, which is a hormone secreted during strong emotionality, regulates the internal organs (increases the heart rate, makes more energy available to muscles and brain, and the like). Its effects are shown behaviorally by a drying of the mouth, pupillary dilation, and other symptoms. In general, its function is to prepare the individual for action. If it could be demonstrated that its effects were mediated by a particular neurological structure, it could be readily inferred that this structure was intimately related to emotion. Rothballer (1956) has succeeded in isolating such an adrenaline-sensitive structure. He demonstrated that intravenous injection of adrenaline in the lower RAS produced and mediated cortical arousal. Furthermore, the adrenaline sensitivity appeared to be limited to the particular portions of the lower RAS.

Other drugs are antagonistic to adrenaline, such as anesthetics, which reduce or abolish emotional activity. Bernhaut and his colleagues (1953) have shown a direct correlation between the degree of anesthetization in the lower RAS and arrest of the activation response. This observation again points to the RAS as a mechanism of emotional control, since emotionality is decreased through the use of anesthesia.

Further data reveal that brain-stem activation is capable of blocking cortical responses which are considered to be important in associative learning. Duncan (1949) administered traumatic shock to the hind legs of rats at different intervals during a learning task. Four groups were used and after each trial the voltage was applied at one of the following intervals: 20 seconds, 60 seconds, 4 minutes and 45 minutes. At the end of the experiment there was no significant difference between the 45-minute, 4-minute, and 60-second groups in the time it took the subjects to learn the task, but the 20-second group performed at a level below these groups. Thus, there appeared to be an optimal response-shock interval for the emotional impairment of learning, and the above data suggest that the closer the emotionality occurs to the event the greater the impairment.

Additional evidence of the inhibitory effects of the RAS is provided by an experiment by Mahut (1957). He ran hungry rats in a maze for ten trials a day. Following each trial, the subjects were stimulated in the upper RAS region by an electrical current while they were eating in the goal box. When these subjects were compared with subjects which had not been stimulated, they showed a lesser degree of learning. These results cannot be attributed to any direct effects of the shock on consummatory processes since examination of behavioral responses failed to reveal any visible disruptive effects on eating. Mahut interpreted these results as demonstrating inhibition of the establishment of associative memory traces.

The above relationships could well explain why many people fail to notice particular events during periods of emotional arousal—the RAS either kept the specific impulses from ever reaching the cortex, or interfered with the formation of associations, or blocked the activation of associations previously made in the cortex. The fact that stimulation of the RAS can impair learning and discriminative capacities provides a plausible physiological basis for the behavioral counterpart of failure to respond "rationally" or "normally" under emotional duress.

HABITUATION AND SELECTIVE ATTENTION

The RAS is also related to selective attention and habituation. Everyone has noticed at one time or another that the senses habituate or adapt to a stimulus when it occurs for a long period of time. For example, a barking dog is heard when it first begins to bark, but after a while a person no longer "pays attention" to it; and, unless the event is called to his attention he is no longer aware that the dog is barking. The factory worker becomes so accustomed to the sounds of the factory that he is no longer aware of them, but an "outsider" is very much aware of the din. The process of habituation or sensory adaptation to repetitive stimuli is believed to be a function of the RAS. Sharpless and Jasper (1956) found that cats with chronically implanted electrodes habituated to a particular tonal pattern and that changes in the pattern were effective in producing dishabituation. A similar finding was reported by Galambos, Sheatz, and Vernier (1956), using discrete auditory clicks with cats. After the clicks had been presented for a duration of time, all evidence of impulses from the auditory fibers disappeared. The role of the RAS in these experiments was to block or inhibit the neural messages from reaching the brain.

It is not at the present time entirely clear whether this inhibition occurs in the pathways leading to the brain or in the sense organs themselves. But some data reported by Hernandez-Peon, Sherrer, and Jouvet (1956) indicate that the latter is the case. This study also vividly illustrates how the RAS can determine selective attention—the attending to one stimulus while ignoring another. Hernandez-Peon and his colleagues implanted electrodes in the auditory sensory pathways of a cat and recorded neural impulses to auditory clicks. Then they suddenly placed a bottle containing two mice in front of the cat. Immediately, the neural firing from the auditory nerves stopped, only to return when the bottle was removed. Here the RAS was able to accomplish two functions—it inhibited the firing of the auditory nerves by some type of a feedback system between the nerves and the reticular system and simultaneously permitted the cat to pay attention to the mice. These data also indicate that the nervous system is arranged in an adaptive manner so that a subject will attend to those stimuli which are the most important to the subject.

INTRACRANIAL SELF-STIMULATION AND THE LIMBIC SYSTEM

Work in the field popularly referred to as *intracranial self-stimulation* (ICS) is currently vying with the RAS for honors as the "hottest" area in physiological psychology. The discovery that an animal will perform an instrumental act to obtain intracranial electrical shock in certain brain areas was startling. Moreover, it was an accidental finding resulting from a misimplanted electrode in an experiment originally designed to study the RAS. In the words of the "misimplanter" (Olds, 1955a, p. 83–84), "The result was quite amazing. When the animal was stimulated at a specific place in an open field, he sometimes moved away but he returned and sniffed around that area. More stimulation at that place caused him to spend more time there. Later we found that this same animal could be 'pulled' to any spot in the maze by giving a small electrical stimulus *after* each response in the right direction. This was akin to playing the 'hot and cold' game with a child. Each correct response brought electrical pulses which seemed to indicate to the animal that it was on the right track."

This finding was indeed remarkable, since from all that was known about shock one would expect it to produce an aversive rather than appetitive reaction. The effect is even more striking when it is realized that an animal can be given a strong enough jolt to produce convulsive behavior (frothing at the mouth, and so on) and yet will still return for more. An electrode is chronically (that is, permanently) implanted in such a manner that the end which protrudes through the top of the skull is readily accessible to the experimenter. The exposed end is so constructed that an electrical cord which passes current in the range of a few microamperes can be easily connected. Usually this wire is connected only when the subject is being tested and is removed when the subject is returned to its home cage. After sufficient time for recovery from the operation, the subject may be placed in a variety of test situations.

Subsequent experiments have demonstrated equally amazing behavior. For example, Olds, Travis, and Schwing (1960) have demonstrated that animals will barpress for shock alone at a rate up to 8000 barpresses per hour, and Lilly (1958), using shorter durations of ICS with monkeys, has observed as many as 17 barpresses per second. Olds (1958b) has also shown that subjects will continue self-stimulation up to 48 hours, at which time they cease pressing because of exhaustion.

Another method for assessing the effects of electrical self-stimulation is the obstruction box, in which the subject has to cross an obstruction—an electrified foot grid—in order to obtain reward. Subjects which are 24-hours hungry will not cross a grid with more than 60 to 180 microamperes foot shock to gain food reward, but ICS rats crossed the grid carrying as much as 425 microamperes in order to barpress for self-stimulation.

EXPERIMENTAL RESULTS

BRAIN MAPPING

Olds has done a considerable amount of work in mapping the areas of the brain collectively referred to as the limbic system (the septal area, amygdala, hypothalamus, hippocampus, and parts of the thalamus) and has found that different areas produce different levels of responding. The different rates are not only found among species but also among animals within the same species. Irrespective of these individual differences, an animal quickly reaches a very stable rate of performance. This property of a steady response state is extremely important, for once established it has been found to be very sensitive to the manipulation of many different independent variables.

PHARMACOLOGY

Pharmacological implications of ICS for those drugs that come under the heading of tranquilizers and antidepressants were immediately grasped. Olds (1962) has summarized the results of such studies. Tranquilizers (phenothiazine type) have been found to eliminate the ICS effect by acting to raise the threshold, while antidepressants of the amphetamine group facilitate self-stimulation by lowering the threshold.

AVERSION

There is evidence that stimulation becomes noxious if too much ICS is administered during a given time period. If the intensity of shock is increased from an optimal level, the subject immediately responds more slowly; if it is then decreased, an increment in response rate occurs. Bower and Miller (1958) hypothesized that long durations of ICS may be punishing. To test this, they programed the shock so that its duration was equal to the period of time the bar was held down; the initial depression of the bar began the shock and release of the bar terminated the shock. Rats were also stimulated with a predetermined duration of shock which was independent of the amount of time the bar was held down. Their major finding was that the onset of the stimulation was rewarding but that continued stimulation became aversive. Also, animals which had been forced to receive a long-duration stimulation subsequently showed a preference for short bursts of stimulation.

PRIMARY DRIVES

Another area of interest is the interrelationship between ICS and different primary drives. Animals on food deprivation, when compared to satiated animals, demonstrated a higher ICS response rate. Moreover, when thirsty subjects were simultaneously provided with two bars, one giving ICS and the other giving water as a reward, a decrement in performance on the water bar was accompanied by a similar decrement on the ICS bar, presumably because of satiation on the former (Brady, 1957; Brady and colleagues, 1957). Olds (1962) has suggested the possibility that in systems or centers associated with drive, stimulation of extremely low intensity lowers the threshold for associated consummatory and instrumental acts, while, at higher intensities, positive reinforcement of preceding behavior is produced. Deutsch (1960), on the other hand, believes that two separate pathways exist, one for motivation and one for reward. Both of these accounts have been able to predict some behavior but also have had to resort to ad hoc explanations in other cases.

SPACING OF TRIALS

At least two general findings have been somewhat perplexing when compared to other psychological data. One of the first facts an introductory experimental student learns is that spaced trials produce quicker and more permanent learning than do massed trials. However, the results with self-stimulation indicate an opposite relationship. When rats were trained to run down a runway and press a lever for self-stimulation, it was found the subjects who had a short intertrial interval steadily improved with time, but when the intertrial interval was increased to approximately 15 minutes no such improvement was found. Additional information is provided by Olds (1958a), who observed that when ICS rats were run on successive days the first trial was always *slower* than the last trial on the previous day. This behavior is contrasted to that of food-rewarded rats, whose first trial is *faster* than the one on the preceding day.

EXTINCTION

The number of unrewarded (nonstimulated) trials that it takes to extinguish the response is extremely small—as few as three or four trials. It may be tentatively concluded that self-stimulation produces highly motivated behavior, but that its absence leaves little residual motivation. This conclusion suggests that in order for the ICS to be effective it must follow in close proximity to the response which the experimenter is trying to establish, and when it is absent for only a few trials the animal stops responding. Further studies have shown that these temporal parameters are among the most critical variables determining ICS effectiveness.

Several studies have used different schedules of reinforcement in conjunction with self-stimulation (Sidman and colleagues, 1955; Brady, 1960; Brady and Conrad, 1960). All of these studies indicate the inability of the subject to maintain either a high-ratio or long-interval schedule of the sort which can be achieved by using the more conventional consummatory rewards. (For a discussion of ratio and interval schedules, see Chapter 6.)

Howarth and Deutsch (1962) report extinction data in support of this temporal-immediacy hypothesis. One group of rats (A) had the bar removed for 7 seconds at the beginning of each extinction session, while a second group (B) was allowed to barpress during this period of time. Both groups extinguished at the same time even though group B produced more barpresses. These investigators concluded that resistance to extinction is a function of the duration of time from the last stimulation, and not the number of unreinforced barpresses. Another way of stating this conclusion is that extinction is a function of motivational decay. Olds and Milner (1954) have shown this motivational decrement can be readily reversed by administering a few shocks after extinction, thus increasing the amount of motivation and correspondingly reinstating the previous response rate.

HUMAN SUBJECTS

Not all of the ICS data come from infrahuman studies. A search of the psychological literature reveals several studies with human subjects. These are investigations of possible therapeutic applications. For example, Heath and Micklé (1960) summarize seven years of brain-stimulation work using schizophrenic patients with the statement that stimulation of certain parts of the limbic system results in an alerted patient, with an increased ability to verbalize. Moreover, several patients were reported to have expressed a wish for repeated limbic stimulation. The clinical reports provided by Sem-Jacobsen and Torkildsen (1960) give further data on the subjective experience produced by limbic stimulation. Feelings of relaxation, pleasure, and joy accompanied by overt signs of smiling and laughter have been reported. Subjective reports and related behavior, however, cannot always be accepted at face value. For example, Sem-Jacobsen and Torkildsen report that "One patient laughed with joy in response to each stimulation. After several days with stimulation we learned what really took place. The stimulus evoked a fluttering in a muscle group in the pelvis which tickled the patient and she responded with joy and laughter" (p. 284). Sem-Jacobsen and Torkildsen also found a great deal of variability among patients, some preferring many stimulations with short temporal intervals between them, others liking longer periods of continual stimulation. It was determined that the fastest rate of self-stimulating pressing, which was far below that of animal subjects, occurred when ICS altered the patient's level of awareness, suggesting some type of a feedback system influencing the limbic system. Futhermore, stimulation of certain areas was found to produce convulsions. Following these convulsive states the patient was relaxed rather than restless and nervous as is characteristic of other convulsive techniques. The same therapeutic effect has been obtained in other cases where shock intensity was below the convulsive threshold. One further example from the Sem-Jacobsen and Torkildsen report shows the extent to which such a technique can be used to control behavior. In a patient with multiple implantations, stimulation at a particular electrode produced a sudden and intense desire to urinate, and he asked to be excused. The doctor then stimulated another area previously found to produce relaxation. Following this sequence the doctor asked the patient if he still wanted to be excused. The patient answered, "Oh, sure I wanted to go to the toilet, but I am in no hurry. You just continue; I'm in absolutely no hurry" (p. 287).

What do all these findings mean? Obviously the limbic system is intimately connected with both motivating and reinforcing properties. It also seems reasonable to infer that this stimulation is tapping the pathways which project to certain "centers" in other parts of the brain. What, where, and how these "centers" operate is an important experimental problem. Until these centers are located and investigated it is only speculation to say that a pleasure or pain center exists. Even so, evidence from both human and infrahuman subjects indicates that ICS produces some type of pleasurable or satisfying state of affairs.

HUNGER AND THIRST

The underlying physiological mechanisms which control the drive states of thirst and hunger are treated in a single section for two reasons: First, it has been demonstrated that both drives have similar hypothalamic "centers" which are sensitive to somewhat the same internal and external sources of stimulation; second, parallel approaches have been employed in investigations of their characteristics. These approaches may be categorized by the degree of theoretical and experimental emphasis directed toward one or more of the following areas: (1) *peripheral,* those organs or cavities which lie near the exterior of the organism (as do the mouth and the stomach); (2) *central,* the brain and central nervous system; and (3) *general,* the systems or structures lying between the peripheral and central areas (such as the circulatory system and the cellular structures).

PERIPHERAL FACTORS

THIRST

The peripheral studies of thirst are chiefly concerned with the oral cavity. Such an emphasis originated from the commonsense conception that the sensation of dryness in the mouth and alimentary canal, associated with thirst, regulates water intake. The best-known proponent of this "dry mouth" hypothesis was the physiologist W. B. Cannon (1918, 1939). The basic principle underlying this approach is that thirst and a dry mouth are always coexistent. From this assumption, the hypothesis that thirst should not occur when the oral cavity is moist or wet is readily derived. If this hypothesis is correct, thirst and the activity of the glands which secrete moistening agents (salivary glands) should be correlated. That is, the greater the secretion the less the subject should drink, and vice versa.

Supporting evidence for this notion was supplied by Bidder and Schmidt (1852) in an experiment in which they prevented saliva from being secreted by tying shut the salivary ducts. Their results indicate that this treatment greatly increased water consumption, as compared with treatments which allowed normal salivation. Moreover, the experimental subjects had a great deal of trouble digesting dry food.

Cannon himself reported several experiments in support of the local hypothesis. In one study, he subjectively reported a sensation of thirst following the injection of a salivation-inhibiting drug. In another experiment, he measured his saliva production at one-hour intervals while depriving himself of water. Thirst occurred approximately at the same time salivation terminated—four hours after the beginning of the deprivation.

However, a wealth of evidence has now accumulated which renders the "dry mouth" theory untenable as an explanation of thirst. For example, the same subjective source of evidence used by Cannon also reveals, upon a more detailed search, that thirst in some cases does occur when the mouth is moist, and that a moistening of the oral membranes does not dissipate thirst but only alleviates the dryness of the mouth. Austin and Steggerda (1936) reported a particularly devastating piece of evidence. They discovered a so-called "freak of nature"—a man who was born without salivary glands; yet, his water intake and sensation of thirst appeared in all respects to be no different from those of a normal person.

Much earlier, Bernard (1856) had diverted the esophagus of a horse so that ingested water was expelled between the front legs rather than reaching the stomach. The horse drank continually until fatigued, then rested and drank again until fatigued. Bernard repeated this procedure, which has subsequently become known as "sham" drinking, with a dog who had a fistula (opening) in its stomach; he reported the same general results even though the water entered the stomach before it was expelled.

One final source of damaging evidence is the inability of the "dry mouth" to regulate the volume intake of water. As Wolf

(1958, p. 64) mentions, "the volume drunk, per se, has no necessary relation to the local moistening produced . . . e.g., a small volume of water held in the mouth and gargled, or sucking a piece of ice should wet the throat more thoroughly than a large volume of water quickly swallowed." It may now be concluded that true thirst resides "deeper" in the organism and the dryness of the mouth is nothing more than a false or pseudo thirst, a symptom of thirst rather than the cause or regulator of thirst.

HUNGER

Cannon also held a prominent theoretical position in the area of hunger. In essence, he extended his peripheral position to include the stomach. He believed that stomach contractions (hunger pangs) were the principal factors controlling appetite and hunger. The first direct observation of the mechanics of the stomach was achieved by Beaumont (1833) in the famous clinical case of Alexis St. Martin, a French-Canadian hunter who was the victim of a shotgun accident. The opening in his stomach caused by the blast never completely healed. In fact, a small natural tube or fistula remained through the wall, permitting Beaumont to observe the process of digestion and the variables which affect it. During some of his observations, he noticed that the contractions of the stomach walls occurred in the absence of food but not when the stomach was full.

Cannon and Washburn (1912), in a unique study, demonstrated a positive relationship between hunger pangs and stomach contractions. Washburn swallowed a small balloon attached to the end of a hollow tube, and air forced through the tube inflated the balloon in his stomach. By means of appropriate recording instruments, the stomach contractions could be recorded. In addition, Washburn recorded his subjective sensations of hunger by pressing a key each time he experienced a hunger sensation. When these two records were compared, a high correlation between the occurrence of stomach contractions and reported sensations of hunger was evident. Carlson (1916) presents an impressive array of data supporting this view. In more than 50 human cases, he found that an empty stomach invariably resulted in stomach contractions and the sensation of hunger. He further isolated the stomachs of dogs from other influences by severing all neural connections and found that even in the absence of neural influence the characteristic contractions obtained.

More recent investigations have demonstrated that the results of these earlier studies may be attributable to the technique employed (Gianturco, 1934; Martin and Morton, 1952). It was demonstrated that a balloon introduced into an empty stomach *increases* the stomach's activity, and that an "empty" stomach was not really as empty as once believed. When stomach activity was measured without the balloon, relatively little activity occurred (Gianturco, 1934). In 1957, Garafolo and Davis performed an experiment in which they measured the gastrointestinal activity without introducing a foreign object into the stomach. They failed to find the large slow contraction which Cannon and others believed to accompany hunger. By measuring consummatory activity rather than using verbal reports, investigators showed that the local-stimulation theory was inadequate. Organisms continued to eat or drink the same amount in the absence of local stimulation (as when the stomach or salivary glands are removed). Also, clinical observations (Wagensteen and Carlson, 1955) indicated that patients perceive hunger normally even when all of the stomach had been removed. While local sensations may make one conscious of needs, local or peripheral stimulation is not necessary in the regulation of hunger. Therefore, even though hunger pangs may serve as internal cues for the initiation of food intake, we must go further into the organism to find the specific controlling centers. Furthermore, stomach contractions constitute only one of the multitude of cues which may serve to indicate the presence of hunger.

In spite of contradictory evidence, these local-stimulation theories have continued to be influential in some areas. Rosenzweig (1962) states three reasons why they have persisted, not only in the case of hunger but in other areas as well: (1) the theories corresponded well with common-sense concepts, (2) they were advanced by authorities within the field, and (3) it was difficult to formulate a better view—that is, the local-stimulation hypotheses for both thirst and hunger were accepted, even though the inadequacies were known, for the want of a better explanation.

CENTRAL FACTORS

In both thirst and hunger the vast majority of recent investigations have concentrated on the hypothalamic portion of the brain, and there is considerable evidence that thirst and hunger "centers" are located within this region. The use of the word *center* is an expository device used for convenience and should not be construed to mean strict anatomical isolation. Such an interpretation, which may eventually prove to be correct, is a dangerous one, for it tends to impede research on other possible centers as well as on the variables influencing them.

One of the first experiments on central factors was performed by Bailey and Bremer (1921). Employing the rather crude technique of exposing the hypothalamus and lesioning it with a probe, they found that the lesion greatly increased the quantity of water and food ingested. Since that time, more refined techniques have been developed, enabling physiologists and psychologists alike to localize the centers more precisely.

THIRST

Reduction or abolition of thirst (adipsia) has been achieved in several studies. Witt and colleagues (1952) found that lesions in a dog's hypothalamic area produced a partial or complete abolition of thirst. Montemurro and Stevenson (1955) obtained similar results with lesions in rats. Witt and his colleagues also found that when the entire anterior hypothalamus was removed the dogs ceased to drink and could be kept alive only by artifically providing water. Partial lesions of the anterior hypothalamic regions have also been reported to produce permanent adipsia. Other studies, lesioning similar areas, have found evidence of a temporary rather than permanent adipsia.

Stimulation of the hypothalamus has been shown to produce the opposite effect—incessant drinking or polydipsia. Greer (1955) stimulated the hypothalamus by means of radiofrequency activation transmitted through implanted electrodes. The stimulated animal began licking in the absence of appropriate external stimulation, stood on its hindlegs, lunged, and licked the glass enclosure. Increases and decreases in the amount of stimulation produced corresponding amounts of licking behavior. When water was placed in the cage, the random lick responses ended and the animal ravenously consumed water. When the water was withdrawn, the licking behavior recurred. When a 5-per-cent salt solution was substituted for the pure water, the animal began drinking as before but quickly stopped and demonstrated avoidance behavior. However, the subjects could not resist this distasteful solution for more than a few seconds before returning to their compulsive drinking.

Andersson (1952, 1953) injected small quantities of sodium chloride (salt) into the anterior hypothalamus of goats; immediate increase of water consumption followed. In later experiments, Andersson and McCann (1955) found that electrical stimulation produced similar results, with one difference—electrical stimulation could be repeated more frequently than the salt stimulation. Apparently, the "center" is more resistant to habituation to electrical stimulation than to sodium-chloride stimulation. Polydipsia occurred to such an extent that the subjects could be induced to drink up to as much as 40 per cent of their bodily weight. Other types of stimulation, such as chemical (Epstein, 1960; Grossman, 1960), have produced similar results. Although there is currently some question as to the exact portion of the hypothalamus which is sensitive, it is sufficient for our purpose to conclude that within the hypothalamus there are some fairly well localized areas which appear to initiate and regulate water intake.

HUNGER

The quest for hunger centers has had a longer history, and more knowledge has accumulated. Centers relating to hunger and food appetite have been more precisely localized in the hypothalamus. Hetherington and Ranson (1940) were probably the first to establish clearly the involvement of the hypothalamus in eating. They lesioned different hypothalamic areas, producing obesity in the rats. The obesity was caused by overeating (hyperphagia) and has since been produced in a wide variety of animals, among them rats, mice, dogs, and monkeys. Moreover, when hyperphagic rats were "trimmed" down to normal weight by deprivation and then given access to unlimited food they overate *as if* ravenously hungry and quickly became overweight.

Stimulation of the medial section of the hypothalamus (Anand and Dua, 1955) produced a slight decrease in the amount of food intake, but never complete cessation. Olds (1955b) and Hoebel and Teitelbaum (1962), using ICS, corroborated these results and added one observation. During periods of satiation there was a decline in the amount of self-stimulation, but during deprivation there was an increase in self-stimulation. In view of these findings it may be reasoned that the medial portion of the hypothalamus is an inhibiting or "satiety" center. That is, its chief function is to inhibit eating. When this area is destroyed, the subject is freed of the inhibition and becomes hyperphagic.

If there is a satiety center, there must be a corresponding hunger center which initiates feeding and upon which the satiety center exerts its inhibition. Anand and Brodbeck (1951) first clearly demonstrated such an anatomical area in the lateral portion of the hypothalamus. Removal of the lateral region resulted in an aphagia (cessation of eating) which was so pronounced that the subject had to be kept alive by direct feeding. On the other hand, stimulation of the lateral areas results in "eating automatisms"—chewing, swallowing, and the like. Morgane (1961), in addition, found that lateral stimulation increased motivation so that rats crossed an electrical grid to perform a previously learned instrumental response, and that food-satiated but thirsty subjects upon lateral stimulation left a source of water and performed a similar instrumental act.

GENERAL FACTORS

Although we have seen that different areas of the hypothalamus control drinking and eating behavior, the various inputs which stimulate or inhibit these centers still remain to be determined.

The most likely candidates for thirst are different types of receptors (heat, osmotic, pressure, taste), while for hunger the field is replete with such possibilities as thermostatic, gastrointestinal, and hormonal regulators. It must be understood that there is a multiplicity of heterogeneous stimuli which may and do affect the previously mentioned centers. The osmoreceptors, which are located in the hypothalamus and other parts of the body and are sensitive to changes in salt content, have been selected for discussion as representative of the general factors.

THIRST AND SALT

There is an optimal concentration of salt for body functions. When this level is exceeded, the body normally increases its intake of water and thereby decreases the concentration of salt. When the salt content falls below this optimal level, there is a corresponding decrease in the intake of water.

Reports of sailors who experience greater thirst after they have ingested sea water provide anecdotal evidence of how salt can induce thirst. This effect has been independently verified by several experiments. For example, Wolf (1950) intravenously injected different amounts of salt water and observed corresponding increases in thirst. It will also be recalled that stimulation of the drinking center in the hypothalamus is accomplished both by electrical stimulation and by injections of salt water. Gilman (1937) concluded from experimental evidence that cellular dehydration is a principal drinking stimulus for water intake.

Termination of drinking may be controlled by nerve impulses sensitive to changes in either water or salt content (Zotterman, 1956). The rate of neural impulses increases as the concentration of salt increases or as the amount of water decreases. This finding explains the rather remarkable ability of animals to maintain a precise water balance, as reported by Adolph (1939) and by Robinson and Adolph (1943). A deficit in water of as little as 1/2 per cent activated drinking in dogs, and if water was totally withheld the amount was made up later by longer periods of drinking.

SEXUAL BEHAVIOR

The purpose of the following discussion is to familiarize the reader with an experimental approach to the study of sexual behavior which has been far less publicized than the popular psychoanalytic and clinical endeavors. The clinical technique pivots around the interview, relying heavily upon the verbal report of the patient. Being largely speculative, it seldom achieves an adequate degree of quantification. The experimental approach is concerned with manipulating both external and internal stimuli, quantification of the data, and establishing relationships between different empirical findings rather than generating untestable theories. The clinical approach deals exclusively with human subjects while the experimental approach, because of the nature of the experimental manipulations, primarily studies infrahuman species. However, these two approaches are not mutually exclusive. In spite of the differences, their results often dovetail into meaningful generalizations.

A major figure in the experimental movement is Frank A. Beach (b. 1911). Most of the following section has relied heavily upon his books and articles. Only a glimpse of the vast amount of work that has accumulated will be given, and even this will be limited to mammalian species.

MOTIVATIONAL PROPERTIES

Several laboratory studies have demonstrated the motivational properties of sexual incentives. For example, Schwartz (1956) used receptive female rats as rewards in establishing barpressing in male rats and found that the subjects learned this instrumental task. However, their response rate was lower than that obtained with hungry or thirsty rats appropriately rewarded. Jenkins (1928) indicated the influence of prior experiences and sexual practice as determinants of sexual behavior. He demonstrated that male rats which had been sexually isolated failed to cross an electrified grid as readily as subjects raised in a heterosexual environment. Beach, Conovitz, Steinberg, and Goldstein

(1956) incorporated a "shock harness" through which different voltages of electricity could be passed. Strong shocks given at the time of intromission produced sexual avoidance and failure to mate on subsequent trials. Apparently the shock places the subject in a conflict situation in which the aversiveness of the situation is more powerful than the sexual motivation provided by the receptive female.

Furthermore, Beach (1956) reports that in many mammalian species successful copulation is followed by periods of sexual unresponsiveness analogous to the satiation effects that occur with other appetitive rewards such as food and water. Mating tests showed that with increased temporal periods between copulations there was a corresponding increase in the number of possible ejaculations, the maximum appearing after about 10 days of rest.

A second measure of sexual motivation was the latency between intromissions. One would expect highly motivated subjects to have a shorter latency for the initial sexual contact than subjects with a lesser degree of motivation. This supposition is supported by the fact that after a period of 1 day's rest, about 10 hours preceded the first contact, compared to 623 seconds after 3 days' rest, 135 seconds after 6 days, and 18 seconds after 15 days.

The results of these studies clearly demonstrate the motivational properties of sex and, more importantly, show how the manipulation of environmental conditions can influence the sexual drive. The nature of the physiological mechanisms that mediate sexual behavior remains to be explicated. These can be divided into *neural* and *hormonal components,* which for pedagogical purposes will be treated in separate sections. The separate expositions are not intended to convey the impression that these components are separate and unrelated. Quite to the contrary, they are very clearly related indeed.

NEURAL MECHANISMS

The elementary reflexive responses which compose the integrated mammalian sexual patterns have been shown to be controlled by spinal mechanisms. For example, Beach (1951) reports that electrical stimulation of parts of the spinal cord, previously severed from the higher parts of the brain, results in erection and ejaculation in rodents, rabbits, and dogs. In dogs whose spinal cords have been severed and transected above the lumbar region (small of the back), sexual responses are still exhibited when the sex organ is directly stimulated. Humans suffering similar transections from tumors or gunshot accidents often respond to sexual stimulation with gross pelvic movements similar to those present in intercourse (Riddoch, 1917). In all of the above cases, the transections completely abolished voluntary muscular control and the sexual responses are entirely mediated by involuntary or autonomic control. Even so, men with severed spinal cords are capable of fertile copulation, as evidenced by their impregnated wives. Similarly, women with spinal sectioning still exhibit receptive posture movements as well as the usual estrous cycles.

These results are not really too striking since one would expect reflexive behavior to be controlled by the lower parts of the nervous system. However, as animals have evolved they have become more dependent upon the higher centers of the brain (cerebral cortex) for the integration of activities and one might expect that removal of these regions in the higher species would produce relatively greater interruption of efficiently motivated sexual behavior in comparison to the lower species.

Not only has it been clearly demonstrated that the neurological mechanisms controlling the integration of sexual behavior are different between species, but it has been further shown that different neurological mechanisms control sexual behavior. For example, Beach (1940, 1941) has compared the effect of different-sized cortical lesions on sexual patterns in the adult male rat. When less than 20 per cent of the cortex was destroyed, sexual behavior was relatively unaffected. If 20 to 50 per cent of the cortex was removed the postoperative behavior showed mating in some but not all subjects. When 60 per cent of the cortex was removed, postoperative mating was abolished in all cases. In general, there was an inverse relationship between mating and the amount of tissue removed. The interesting finding, however, is that when copulation did occur its pattern was not noticeably different from the preoperative pattern. Since the motor pattern was judged normal, the reduction in activity was related to a decrease in the sexual excitability or motivation of the rat. Subsequently Beach (1951, p. 401) concludes, "These findings suggest that the cortex is not directly involved in the organization of sexual responses in the male rat but serves to maintain the excitability of lower centers that are essential to the integration of mating behavior. In the absence of facilitative support from the cortex, these hypothetical executive mechanisms become relatively unresponsive to exteroceptive stimuli."

Beach (1943) also studied the female rat's sexual response with similar cortical lesions. He found that 100-per-cent decortication did not eliminate female mating with an active male. In some cases such decorticated females showed greater sexual excitability than normal females. Yet certain behavior deficits were noted, such as the inability to direct responses toward the male. Furthermore, the decorticated subjects often needed physical contact before the sexual position was elicited. Close examination of the female response revealed a somewhat disorganized motor pattern, with the female often maintaining a particular sexual position rather than organizing different responses into the common sexual patterns. Nevertheless, the response was sufficiently coordinated to permit conception. Thus, in contrast with the male, it appears that the female's cortex is intimately involved in the coordination of responses and ability to solicit the attention of the male, but it does not occupy a dominant role in sexual receptivity and excitability.

Beach (1943) ingeniously verified these differences between cortical control in single subjects. He noticed in the course of his investigations that some species of female rats display *both* masculine and feminine mating responses (bisexual behavior) in appropriate conditions. After removal of varying percentages of cortical tissue the females were placed in different cages: first with a receptive female, and second with an active male. The females' behavior was then compared to preoperative responses previously recorded in similar situations. The results showed that with increased decortication the masculine mounting of the other females was reduced and finally eliminated. Yet no reduction was shown to exist in the feminine response when these females were mounted by the males.

A similar series of studies was performed on male cats (Beach, Zitrin, and Jaynes, 1956a, 1956b). Cortical removal produced gross motor dysfunctions which were most apparent when frontal lobes were eliminated. However, little decrement in excitability, as revealed by the extent to which the male cats followed and tried to mate with females, was evident. The subjects' copulatory pattern showed the following changes: a decrease in the number of mountings and intromissions with an increase in the clasping response, delays prior to initiation of copulatory behavior, and awkwardness and uncoordinated body movements resulting in fewer successful acts. Thus, unlike rats, male cats retain their excitability but lose control of the motor components necessary for successful mating.

If these findings are projected to even higher species where few or no controlled data are available, it is evident that the cortex holds a more dominant position in the timing and integration of sexual behavior. Cortical control is vastly important, for cortical functions are not limited solely to sensorimotor control. The cortex is also the "seat" of the higher intellectual capacities such as thinking and reasoning. It provides the basis for explaining how human sexual behavior is so readily adaptive, not only between cultures, as the anthropologists have demonstrated, but even within a single society. The omnipresent mores and values with which people have been inculcated since their birth are, loosely speaking, located in the cortex and exert influence from it. Because of this location, human sexual behavior, as well as most other types of human behavior, is freed from purely reflexive and involuntary dominance and is guided by learned as well as innate factors. But neural control explains only part of sexual behavior and its physiological basis. Hormonal control is an equally important, if not a more important, determinant.

HORMONAL CONTROL

In the lower mammalian species, hormones secreted by the sex glands (ovaries of the female and testes of the male) have important motivational implications. Sexual behavior in female rats is highly correlated with the production of estrogen (hormone of the ovaries) and mating does not usually occur until estrogen is secreted into the blood stream. Moreover, estrogen controls the rhythmic sexual cycles of those lower mammals such as the dog and cat. At intervals, commonly twice a year, bitches come into heat or *estrus,* and only at this time are the females sexually attractive or receptive to the males of the species. This attraction is predetermined by the hormonal level and is usually unaffected by fertile copulation.

When the ovaries of the female are removed during infancy, mating behavior fails to develop at puberty. If the operation occurs during adulthood the female entirely ceases sexual mating (Beach, 1942a, 1942b; Hertz, Meyer, and Spielman, 1937). Furthermore, Nissen (1929) has demonstrated that ovariectomized rats show a greater reluctance to cross an electrified grid in order to reach a male than normal rats, indicating a reduction in their motivation to seek out members of the opposite sex.

Other investigators (Moore and Price, 1938; Boling, Young, and Dempsey, 1938) have established sexual receptivity by hormone therapy. If the ovariectomized animals are injected with various amounts of hormones a resurgence of the mating response occurs. Beach (1942c), using a similar method, further demonstrated the importance of estrogen by producing adult mating patterns in prepuberal females. His study also indicated an interesting developmental relationship between neural, muscular, and hormonal components of the sexual pattern. Normally, the first two components are sufficiently well developed and integrated *prior* to the natural release of the hormonal stimulants. This observation is true for both sexes of a given species.

A marked reduction in hormonal control is evidenced in organisms higher on the phyletic scale, such as primates and humans. Carpenter (1942) illustrated this fact in an experiment with monkeys, whose motivation for sexual intercourse was found to be independent of their estrous cycle. Corroboration of this result is provided by Yerkes and Elder (1936), who intensively studied the mating of chimpanzees and concluded that a female will sexually present herself and receive males at any time. They qualify this generalization by adding that the greatest number of copulations occur when estrogen is at its highest level (between menstrual periods), producing not only the greatest sexual motivation but also the optimal time for conception. Clinical results from human patients substantiate the assumption of their relative independence from these effects of estrogen. Filler and Drezner (1944) studied the effects of ovariectomy in 40 women without finding a significant reduction in sexual desires; in fact, they often noticed an increase in sexual motivation despite the presence of such typical menopausal symptoms as depression, sweating, fatigue, crying, and irritability. However, other studies have reported a decrease in sexual desire, indicating a considerable amount of variability probably related to psychological effects upon behavior.

Davis (1929) and Terman (1938) interviewed a large number of women as to when the greatest sexual desire occurs. The replies definitely indicated greater premenstrual or postmenstrual sexual motivation, coinciding with the lowest levels of estrogen. This finding is in direct contrast to that of Yerkes and Elder (1936). Beach (1951) explains the lack of correspondence between chimpanzees and humans by appealing to cultural taboos and restrictions. That is, in most societies intercourse is forbidden during the actual menstrual periods, producing a condition of sexual deprivation and a concomitant increment in motivation exhibited when the social gates are lowered following menstruation. The premenstrual desire may be viewed as an attempt to "store up" satisfaction for the forthcoming deprivation period.

Male rats will normally display prepuberal sexual behavior such as mounting and clasping. But not until androgen (the male hormone) is secreted are erections and ejaculations evidenced. However, in contrast to females, males show some elementary prehormonal sexual responsiveness. It has also been established that in many species males do not possess rhythmic sexual cycles but are sexually active throughout the year. Exceptions are seasonal breeders, like the Alaskan fur seal, some deer, and squirrels. The activity of these males is definitely linked to the level of hormones secreted by the testes, which regress and are quiescent except during mating seasons.

The effects of castration (removal of testes) are varied and depend largely on the age and species of the animal. In rats a marked decrease in adult mating results when castration occurs at birth or during early infancy (Beach and Holtz, 1946). A quantitative study of postcastrational mating in rats was performed by Stone (1927). He found the following decreases in copulatory behavior as a function of castration: 33 per cent after 1 month, 45 per cent after 2 months, 57 per cent after 3 months, 74 per cent after 4 months, 79 per cent after 5 months, and 91 per cent after 6 months. He also found a differential rate of decrease between ejaculation and copulation—ejaculation was the first component of the response to be eliminated whereas copulation, when it was eliminated, disappeared at a much later time. Thus, the sexual motivation did not abruptly dissipate but was gradually reduced as a function of time. Furthermore, Beach (1951) states that in all species investigated an increment in sexual interest and reinstatement of the behavioral component was produced following injections of androgen.

When older infraprimate mammals are castrated the responses are varied but generally follow the same pattern. The ejaculatory response drops out first, followed by the rest of the components. However, in some cases the elementary reflexive behavior fails to be abolished.

As in the case of females, except that the difference is accentuated in males, a reduction in the degree to which hormones dominate the male's behavior is a function of phyletic position. In young apes and chimpanzees sexual behavior occurs with greater frequency and variety than in lower species. Clark (1955) castrated a young male chimpanzee and observed little evidence of abnormal sexual behavior or reduced copulation in later adulthood. Several other authors report that castration in humans fails to eliminate copulatory activity. In summarizing the literature, Beach (1951, p. 275) states "the only element in the sexual repertoire which seems to necessitate androgenic support is the ejaculatory reflex." In spite of the impotency castration causes, castration by itself does not necessarily prohibit normal sexual motivation in humans or the ability to perform most of the responses necessary for the reduction of that motivation.

Suggested Readings

Beach, F. A., ed. 1965. *Sex and behavior.* New York: John Wiley and Sons.

Morgan, C. T. 1965. *Physiological psychology,* 3rd ed. New York: McGraw-Hill Book Co.

Olds, J. 1955. Physiological mechanisms of reward. In M. R. Jones, ed., *Nebraska symposium on motivation.* Lincoln: University of Nebraska Press, pp. 73–139.

Rosenzweig, M. R. 1962. The mechanisms of hunger and thirst. In L. Postman, ed., *Psychology in the making.* New York: Alfred A. Knopf.

Chapter 6

MOTIVATION AND LEARNING

The centrality of the concept of motivation in learning should be self-evident. Apart from the question of the role of motivation in the acquisition of behavior as such, it is clear that learning without appropriate motivation to respond is of little practical value. An analogy to this facet of the learning-motivation relationship may be found in the operation of the gasoline engine. No matter how well built and finely tuned an engine may be, it will not operate without fuel. Similarly, even the best-developed habits do not function without relevant activation—or motivation.

The role that motivation plays in the education process is treated in the next chapter. In the present chapter we are concerned with the relationships between learning and motivation from a fundamental point of view. That is to say, we are concerned more with theoretical problems than with practical ones. Accordingly, our treatment in this chapter begins with a brief methodological section and review of the basic types of learning processes as psychologists have identified them. Thereafter we proceed to discuss the drive concept and then a number of specific problem areas in which motivation plays a large part (schedules of reinforcement, magnitude of reward, delay of reinforcement, and secondary reinforcement).

The motivational bases of learned responses, or habits, are usually rather difficult to pinpoint. Moreover, they often are transformed, during or after learning has occurred. To take a common example, nailbiting is a habit whose motivational bases apparently change radically from its inception to its later development. Let us suppose that this particular habit is initially reinforced by "tension" reduction, at a time, say, of special stress (perhaps induced by school pressures, social expectation, or some other similar situation). Nailbiting helps to relieve the tensions then acting upon the individual, and so the habit is strengthened and maintained. It tends to reappear whenever these particular tensions recur or when, through stimulus generalization, any similar tensions occur. Gradually, however, nailbiting comes to acquire either its own intrinsic motivational bases (becomes, as Allport [1937] put it, "functionally autonomous") or to occur in stimulus situations greatly different, in quantity as well as kind, from the original initiating ones. This kind of motivational transformation, although most marked in habits like nailbiting and "drinking," is presumably characteristic of a wide variety of responses.

Many acquired responses involve an intimate relationship between physiological mechanisms and learning. Here the role of motivation is especially difficult to unthread. A good example is the case of drug addiction, which has both unlearned physiological bases as well as learned bases. Another example is the phenomenon called "imprinting"—a term which refers to the permanent attachment of certain animals, notably chicks and ducklings, to objects or persons encountered during a very early and critical period in life. For example, ducklings which normally follow their mother can be easily induced to follow a human being, if that stimulus happens to be present during the imprinting period. The precise role of learning in this kind of behavior remains to be explained, but most students of imprinting agree that it is different from ordinary learning.

METHODOLOGICAL ISSUES

The fact that psychologists in investigating learning phenomena have very largely utilized infrahuman subjects, mainly laboratory rats, is much misunderstood and deserves some attention. It is interesting that few people object to utilizing animals in medical research, where their role is generally well accepted, but many people are likely to voice strenuous objection to their utilization in behavioral research.

Animals are widely used in behavioral research for several key reasons, reasons more or less the same as those for which they are used in medical research. Foremost among these is the fact that it is possible to achieve a higher degree of control over conditions with animals than with humans. An investigator can manipulate animal subjects in ways in which human subjects cannot be used. Animal subjects are generally inexpensive to maintain, are readily available for experimentation, and may be used for long periods of time. Finally, a great deal of information has been built upon some animal species, such as the laboratory rat, and this accumulated knowledge makes it easier to plan further and more refined studies with these subjects.

Note that we are not advocating anything like exclusive dependence upon animal subjects, of any kind. We believe that all kinds of subjects, and all varieties of problems, should be scientifically investigated. We do deprecate the marked tendency, among students as well as laymen (and even sometimes in professional people, to be sure), to downgrade behavioral research that is performed with animals in general or with some particular species. It is useful to consider here, briefly, the most common reason advanced for this downgrading—the difficulty of generalizing from the more lowly of animal forms to man.

Generalization from animal subjects to humans is admittedly very tenuous, and should be done only with the greatest of caution. But this problem is not one that occurs only with regard to this kind of transfer. Generalizing among human subjects is difficult enough, in many cases, and as a matter of fact it is not even safe to risk generalizing from one situation or time to another within the same human individual! Once this problem is recognized as one of degree, it is easier to put it into proper perspective.

Another consideration that is involved in the generalization issue is the fact that many behavioral investigators, perhaps most of them, are primarily concerned with particular problems. These may be general ones like learning or motivation, or more specific ones like level of aspiration or stimulus generalization. For this kind of person the type of subject used is of distinctly secondary importance. His central concern is with the relationships among variables, and he uses whichever kinds of subjects are available and appropriate to the problem at hand. The question of applicability of his results to various other species is an interesting but less important one to him. Analogous points of view are quite common in the biological sciences (in genetics, for example), where the focus of research tends to be on the problem. It is important to remember that the question of the extent to which generalizations are possible is always an empirical one, and one that cannot be resolved in advance of gathering the data.

With regard to the present issue, it is indeed unfortunate that so little has been done on the motivation-learning problem with human subjects. One reason for this relative lack of research, especially conspicuous because of the critical nature of the problem, is that it is so difficult to manipulate human motivation meaningfully in the laboratory—and so difficult to measure learning carefully outside of the laboratory. The kind of research that is most relevant to human learning is verbal learning. While this field has indeed seen a marked resurgence in recent years (see Melton, 1964), there has not been anything like a corresponding increase in manipulation of relevant motivational variables.

It is quite clear that there is a great need for investigators who do want to apply fundamental research principles and techniques to everyday-life problems, such as those of formal education. It seems to us that, for better or worse, it will be up to those who desire the applied-science type of information to bridge the gap between the pure scientific investigation on the one hand and the strictly applied-science type of research on the other hand. It is thus up to them, mainly, because few "pure" scientists are directly interested in the applied-science type of problem. As a consequence it is necessary for the person who is so interested, say the educational researcher, himself to master enough of the principles and techniques of learning research so that he can meaningfully adapt them to his own more immediate problems, such as those involving classroom learning. We return to this issue in Chapter 8, where we treat problems in educational research.

TYPES OF LEARNING PROCESSES

Learning as it is viewed by psychologists is not something tangible, but is rather a concept inferred from behavior—a construct intervening between independent and dependent variables. When we say that something is learned we mean that in observing a person's or an animal's behavior we notice a change which is related in some manner to specific antecedent conditions. More specifically, "learning refers to a more or less permanent change in behavior which occurs as a result of practice" (Kimble, 1961, p. 6). The qualifying phrase, "as a result of practice," is intended to exclude behavior resulting from "instincts," maturation, or physiological variables such as fatigue and drug action. The definition also suggests that learning is related to objective features of the environment, since both antecedents (stimuli) and consequents (responses) can be quantified. The term *stimuli,* as used here, refers to any changes in the environment (lights, shock, voices, or other). The word *response* is given an equally broad meaning and is more or less synonymous with behavior, but usually refers to modifiable behavior.

The learning situation is generally structured so that the experimenter changes the stimulus conditions in a particular manner and records the subject's responses, only one of which is "correct." For example, a person is shown different lists of words rated in terms of difficulty and required to learn them. Here the stimuli are the words, with their various degrees of difficulty, and the response is verbalization of the different words. Another example is presenting a piece of candy to a child whenever he presses a bar while a red light is on. If he presses the bar at any other time, he does not receive any candy. The stimulus condition is either light-on or light-off, the response is the barpress, and the learned behavior is the discrimination between the differences in stimulus condition.

The fact that a response followed by a reward tends to be strengthened—that is, reinforced—was originally formulated by Thorndike (1911) as the *law of effect.* The terms *reinforcement, reward,* and *incentive* are used more or less interchangeably throughout our text without implication for any theoretical position. Within this framework, *positive* reinforcement is marked by the increase in probability that a given response will occur on subsequent trials. For example, when a hungry subject is given food for making a particular response, food is viewed as the positive reinforcement, since the probability of the subject's making the response under similar conditions increases. *Negative* reinforcement refers to the decrease in the probability of a given response on subsequent trials. Shock is a commonly used negative reinforcer. *Negative reinforcement* can also be defined as a stimulus whose removal increases response probability.

CLASSICAL CONDITIONING

Within the area of learning two broad types of situations are distinguished: classical (respondent) conditioning, and instrumental (operant) conditioning. *Classical conditioning* was discovered around the turn of the century by Ivan Pavlov (1906), the eminent Russian physiologist. In the course of feeding his experimental dogs he noticed that the sight and sound of food being carried to the pen tended to elicit the dog's salivation response. Futher observations revealed that when a neutral stimulus such as a tone was paired with the food, the tone eventually would, by itself, be able to produce the salivation. Pavlov (1927 translation) called the food an *unconditioned stimulus* (UCS) since it naturally produces salivation, which he called the *unconditioned response* (UCR). The tone was referred to as the *conditioned stimulus* (CS), defined as any previously neutral stimulus which, through its pairing with the UCS (food in this example) takes on the eliciting powers of the UCS. The response to the CS is referred to as the *conditioned response* (CR). The CR is very similar to the UCR but differs from it, especially in terms of intensity. The various classifications of classical conditioning are based on temporal relationships between UCS and CS (see a text such as Kimble [1961]).

In addition to its role as a particular type of learning process, classical conditioning has had a long history of utilization by various behavior theorists. Perhaps because of the great simplicity of its basic paradigm, it has very often been cited not only as the basic kind of learning, but also as the basis of other more complex learned behaviors. For example, Watson (1925) found it convenient, in advancing his behavioristic doctrine, to assume that all learned behaviors consist of simple conditioned reflexes, tied together in varying degrees of complexity. Hull (1943) used the conditioned reflex as the prototype of other more complex kinds of learning, and felt that its analysis would yield valuable information that would be applicable over a much wider range of learning phenomena. More recent versions of learning theories reveal frequent recourse to classical conditioning as a fundamental process (see Hilgard, 1956). In the present chapter we relate classical conditioning to the motivational aspects which occur in the phenomena of aversive conditioning and secondary reinforcement.

INSTRUMENTAL CONDITIONING

Instrumental or *operant conditioning* is selective learning—the strengthening of one among many possible responses. This occurs when some particular response in a stimulus situation is followed by reward. For example, the subject is placed in a situation where barpressing is followed by reward.

Two basic types of operant conditioning may be distinguished on the basis of whether the subject is free to respond all of the time or has some restriction placed upon its responses. The former situation is called a *free-operant situation* and the latter is referred to as a *controlled-operant situation*.

The free-operant situation has been extensively employed by B. F. Skinner, who has been the prime mover in the development of operant-conditioning methodology. The experimenter places a subject in an operant-conditioning apparatus, usually a box or chamber, which contains some type of manipulandum (such as a bar) that is continuously accessible. He then records the subject's level or rate of response over relatively long durations of time.

A controlled-operant situation is one in which the subject's behavior is restricted so that it is only able to respond at specific times. The runway provides a typical example. The subject is placed in the closed startbox. After the startbox door is opened, the subject is allowed to traverse the runway. After each traversal (trial), the subject is removed from the runway and again placed in the closed startbox. Another example is the situation where the subject remains in the box but the manipulandum (perhaps a retractable bar) is presented only at specific times. In both of these examples, the subject is prevented from responding "freely" by some operation of the experimenter.

COMPARISON OF CLASSICAL AND INSTRUMENTAL CONDITIONING

The distinction between classical and instrumental conditioning is an important one. Since we will refer to both of these paradigms in different experiments, their distinguishing characteristics are here summarized. Parenthetically, however, it should be noted that these characteristics are based upon procedural differences and do *not* necessarily indicate the existence of two types of learning, for this is still very much of an unsettled question.

In classical conditioning, the response is directly under the control of the experimenter in that it is the normal response to the UCS. In other words, the response is elicited (drawn out) by the stimulus. In operant conditioning, since the stimuli do not naturally elicit the desired response, the experimenter cannot directly control the response; he must wait for it to occur. That is, the response is *emitted* rather than elicited.

Closely related to this distinction is the fact that the UCR is already one of the responses in the subject's repertory, while in the operant situation the response (such as a barpress) may be new. Also, the UCR is typically mediated by the involuntary nervous system rather than the voluntary system, which controls the operant response. The stimuli in the classical situation which elicit the response are extremely well defined, but it is commonly agreed that there are no readily observable "response-producing" stimuli in operant conditioning. Moreover, stimulus substitution (CS for UCS) is a basic component in classical conditioning but is not emphasized in operant conditioning. Finally, in classical conditioning, the response prepares the subject for the reward, but the response does not actually produce the food. In operant conditioning, the response "operates" on or manipulates the environment and in this sense the response actually produces the

reinforcement. Thus in instrumental conditioning the reinforcement is contingent upon the response, while in classical conditioning no such contingency relation exists.

THE LEARNING-PERFORMANCE DISTINCTION

Generally, it may be said that learning underlies performance,
sets the upper limits for performance, and is more enduring and
permanent than performance. Although changes in performance
are the basis for inferring learning, performance may be affected
by motivational factors such as the size of the reward and the
physiological state of the organism. Not all performance changes
are related directly to learning.

One way to assess motivational factors in performance is by
measuring *resistance to extinction*. This term refers to the persistence of responding in the absence of reinforcement. Extinction is
said to occur when the same S-R relationships are repeated in the
absence of reinforcement and the response diminishes and eventually ceases. Forgetting, which is often confused with extinction,
is related to the failure of the response to occur (that is, absence
of practice). Extinction thus emphasizes the lack of reinforcement for the repeated occurrence of the response whereas forgetting stresses the nonoccurrence of the response.

The importance of extinction, from the present point of view,
is that it provides a relatively sensitive gauge of motivational
factors. Once reinforcement, as manipulated by the experimenter, is removed, the persistence of performance is measured in two
main ways. It is measured mainly as resistance to extinction in
terms of trials to some criterion of nonperformance, but also
secondarily by latency and speed scores in the early extinction
trials. Subtle influences of training variables, perhaps not expressed as clearcut determinants of performance during reinforced trials, may be expected to have more powerful effects after
reinforcement ceases. Knowing the laws influencing performance,
the investigator could then compare these curves with others
obtained in different situations and any differences would be
related to learning. However, Kimble (1961, p. 117) has listed
four reasons why this comparison is difficult to achieve: (1) most

factors influence *both* learning and performance, (2) the same variables probably exert different amounts of influence in dissimilar situations, (3) various response measures are differently influenced by the same variables, and (4) methodological techniques for separating performance and learning variables have not been developed.

In view of these difficulties, two "rules of thumb" are generally followed. First, performance at the beginning of a test session is usually taken to reflect learning rather than other factors. This early performance is referred to as *"preasymptotic" behavior* or *acquisition performance*. An asymptote is that point at which the performance reaches a relatively maximal stable or flat level.

Second, if a new condition is introduced into the experimental session and a *rapid shift* in performance occurs, that variable is assumed to have affected performance rather than learning. This reasoning rests upon the assumption that learning is viewed as an incremental process which develops slowly. Any rapid shift in behavior accordingly reflects pure performance, or motivation, rather than learning.

The distinction between learning and performance, with the interaction of motivation and learning seen as the critical factor, has been generally accepted. This distinction has typically been applied to the problem of the strength of the consummatory habit. An attempt to make a comparable distinction for instrumental responses may be found in Marx (1966). The concept of *instrumental motivation* was devised to represent the joint operation of activating and associative conditions at an instrumental-response level. The basic proposition is that much of what is commonly called "learning" in the strengthening of an instrumental response (such as, running or barpressing) is in actuality an increment in the activating, or motivational, component of the habit rather than in the associative, or learning, component.

THE DRIVE CONCEPT

HISTORICAL REVIEW

The term *drive* has been used in a general way to refer to internal motivational factors, more or less directly physiological.

After the rise and fall of the instinct doctrine, in the late 1920's, it became for a time fashionable to utilize the concept of "drive" as a kind of substitute for "instinct." Whereas formerly each major type of motivated behavior had been attributed (by some) to an innate factor usually called an instinct, now somewhat the same attribution was made to the concept of drive, as a more generalized kind of intraorganismic activation. The seemingly endless proliferation of a variety of drives disenchanted many psychologists, for a concept that can explain everything is very close to explaining nothing. In a similar manner, the plethora of instincts had hastened the demise of the instinct concept as an explanatory mechanism. A contemporary example may be found in the concept of "anxiety," a hypothetical organismic state which is used to explain such a vast array of behavioral phenomena that its usefulness as a term in the language of science is highly questionable. While such terms may at times be necessary in theory building, the actual creation of useful data demands a language with a high degree of specificity.

Because internal activating factors play too powerful a role to be long neglected, there has been a resumed interest in drives and drivelike phenomena. This resumption has taken many forms, ranging from the monolithic drive theory of Hull (1943), in which the term *drive* comprises the *totality* of internal activating factors, to many variations of more specialized developments in which a number of separate kinds of processes are posited. One of the more important and interesting of these latter developments is the relatively recent emphasis upon such superficially nondrivelike phenomena as curiosity and exploration. However, as Fowler (1965) has recently demonstrated in an interesting theoretical essay, the concept of "drive" can be brought to bear even upon these topics.

"Drive," like "learning," is a concept which is identified with a given set of experimental operations inferred from behavior. In either case, it is intangible. *Primary drive,* as we are using the term, refers to those physiological drives such as hunger and thirst which are defined in terms of deprivation conditions in order to distinguish them from the learned or secondary drives discussed later in this section. Thus, hunger is defined in terms of the organism's being so many hours without food, and thirst in terms of the number of hours without water. Although the concept of "drive" has recently been the subject of much psychological criticism, it is undeniable that drives do motivate behavior in the sense of initiating and, possibly, directing behavior. In addition, drives may in some instances also contribute to learning, although this statement is more questionable. However, primary drives do *not* constitute the only source of motivation—some behavior is *not* built upon drives. Futhermore, there is no intent on our part to propose that need or drive reduction is a necessary condition for motivation.

PROPERTIES AND INTERACTIONS

PERFORMANCE EFFECTS

Drives have been shown to exert their greatest influence upon performance after a task has been learned. This major function is usually referred to as the energizing effects of drive, as opposed to the directional properties. The typical design used to evaluate this energizing function is to train a subject under a given level of drive and then test it under different drive conditions.

An early study in this area was performed by Yamaguchi (1951). He found that as deprivation increased from 3 to 72 hours during test there was a corresponding increase in the number of nonreinforced (extinction) barpress responses. Cotton (1953) and King (1959) varied the deprivation conditions from 0 to 72 hours and found essentially the same relationship. However, in their studies, the data were analyzed in a slightly different manner. For each deprivation condition they considered not only the total time required to traverse the maze, but also the total time minus the time required for activities which were not directly concerned with forward movement—competing responses such as sniffing, stopping, or grooming. When these two curves were compared, the curve without competing responses was relatively flat (showed little change between the drive conditions), while the other curve, including the competing responses, showed a steep function—as drive increases, competing responses decrease and the change in effect produces better performance. Consequently, it may be concluded that performance under certain conditions is increased by increases in drive and that in large part at least this change is attributable to the dropping out of responses interfering with the instrumental response. Lawson (1960, pp. 334–335) states a similar principle in respect to the general nature of response variability: "As drive strength increases, most subject's Rs show less variability from observation to observation. Under low drive there is typically a great deal of intra-subject variability—sometimes the organism will make a given response quickly, only to make it sluggishly the very next time; and as we increase drive, however, we decrease such inconsistencies."

DIRECTIVE PROPERTIES

A second and perhaps more interesting question is whether or not drives, in addition to their energizing aspect, have directing properties. Although this question is far from settled, there are several sources of data which indicate that drive, *under some conditions,* may exert an executive or directive function. In classic studies, Hull (1933) and Leeper (1935) independently reasoned that if drive can direct behavior, then it is possible to train a rat to do one thing under one type of drive (say hunger) and another thing under a second type of drive (say thirst). They found that if a sufficient number of trials was used, subjects could be trained in a T-maze to turn left for water when thirsty and to turn right for food when hungry.

These results can be explained by the assumption that drives produce certain distinctive cues which can be conditioned to responses much in the same way that any S-R relationship can be established. Reflection reveals that this directional property makes good sense when viewed from an evolutionary or adaptation position. That is to say, how could organisms learn to go to water when thirsty unless the deprivation-of-water stimuli produced cues which had somehow become attached to appropriate responses? "Survival value" thus resides in the fact that an organism's behavior conforms to its previous reinforcement history.

Kimble (1961, pp. 414–415), in summarizing the experiments concerned with the effects of drive level upon learning, reports that about half of the studies support the conclusion that learning and drive are related—that drive determines the strength of the habit—and that half do not support such a conclusion, but rather indicate that drive is solely a performance or motivational variable. Campbell and Kraeling (1954) observed that the behavior of rats trained under different drives was different, with the high-drive group leaving the startbox faster than the low-drive group. A moment's reflection will reveal the similarity between the Campbell and Kraeling observation and the conclusion advanced previously that increased performance may be the result of a decrease in competing responses. It may be that drive influences learning indirectly rather than directly. That is, it is quite possible that the most efficient learning occurs under that drive level which produces the type of behavior most readily adapted to the particular situation. Thus both variables—drive level with its correlated behavior and the complexity of the task—must be considered in relation to learning a task; any generalization omitting either of these two factors may indeed fail to account for most of the data. A general rule of the thumb is provided by the Yerkes-Dodson Law (1908)—as the complexity of the task increases there is a decrease in the level of the most effective drive.

AVERSIVE DRIVES

So far, we have been concerned only with the effects of primary appetitive drives. Let us now briefly consider the aversive drives and how they may motivate behavior.

AVOIDANCE CONDITIONING

In general, it may be said that aversive stimulation (such as shock) produces either active or passive avoidance behavior. The manner in which the noxious stimulus is presented determines which of these two forms of behavior will occur. In *active avoidance*, the subject must learn to make a response to avoid the onset of the shock. For example, a light is paired with a shock and a rat must learn to turn a wheel when the light occurs in order to avoid the shock. Only one particular response (determined by the experimenter) will achieve this goal. In *passive avoidance* (which may be related to punishment), the subject must learn *not* to do something in order to avoid the shock, and all responses but one serve his purpose. That is, the subject in training is punished for making a particular response, whereas in the active-avoidance situation the subject is shocked when it fails to make a particular response. An example of passive avoidance occurs when every time a rat presses a bar he is shocked, and the only way to avoid the shock is to learn not to press the bar. What is important here is to determine how shock can motivate behavior when it is not present at the time the behavior occurs.

When shock has been paired with some neutral cue, that cue takes on the properties of the shock—it is a "secondary motivator." Thus, a light (CS) associated with shock (UCS) has the functional properties of the shock and becomes able to elicit the UCR. Here is the crux of the matter—what is the UCR in aversive conditioning? The answer most widely accepted by psychologists is that some type of fear is the natural response to shock. If this is true, as the evidence appears to indicate, then the CS is able to produce this fear through its prior association with the shock, and it produces a secondary or learned drive.

THE ROLE OF FEAR

Our question is still not answered, for we have not discovered how the actual avoidance response to fear is strengthened. One possible answer lies in the fact that when the avoidance response occurs, it *reduces* the fear of future shock, and it is this fear reduction which is the reinforcer. Since fear reduction occurs after the avoidance response, it tends to strengthen the avoidance response. Stated slightly differently, that which produces the termination or offset of any drive is a reinforcing event (thus, food decreases hunger and avoidance of pain reduces fear).

The above analysis will perhaps be a little clearer through the following example. A rat always shocked in the presence of a light is taught to avoid the shock by pressing a bar which turns off the light and prevents the shock. Then the experimenter turns off the shock so that only the light is terminated by the response and, though the UCS will no longer occur, the subject continues to perform the barpress response. Thus, (1) the light becomes conditioned to fear, (2) fear is a secondary drive which motivates the subject, (3) the barpress reduces the fear, and (4) fear reduction reinforces the barpress behavior.

Miller and Kraeling (1952) have amply demonstrated that fear can be associated with a previously neutral cue and that this association produces an avoidance response in the absence of shock. All subjects were originally trained to run to food in a straight runway. Then they were shocked in the goalbox until they refused to eat. The subjects refused to eat even when the shock was discontinued on subsequent trials. Subjects were also tested on two other alleys progressively different from the original one. On the original runway only 23 per cent of the subjects went to the goalbox; on the runway rated as being intermediate in similarity, 37 per cent went into the goalbox; and on the runway least similar to the original, 70 per cent of the subjects entered the goalbox. Thus, the greater the degree of similarity to the original fear-producing cues, the greater the avoidance behavior.

In a classic experiment, N. E. Miller (1948) has shown how fear reduction can reinforce behavior. Miller associated a white compartment with shock and an adjoining black compartment with escape from the shock. Eventually, the subject learned to run from the white compartment to the black compartment. Then, Miller arranged the conditions to demonstrate how a new response not previously associated with shock termination could be acquired on the basis of fear reduction. He achieved this by placing a door between the two compartments which the rats were able to learn to open by pressing a bar or turning a wheel. It must be noted that at no time during this barpress or wheelturn training was shock ever associated with these responses. Thus, learning the responses was held to have been mediated by the fear reduction.

Amsel and Cole (1953) further demonstrated that not only may fear produce learning but it may also inhibit behavior. They paired a light with shock which the subjects were unable to avoid by any overt response. After training, the subjects were placed on water deprivation and then allowed to drink. After several sessions, when a stable drinking rate had become established, the light was introduced in the drinking situation without the shock. Immediately the rate of water consumption decreased. Again, it would appear that the presence of the fear-producing light could explain the disruption of the drinking rate.

In all of the above examples, the previously neutral cues, when associated with the onset of noxious stimulation, were able to "take on" some of the properties of the noxious stimuli and were called secondary motivators or drives. We will later discuss what happens when cues are associated with the termination of drives (the phenomenon of "secondary reinforcement").

RESEARCH PROBLEMS

SCHEDULES OF REINFORCEMENT

There are several different basic types of variation in the presentation of reinforcement. These schedules of reinforcement, which can be divided into two broad categories, are continuous and noncontinuous (or intermittent) reinforcement. In *continuous reinforcement* every response is reinforced, while in *noncontinuous reinforcement* either a prescribed number of responses must occur or a particular interval of time must elapse before the reinforcement is presented. Reinforcement which is provided in a random schedule with no particular relationship either to time interval or response rate is termed *adventitious reinforcement*. Ferster and Skinner's *Schedules of Reinforcement* (1957) is devoted to the effects of these different schedules using free-operant techniques.

Reinforcement may be considered to be, basically, a means of motivating or activating the organism to make a given response, apart from any role it may have in establishing habits. From this point of view, as a matter of fact, most if not all of the reinforcement manipulations utilized in operant-conditioning research may be seen as essentially motivational in character, with rate of response as the major and often the sole measure of performance.

THE CUMULATIVE RECORDER

The subject (usually a rat or a pigeon) is typically placed into an operant-conditioning box equipped with either a bar (metal rod) for the rat to press or a key (a small plate, usually lighted) for the pigeon to peck. Each barpress or keypeck activates a recording pen which makes a vertical movement on a continuously moving roll of paper. This device is called a cumulative recorder. If the subject does not press the bar or peck the key, a horizontal movement is recorded. Thus, the pen actually moves horizontally except when a response occurs. The steeper the curve the greater the response rate. This type of a graph is called a cumulative curve to distinguish it from the more conventional curve in which the number of responses per unit of time or trial is plotted. By comparing different graphs from different schedules, the experimenter can determine whether a given schedule produces any particular pattern of response. Usually, a limited number of subjects are studied intensively and few or no statistical analyses are performed on the data.

The relatively simplified free-operant conditioning situation is an especially good one for reflecting motivational strength, since a fairly reliable baseline can be readily achieved. That is, a stable level of responding can be established before manipulation of the independent variable is begun. Deviation from this baseline may then be taken as an index of motivation. For example, the baseline can be established for a given level of reinforcement and then the amount of reinforcement can be varied. If the rate of responding increases with an increased amount of reinforcement it is reasonable to think that the increase in reinforcement may have produced an increase in motivation to respond. (For this same reason the free-operant technique also provides an especially effective measure of the behavioral effects of drugs; as a matter of fact, it is such an extremely sensitive measure that effects of minute dosages can sometimes be detected behaviorally even when the ordinary physiological measures fail to reveal any effect.) The absence of competitive responses of the sort that are found in all more complex learning situations also has the dual effect of channeling all of the motivational factors into one response while at the same time reducing the learning (that is, stimulus-response associative) factor to a minimum (see Marx, 1966).

CONTINUOUS REINFORCEMENT

A continuous-reinforcement schedule results in a cumulative curve which is negatively accelerated and is fairly stable after the first few responses. Later in a given experimental session, the response rate may decrease because of satiation factors. This property of reasonably rapid satiation makes the CRF schedule inappropriate for use in studies of long duration. The rate is also affected by other variables such as amount and quality of reward, but these are topics in themselves and will be treated separately.

INTERMITTENT REINFORCEMENT

The intermittent or noncontinuous schedules can be divided into time-based (interval) and response-based (ratio) schedules. These can be further divided depending on whether the reinforcement is delivered regularly (fixed schedule) or irregularly (variable schedule). Thus, in total we have four basic noncontinuous schedules: *fixed-ratio* (FR), *variable-ratio* (VR), *fixed-interval* (FI), and *variable-interval* (VI).

FIXED RATIO

On a fixed-ratio schedule, reinforcement occurs regularly after a specific fixed number of responses have occurred. A 4-1 FR means that every fourth response is reinforced; a 1-1 FR is continuous reinforcement. The FR schedule may produce a very rapid response rate; the subject tends to respond at a maximal rate or not at all. That is, the records are characterized by bursts of responses followed by periods of inactivity that usually occur after the reinforcement. The subject "knows" it never receives a reward immediately following a previous one, so it stops responding after the reinforcement. However, when it begins to respond it does so at a maximum rate to decrease the time necessary for completing the required ratio and the slopes of the cumulative record increase in steepness as the ratio increases.

VARIABLE RATIO

In a variable-ratio schedule the required number of responses is changed between reinforcements. Thus, for the first reinforcement five responses may be required, for the second seven responses, for the third two responses, and so on. This schedule tends to produce a steady and relatively invariant response rate without the bursts of activity between the reinforcements found in the FR schedules. The premium is on the persistence of a response and the subject has no way of "knowing" when the next reinforcement will occur. Consequently, the subject is motivated to employ the most efficient mode of response—a constant and persistent rate. This is the schedule commonly used with slot machines and pinball machines, for obvious reasons.

FIXED INTERVAL

Fixed-interval (or periodic) reinforcement is that schedule in which the first response after a specified period of time is reinforced. Thus, on a one-minute FI, the subject is reinforced for the first response which occurs after one minute has elapsed from the last reinforcement.

This schedule generates a characteristic response pattern called *scalloping*—the rate following the reinforcement is low and increases gradually until the interval is almost terminated at which time sudden rapid responding occurs, *as if* the subject can tell time. Deese (1958) states that an animal will emit a constant number of responses per reinforcement for any fixed interval, and the general rule is that the rate of responding is inversely proportional to the interval between reinforcements. Thus, if an animal is found to produce an average of 20 responses per reinforcement, the average rate of response for a 1-minute FI will be 20 per minute, while on a 2-minute FI, the average rate will be 10 per minute, although in each case most of these responses occur near the end of the interval.

One interesting sidelight of a fixed-interval type of schedule is the development of what Skinner (1948) calls "superstitious" behavior. Since the reinforcement occurs at temporal intervals, it very often follows, quite adventitiously, some behavior which is entirely irrelevant to the situation. For example, a pigeon might happen to turn its head just before the grain is presented. A single such reinforcement can increase the probability of the response, so that one or more subsequent associations of the response and reward will be more likely. Eventually this reponse may thus become part of the behavior sequence. Those "natural" responses which occur most frequently were found to develop into "superstitious" behavior quicker than others. The parallel to human behavior should be apparent.

The variable-interval (or aperiodic) schedule is the same as the VR except that the intervals are changed rather than the response-reinforcement ratios. This schedule produces the most stable response rates, the animal responding with almost clock-like precision over long periods of time. Because of this characteristic the VI schedule provides a constant baseline from which the effects of variables such as drugs may be studied.

When the different schedules are compared in terms of resistance to extinction, the greatest resistance is produced by the variable schedules; that is, the variable-ratio and variable-interval schedules appear to result in the greatest motivation to respond in the absence of reinforcement.

MAGNITUDE OF REWARD

The motivational implications of magnitude of reward should be readily apparent. Reward, which reinforces behavior, has motivating or activating properties. These are especially evident in the simpler kinds of "learning" tasks, such as the runway and the barpress situation, where the stimulus-response associative factor is minimal and much if not all of the increment in performance over acquisition trials may be attributed to motivation rather than learning.

The term *magnitude,* as used in this section, will refer to the quantitative manipulation of a given type of reward. Several variations can be used, such as number of pellets, duration of time permitted for the subject to consume the reinforcement, concentration of a solution (for example, amount of sugar per volume of water) and so on.

An experiment by Grindley (1929) is the first reported study in which the amount of reward was systematically varied. He found that chickens reinforced with either 0, 1, 2, 4, or 6 grains of rice ran fastest at the end of training to the 6 grains and slowest to the 0 grains. A host of subsequent experiments with a variety of organisms has substantiated this relationship. Subjects perform at a higher level with greater amounts of reinforcement. One additional factor that should be mentioned is that although the asymptotic performance is higher for the larger incentives, the rate at which this level of response is reached does not usually differ among the different groups (Hutt, 1954; Pubols, 1960). That is, high-incentive groups have a higher level of responding at the end of training than the low-incentive groups, but all groups reached their respective level in approximately the same number of trials. Thus, magnitude has no significant effect upon learning (if it is assumed that learning is reflected in the slope of preasymptotic performance), but rather it exerts its influence upon performance, presumably through motivational effects. According to this view, the magnitude of the incentive does not result in faster learning but produces an increase in motivation which subsequently increases performance. Not that the magnitude of reinforcement never affects learning—it may well increase learning in particular situations of a more complex nature than those discussed above.

The studies previously described have utilized what Lawson (1957) has called the absolute method of comparison—only a single incentive is presented. The following studies have employed the differential method, in which the subject experiences more than one incentive. Several such procedures are possible within the differential paradigm, but we will be interested only in those involving problems where (1) the subjects are given two or more stimulus conditions which are differentially reinforced, and (2) a shift in magnitude of incentives occurs within a single task.

One variation of the first method is to present the subject with a choice between two spatially separated magnitudes of reward. This procedure is usually referred to as simultaneous discrimination. It is well illustrated by Pereboom (1957), who trained rats in a T-maze with five pellets in one arm (positive arm) and one pellet in the other (negative arm). After 10 days of training, the subjects consistently ran to the arm with the larger reward. An interesting experiment by Fay, Miller, and Harlow (1953) used five quantities of preferred incentive (peanuts or bread). They found that the percentage of preference for the preferred incentive increased as the ratio of preferred to nonpreferred incentive (potato) increased. Thus, the greater the contrast or ratio between incentives in a choice situation, the more motivated are subjects to choose the larger incentive.

A second variation of the first design is to present different magnitudes, or different magnitudes paired with distinctive environmental cues, on separate trials instead of simultaneously. This type of procedure is called successive discrimination. It is exemplified by D'Amato (1955), who trained subjects in a straight runway to run either for five pellets or one pellet on different trials. The trials were distinguished by differently colored goalboxes associated with the different magnitudes of reinforcement. After 70 training trials, differential responding occurred; the subjects ran significantly faster on the large-reward trials than on the small-reward trials. Thus, both the absolute and differential situations yield essentially the same results—subjects will perform at a higher level for large rewards than for small rewards.

INCENTIVE SHIFTS

Within recent years a great deal of attention has been devoted to the effects upon behavior of shifting incentives, that is, changing magnitudes of reinforcement. This problem is of interest here mainly because of its relevance for motivation. The basic paradigm for the shift experiment is to maintain groups of subjects at the same level of reinforcement for a large number of trials, preferably until their acquisition performance is asymptotic, after which a substantial increase or decrease in amount of reinforcement is introduced. The general expectation is that a sudden and marked increment in performance will thereupon occur for the upshifted groups and a marked decrement in performance for the downshifted groups. The critical comparison is then between the new level of performance and that maintained by a control group which has been kept on the same amount of reinforcement throughout the experiment. The upshifted group may excel the performance of control subjects which have been on that same (relatively high) incentive level; this phenomenon is called "overshooting." The downshifted group may fall below the performance level of control subjects maintained throughout the experiment on the lower incentive value; this phenomenon is called "undershooting." The similarity of this experimental paradigm to the use of shifts of incentive in industry (say, in factories where piecework pay is employed) should be evident. It is often assumed that increments in motivation, such as slight increases in rate of pay, can improve production levels even after long periods of no improvement. Experiments with proper controls may suggest whether such assumptions are warranted.

The first animal study to employ a shift in magnitude of reinforcement within the same task was reported by Crespi (1942). His procedure was as follows: He trained four groups of rats to traverse a runway with either 1, 4, 64, or 256 .02-gram pellets as reinforcement. After all groups had reached asymptotic running speed they were shifted to 16 pellets. The performance of these groups was then compared with that of another group which had received 16 pellets throughout the experiment and which had reached asymptotic performance. The results clearly indicated that the upshifted group ran faster than the constant 16-pellet group and the downshifted group ran slower than the constant 16-pellet group. That is, subjects which had an increase to 16 pellets tended to "overshoot," while subjects which experienced a decrease to 16 pellets tended to "undershoot" the level of performance of subjects which had always been maintained from the beginning of the experiment on 16 pellets. The phenomena of "overshooting" and "undershooting" were substantiated by Zeaman (1949).

The "overshooting-undershooting" phenomenon is frequently referred to as the Crespi-Zeaman effect, and the rapid shift in performance strongly indicated that this effect is attributable to performance or motivational variables rather than to learning factors. Presumably, the contrast between the two incentives makes the larger incentive following a smaller incentive "more attractive" and conversely, renders a smaller incentive following a larger incentive "less attractive" than are the same incentives when no contrast is presented. "Attractiveness," then, appears to be a function of the difference or discrepancy between subsequent incentives rather than simply a matter of the absolute magnitude of the reward. Thus, a change in incentives appears to produce a greater or lesser degree of motivation depending upon the direction of the shift.

A more direct attempt to separate learning and motivational factors has been undertaken in a first experiment by Collier and Marx (1959) and in subsequent experiments by Marx and Pieper (1962, 1963). These experiments were designed to assess the effects of incentive shifts upon early acquisition rather than strictly on performance. The Crespi-Zeaman procedure, where subjects experience both magnitudes on the same task, was modified so that the subjects did not experience both incentives on the same response. Two interrelated tasks were used, the subject experiencing one incentive on one task and the second incentive on the second task. It was predicted, on the basis of the Crespi-Zeaman studies, that the upshifted subjects should have the highest rate of response, the downshifted subjects should have the lowest rate of response, and the subjects maintained on a constant incentive should be somewhere between the other two groups.

Collier and Marx (1959) trained three groups of subjects to lick solutions of either 4, 11.3, or 32 per cent sucrose from an automatic liquid dispenser which advanced periodically (task 1). After the subjects had received a sufficient amount of training on the feeding device (magazine training), they were then trained to barpress (task 2) for 11.3 per cent sucrose, which was presented by the same dipper. Three groups were used, identified by ratios in which the first number refers to the concentration received during magazine training and the second number refers to the concentration received in barpress training: 4/11.3; 11.3/11.3; and 32/11.3. The magazine training was independent of the subsequent experience with the bar. The results supported the Crespi-Zeaman proposition, with the 4/11.3 group having the greatest number of barpresses, followed by the 11.3/11.3 group. The 32/11.3 group had the lowest number of barpresses.

Three follow-up studies (Marx and Pieper, 1962, 1963; and Pieper and Marx, 1963), using a modified procedure in which barpress training followed magazine training every day, have extended these results. During early barpress training the "under-shooting" and "overshooting" were not evidenced and the groups ranked themselves in order of the magnitude they had received during magazine training irrespective of what concentration they had received during barpress training. However, later in training the classical Crespi-Zeaman effect was found. These results are most readily explained in terms of a dual learning process. Not only must the subject learn to press the bar, it must also learn to discriminate between the different concentrations used in the two different parts of the experiment. That is, only after a discrimination between the concentration used during magazine training and the concentration used in barpress training was established did the results reflect the motivational effects resulting from the contrast between the two incentives. This series of experiments is significant because it demonstrates the importance of structuring situations in such a manner that the effects of motivational variables can be made evident.

EXTINCTION

At the present time no fully definitive statement can be made concerning the relationship between magnitude of reinforcement and resistance to extinction. Some data indicate that resistance to extinction is greater after large magnitudes (Guttman, 1953; D'Amato, 1955; and Tombaugh and Marx, 1965), while other evidence shows that resistance to extinction is less after large magnitudes (Wagner, 1961; Hulse, 1958). The reason for this inconsistency is not immediately clear. Although several interacting variables may account for it, a discussion of them is beyond the scope of this section.

PARTIAL REINFORCEMENT

Even the most cursory analysis reveals that everyday life is seldom characterized by continuous reinforcement—the same response is sometimes reinforced and sometimes is not reinforced. Approximately two decades ago it was discovered (Humphreys, 1939; Skinner, 1938) that offering an organism reinforcement after only some proportion of its responses (partial reinforcement), rather than after all of them as had been customary, produced striking effects on resistance to extinction. We have seen the effects of this type of procedure in the discussion of intermittent schedules of reinforcement, where an intermittent schedule resulted in greater resistance to extinction than a continuous schedule. The present section concerns some of the evidence produced by a discrete-trial rather than a free-operant paradigm. In such a procedure subjects are reinforced on some percentage of the trials (on every other trial, or on two reinforced trials followed by two nonreinforced trials, or the like).

It was generally believed, before the partial-reinforcement experiments, that response strength was directly proportional to the frequency of the reinforcement. Thus, it was predicted that the greater the number of reinforcements, the faster the learning and the greater the resistance to extinction. The part of this assumption related to extinction, like many empirically ungrounded assumptions, was subsequently shown to be incorrect.

ACQUISITION

The majority of studies have yielded consistent results concerning the effects of various percentages of reinforcement on acquisition performance. Subjects (both human and infrahuman) given reward on 100 per cent of the trials perform better than subjects given reward on 50 per cent of the trials. This statement may be generalized to percentages other than 50 per cent and 100 per cent so that acquisition performance may be said to be an increasing or direct function of the percentage of reward. Two qualifications must be appended to this generalization. First, the greatest differences appear early in training. Second, often in later training the differences are slight and many experiments have reported insignificant differences during the performance segment of the curve. In fact, some experiments (Goodrich, 1959; Haggard, 1957; and Weinstock, 1958) found that subjects trained on a *lesser* percentage of reward performed better in later training even though in earlier training their performance was inferior to that of subjects trained on a higher percentage of reinforcement. Thus, in these studies, at least, there appears to be an interaction between number of training trials and percentage of reinforcement. The extent to which this generalization is valid and under what conditions it will obtain is still a matter of empirical demonstration.

EXTINCTION

It is in the extinction situation that the most surprising results have occurred. Humphreys (1939) incorporated 100 per cent and 50 per cent reinforcements into a classical-conditioning situation with human subjects. Although in training the 100-per-cent group demonstrated superior performance, the 50-per-cent group demonstrated greater resistance to extinction. For a while this greater resistance to extinction for a lesser percentage of reinforcement was known as the "Humphreys paradox." As more and more studies demonstrated the same effect, and it became apparent that the phenomenon was not an artifact, psychologists directed their attention toward determining the factors which influence it. The major finding of interest is that resistance to extinction is a decreasing function of the percentage of reinforcement. That is, not only does reinforcement of 50 per cent produce greater resistance to extinction than reinforcement of 100 per cent, but furthermore lower percentages in general produce greater resistance to extinction than do higher percentages. This relationship is now referred to as the partial-reinforcement effect (PRE). A statement by Lewis (1960, p. 2) well illustrates the degree to which the PRE has been established as one of the laws of psychology: "following their review of the pertinent literature, Jenkins and Stanley (1950) arrived at an empirical generalization which stated, 'all other things equal, resistance to extinction after partial reinforcement is greater than after continuous reinforcement.' Nine years and a great deal of research later this generalization still stands, perhaps more firmly than ever."

The PRE obviously poses a real problem for the motivational interpretation of extinction (see Marx, 1966) as well as for most or all of the other more orthodox points of view. Why an organism should respond more strongly in acquisition but less persistently in extinction remains a most difficult problem. If one assumes that superior acquisition performance is typical of a continuous-reinforcement schedule, and thereby indicative of stronger motivation, then it becomes necessary to account for the sharply reduced motivational strength that occurs when subjects are shifted to nonreinforcement. A similar necessity faces most of the orthodox habit-increment types of theories (such as Hull's and Spence's). For this reason, interest in the PRE as a well-established empirical phenomenon, in both rats and humans, has remained at a high level.

The practical implications of the PRE are immense. It is obvious that one can maintain behavior over long periods of time with a minimum amount of reinforcement by interspersing non-reinforced trials between the reinforced ones. This procedure also minimizes the effects of satiation. The fact that learning is only slightly retarded by partial reinforcement may make it advisable to begin training with continuous reinforcement and then shift to partial reinforcement. Moreover, the generalization that partial reinforcement maintains behavior over long periods of nonreinforcement "appears to hold whether one is interested in having a rat press a bar or in maintaining a child's proper toilet habits or table manners" (Jenkins and Stanley, 1950, p. 230).

In spite of the fact that it is not yet possible to make anything like a definitive theoretical or interpretive statement concerning the PRE, its theoretical implications are patently commensurate with its practical implications, particularly for the problem of motivation. It is therefore to be hoped, and expected, that investigators interested in this problem will turn at least some of their energies to experimenting and theorizing on the PRE to accelerate the pace of resolution of the problem—or at least to accomplish the preliminary task of breaking it down into a set of smaller problems, more directly answerable.

DELAY OF REINFORCEMENT

Two types of delay of reinforcement are generally recognized— spatial and temporal. *Spatial delay* refers to the physical distance between the beginning of the instrumental act and reward (perhaps the length of a runway), while *temporal delay* refers to the amount of time which elapses between the completion of the instrumental act and reinforcement (perhaps the time between a barpress and reward, or the interval between goalbox entry and presentation of the reward). Temporal delay has received the most attention since it closely parallels the partial-reinforcement paradigm.

The motivational implications of delaying reinforcement have only recently come into prominence. It is interesting that this increased attention to delayed reinforcement, like the earlier but still somewhat belated experimental and theoretical attention given to partial reinforcement, brings experimentation on reinforcement variables more closely in line with the phenomena of everyday life, where rewards are characteristically both delayed and only intermittently available.

ACQUISITION

Much of the recent research in delay of reinforcement is an outgrowth of partial-reinforcement studies. That is, delay is frequently viewed as a special case of partial reinforcement, with infinite delay at one extreme (viewed as identical to nonreinforcement) and lesser degrees of delay approaching the other extreme of immediate reinforcement. Thus, a procedure analogous to that of partial reinforcement would be to present delayed reinforcement on some percentage of the trials rather than no reinforcement, and immediate reinforcement on the rest of the trials. Wike and his associates have used just such a procedure. For example, Wike and McNamara (1957) found that a 20-second delay presented on 25 per cent of the trials produced faster running than when presented on either 50 per cent or 75 per cent of the trials, and Wike and Kintsch (1959) found that at the end of training the speed of running was inversely related to the percentage of delayed trials when a 30-second delay was used on 0, 20, 50, 80, and 100 per cent of the trials. Thus, partial delay of reinforcement is seen to produce results similar to partial reinforcement. In both cases, acquisition decreases as the percentage of immediately reinforced trials decreases and the percentage of nonreinforced or delay trials increases.

Not only are high percentages of delay trials necessary to retard acquisition markedly, but Wike and Kintsch (1959) cogently point out that long delay intervals are also necessary. This observation leads to the question, "What are the effects of imposing a fixed duration of delay on every trial?" This procedure is referred to as the constant delay of reinforcement to distinguish it from the partial delay of reinforcement discussed above. The majority of constant-delay studies have demonstrated, with a remarkably high degree of consistency, that the longer delays result in inferior acquisition performance than do shorter delays (Warden and Haas, 1927; Perkins, 1947; Grice, 1948; Logan, 1952; Ramond, 1954; and Renner, 1964). Stated in a slightly more sophisticated manner, acquisition performance is a negatively accelerated decreasing function of constant delay of reinforcement.

One of the more interesting variables manipulated in acquisition is the shifting of subjects from one delay condition to another. This is similar to incentive shifting. Seward and Weldon (1953) trained four groups of rats to barpress with the following delays: constant 10 seconds; constant 2.5 seconds; 10 seconds downshifted to 2.5 seconds; and 2.5 seconds upshifted to 10 seconds. The shift groups were trained to asymptote on the first delay, then shifted to the second delay condition. The major finding was that the shift from 10 seconds to 2.5 seconds decreased latencies (increased performance) and that the shift from 2.5 seconds to 10 seconds increased latencies (decreased performance). Similar procedures and results have been obtained by other experiments (Harker, 1956; Logan, 1952; and Sgro and Weinstock, 1963).

These studies, taken as a whole, indicate that a shift from a longer to a shorter delay increases (improves) performance to a level equal to or exceeding that produced by the shorter delay alone, and a shift from a shorter to a longer delay decreases performance to a level equal to or below that produced by the longer delay alone. If delay of reinforcement is viewed as an aversive condition then the contrast between two delays makes the shorter delay following a longer more attractive or more motivating, and renders a longer delay following a shorter delay less attractive or less motivating than the delay condition when the contrast is not present. That is, the motivational increment or decrement produced by the shift is *greater* than that which occurs when the subjects are maintained at a constant delay. Somehow the contrast between the two delays produces motivational changes which cannot be predicted solely on the basis of knowledge of the effects of the constant-delay conditions.

These results are similar to those obtained with shifts in magnitudes of reinforcement—the "overshooting" and "undershooting" phenomena of the Crespi-Zeaman effect. By combining the findings from the studies in delay of reinforcement and those in magnitude of reinforcement, a more general motivational law can be formulated than was possible from the separate consideration of either area: A shift from a more favorable condition (short delay or large magnitude) to a less favorable (longer delay or small magnitude) produces "undershooting," and a shift from a less favorable to a more favorable produces "overshooting."

EXTINCTION

Studies concerned with the effects of partial delay on resistance to extinction have been primarily concerned with generalizing the partial-reinforcement effect to delay of reinforcement. If delay of reinforcement is viewed on a continuum from 0-second delay to infinite delay, as previously mentioned, then infinite delay and nonreinforcement are one and the same. That is, nonreinforcement is the limiting case of delay and lesser amounts of delay, up to a particular value, should produce extinction results similar to those produced by partial reinforcement.

Crum, Brown, and Bitterman (1951) demonstrated that groups which received 30-second delay on 50 per cent of the trials were more resistant to extinction than subjects which received no delay. Two other studies (Logan, Beier, and Ellis, 1955; Logan, Beier, and Kincaid, 1956) indicate that the length of the delay interval is one of the more important factors in partial or variable delay, and that a long delay is necessary to produce performance changes. In order to insure differential-extinction performance in partial delay of reinforcement, delays longer than 10 seconds should be used, at least with rat subjects; probably those in the vicinity of 20 to 30 seconds are advisable.

Another important variable is the percentage of trials on which the subjects are delayed. Representative of experiments which have investigated this variable is the study by Wike and

McNamara (1957). They trained all subjects in a runway on 30-second delay which was present on either 25 per cent, 50 per cent, or 75 per cent of the trials. Their extinction data reveal that the 25-per-cent group had the least resistance to extinction; there were no significant differences between the 75-per-cent and 50-per-cent groups.

At the present time, the data from studies on the partial delay of reinforcement indicate that as either the length of the delay or the percentage of partially delayed trials increases there is a corresponding increase in resistance to extinction. These results, it will be noted, are similar to those found with partial reinforcement. One question is whether this similarity is strictly a function of the time interval that occurs in both situations or is the result of the interval being interspersed with immediate reinforcement. One way in which this problem could be experimentally attacked would be to train and extinguish subjects with constant delay. A finding that longer delays produce greater resistance to extinction than shorter delays would suggest that the temporal interval as such is the critical factor.

Such an experiment was performed by Tombaugh (1965) using delays of 0, 5, 10, and 20 seconds. The data showed that longer constant-delay intervals produced inferior acquisition *and inferior* resistance to extinction than shorter intervals. In fact, resistance to extinction was a linear decreasing function of delay. It will be recognized that this finding is opposite to that found with partial delay and partial reinforcement. It strongly indicates that delay itself is not a sufficient condition to produce the superior resistance to extinction which occurs in the partial-delay studies. This result indicates that the explanation of the partial-reinforcement and partial-delay data is in some manner intimately associated with the variability of the reinforced conditions which occur during acquisition trials. More data are needed before any definite conclusions concerning the relationship between delay and partial reinforcement can be stated.

The Tombaugh study also supports the contention that resistance to extinction largely reflects motivational variables (see Marx, 1966). In addition to the groups which received the same delay in training and extinction, other groups were trained under one delay condition and extinguished under a different delay condition. The results demonstrated that subjects trained under long delays and extinguished under short delays had greater resistance to extinction than subjects trained and extinguished under long delays; and subjects trained under short delays and extinguished under long delays had less resistance to extinction than subjects trained and extinguished under short delays. If delay is assumed to be an aversive condition, then subjects which experience a longer delay in extinction than in training are less motivated to respond because of the increase in aversiveness, while subjects which experience a shorter delay in extinction than in training are more motivated to respond because of a decrease in aversiveness. This same reasoning may be applied to the relationship between the subjects trained and extinguished on the same delay—the longer delays, resulting in more aversiveness, produce less motivation to respond, which is reflected in less resistance to extinction than for shorter delays.

SECONDARY REINFORCEMENT

Up to this point we have seen how different variables have been able to initiate and maintain different behavioral patterns—in short, how they motivate the subjects. However, none of these variables by themselves provide an adequate explanation of performance where there is a conspicuous absence of drive or of primary reinforcement such as food or water. In fact, most of our behavior is directed by factors which *appear* to be independent of the previously mentioned variables. For example, why do people satisfy hunger in a particular restaurant? Or, how is it that money, which can't possibly be viewed as a primary reinforcement in the biological sense, is a much sought-after and desired object in our society?

The answer to these questions is often assumed to lie in a principle called *secondary reinforcement*. This principle states that whenever a previously neutral stimulus is associated with either a primary reward or the termination of a drive, it acquires the functional properties of the primary reinforcement. This result is generally considered to be the counterpart of the secondary motivation or secondary drive. Thus, as acquired drives motivate behavior, secondary reinforcers direct and sustain behavior. For example, if a light is frequently paired with the presence of food in an operant-conditioning chamber, the light can then be used as reinforcement in the absence of the food not only to maintain behavior in that particular situation, but to establish new behavior in another situation.

CLASSIC STUDIES

Early studies on secondary reinforcement were performed by Wolfe (1936) and Cowles (1937), using chimpanzees as subjects. They first taught the chimps to insert a poker chip into a vending machine ("chimp-o-mat") which dispensed raisins as reinforcement. After this habit was thoroughly established, the chimps were then trained to do different tasks in order to obtain the poker chips (secondary reinforcers by nature of their previous association with the raisins), much in the same way humans work for money. The analogy does not stop here, for in subsequent sessions the following occurred: (1) the chimps could be taught to perform very complex tasks for the mere purpose of receiving the chips, (2) when the chip-o-mat was changed so that it would deliver raisins only when 20 chips were inserted, the chimps learned to save the required number of chips, (3) the chimps learned to distinguish between different-colored chips possessing different values (a red chip being worth five white ones, and so on), and finally (4) if the chimps were given a "pension" of 30 chips before an experimental session, they would work only to obtain 3 or 4 chips whereas they normally worked for 30—the free chips appeared to "satiate" the subjects in a manner not unlike primary reinforcement, such as food or water.

From this rather dramatic example of the development and functional value of secondary reinforcers, two salient factors should be noticed and expanded. First, it will be recognized immediately that the manner in which the neutral cues achieved their secondary reinforcing properties is similar to the classical conditioning studies where the CS, through its pairing with the UCS, achieves the power to produce responses formerly elicited only by the UCS. In the above case, the poker chips may be viewed as the CS and the raisins as the UCS. Thus, only the contiguity of a neutral stimulus and a primary reinforcer seems necessary for the neutral stimulus to acquire secondary reinforcing properties. If this statement is correct, then the CS (secondary reinforcement) should be able to be used in a functionally similar manner to the UCS in producing further conditioning. That is, the CS serves as the "UCS" for establishing other "CS-UCS" associations.

The Wolfe and Cowles studies, using the poker chips to establish new behavior, have already exemplified this ability of secondary reinforcement to establish further associative relationships. However, since this was achieved in an instrumental-conditioning situation, let us provide a second example within a classical-conditioning paradigm to insure that this point is clear. When this phenomenon occurs in classical conditioning it is generally called higher-order conditioning, and it was first demonstrated by Pavlov (1906) using the following procedure. First, a bell (CS) was paired with food (UCS) until the bell produced the salivary response. Then the bell (now called the UCS) was paired with a light (CS) in a similar situation until the light was eventually able to elicit the anticipatory salivary response. Thus, the bell served as the secondary reinforcement when paired with the light, as the food had served as the primary reinforcement when paired with the bell.

RESISTANCE TO EXTINCTION

It is obvious from the Wolfe and Cowles studies that the secondary reinforcement was a learned or derived property. It has also been previously demonstrated that partial reinforcement produces greater resistance to extinction than continuous reinforcement. Therefore, if secondary reinforcement is to follow the laws of learning, greater resistance to extinction should occur when the neutral cues are associated with the UCS in a partial-reinforcement schedule than when associated with a continuous-reinforcement schedule. The evidence generally seems to support this deduction, although contradictory evidence can be found. Myers (1957) used three children, aged six, as subjects and found greater resistance to extinction when a stimulus was associated with candy under partial reinforcement than under continuous reinforcement. Saltzman (1949) trained rats to run under either a continuous- or partial-reinforcement schedule to a distinctive goalbox. In a subsequent test he used a U-maze without food being present. The results showed that the subjects which had received partial secondary reinforcement in training made fewer errors in the second task (choice of the previously rewarded goalbox) than subjects which had received continuous-reinforcement training. A further comparison with subjects not having the distinctive goalbox but given food in one of the arms of the U-maze in lieu of the secondary reinforcement revealed no difference between this group and the partial-reinforcement subjects, and both of these groups were superior to the continuous-reinforcement subjects. Notterman (1951) expanded these conclusions by finding that the strength of the secondary reinforcement was directly related to the number of nonrewarded training trials, provided of course that at least some reinforcement was provided.

A series of studies by Zimmerman (1957, 1959) has demonstrated that secondary-reinforcing properties can persist over relatively long durations of time. In surveying the literature, Zimmerman concluded that in many cases secondary-reinforcing properties existed only over short durations of time and that they were very susceptible to extinction. He further reasoned that if an investigator were to present the secondary reinforcer only sparingly in extinction, its effects would persist longer. Hence, Zimmerman devised what has become known as the "double intermittent-reinforcement schedule" in which the neutral stimulus is associated on only a part of the extinction trials. He first placed his subjects on water deprivation and paired the cue (buzzer) with the presentation of a water magazine on a variable-ratio schedule. A bar was then introduced into the situation during test, and its depression produced the buzzer on a variable-ratio schedule. Zimmerman concluded that with this procedure it is possible to establish instrumental behavior which seems to be practically inextinguishable on the basis of secondary reinforcement alone. Zimmerman's procedure stands as an excellent technique for obtaining highly resistant behavior, although his theoretical interpretation, and in particular the necessity of the role of secondary reinforcement, has been seriously questioned in subsequent research (as by Wike, Platt, and Knowles, 1962).

TIME INTERVALS

The principle of secondary reinforcement has been used extensively to explain how an organism can bridge a long time interval between response and reward. That is, it is assumed that cues associated with reinforcement span the interval between the response and primary reinforcement and serve to reinforce behavior during this interval. It has been shown by Wolfe (1934), Perkins (1947), and Grice (1948) that the progressive elimination of secondary-reinforcement cues produces a correspondingly steeper delay-of-reinforcement gradient, indicating that less learning occurs with longer delays.

DRIVE

The relationship between drive and secondary reinforcement may be divided into three facets: (1) the effects of drive upon the acquisition of secondary reinforcement; (2) the effects of drive on performance after the secondary reinforcement has been acquired; and (3) the drive or motivating properties of secondary reinforcement.

J. F. Hall (1951) trained 6- and 22-hour-thirsty rats to run a straight runway with different and distinctive goalboxes used on reinforced and nonreinforced trials. When these goalboxes were later used as arms of a T-maze the results showed that no differences existed in the number of correct choices to the positive goalbox between the 6-hour and 22-hour groups. Thus, drive level exerts little control on the acquisition of secondary reinforcement; this generalization is in keeping with the general findings discussed in the section on the drive concept.

The second area may also be summarized rather succinctly: If subjects are trained under one drive condition and tested under different drive conditions, the greater the drive during test the greater the secondary reinforcing strength as measured by resistance to extinction (see Miles, 1956).

The third area must be considered in greater detail, for it at

first appears rather paradoxical that one operation can produce both secondary-reinforcing and secondary-motivating properties—that a single stimulus has the power not only to reinforce a response but also, under different conditions, to initiate
behavior. Paradoxical though it might appear, several studies
support such a contention. Estes (1943) has shown that a tone
previously paired with reinforcement will increase the level of
response in extinction. Other studies (Dinsmoor, 1950; Estes,
1948; Walker, 1942) suggest that the secondary reinforcers can be
viewed as having the effect of secondary motivators. Perhaps the
clearest demonstration of the dual role of cues is a runway study
by Marx and Murphy (1961). In the first phase of the experiment a buzzer and food were paired for the experimental subjects
but were presented separately for the control subjects; the purpose of this differential treatment was to establish the buzzer as a
cue for food-oriented behavior for the experimental but not for
the control group. All subjects were then given runway training
with food as the reward. Beginning from the sixteenth extinction
trial and on every subsequent fifth trial, all subjects received an
intermittent presentation of the buzzer prior to the actual opening of the startbox door. Presentation of the buzzer increased the
start speed for the experimental subjects. Furthermore, these
subjects also showed greater resistance to extinction. This demonstration gives the theorist one of three possible ways to view the
pairing of a neutral stimulus with a primary reinforcer: (1) as a
secondary reinforcer, (2) as a secondary motivator, or (3) as
both (or either) a secondary reinforcer and/or a secondary motivator, depending upon the temporal-spatial relationship of the
stimulus to the response.

Suggested Readings

Deese, J., and S. Hulse. 1967. *Psychology of learning,* 3rd ed. New York:
    McGraw-Hill Book Co.
Henry, N. B., ed. 1942. *The psychology of learning.* Yearbook of the
    National Society for the Study of Education, 41, Part II.
Kimble, G. A. 1961. *Hilgard and Marquis' conditioning and learning,*
    2nd ed. New York: Appleton-Century-Crofts.

Melton, A. W., Ed. 1964. *Categories of human learning.* New York: Academic Press.

Millenson, J. R. 1967. *Principles of behavioral analysis.* New York: The Macmillan Co.

Chapter 7

A SURVEY OF
MOTIVES IN
EDUCATION

Our concern in these final chapters is with the all-pervasive problem of motivation in the educational process. The present educational structure is largely irrational because it has grown from traditional concepts and without adequate regard for motivational considerations. The following pages present, therefore, the beginnings of a conceptual framework for the design of an educational system from a motivational point of view.

It is remarkable, in view of the basic importance of motivation, that so little direct and explicit attention has been paid to it in the literature. With the exception of a relatively small number of excellent recent works, some of which are cited in later sections of this chapter and in the reading list, there have been few serious attempts to assess realistically the motivational status of the pupil.

Motivational principles as they relate to the educational scene constitute an example of the application of theory and research to practical problems. These principles could likewise be applied to a wide range of social systems, such as the military or industrial organizations. Our present focus on the educational system is a logical choice, partly because of its importance and partly because psychology traditionally has been interested in the problems of education. And learning, of course, though hardly confined to educational settings or even to human organisms, is the avowed primary business of education and of many psychologists as well. For these and perhaps other reasons, the educational setting appears to be a particularly relevant target of a motivational analysis.

Our treatment will be based on the eight following primary propositions:

1. *An insufficient amount of attention has been paid to the motivation of students in the classroom at all grades and levels.* Appropriate motivation all too often appears to be assumed. Such an assumption is not a safe one to make. There are, it is true, investigations of a number of problems involving motivation in one way or another. For example, there is a persistent concern with the problem of examinations and grades, considered both as incentives and as measures of achievement. Interest in the measurement of achievement motivation, in students as well as in others, has also recently developed (McClelland and colleagues, 1953; Atkinson, 1958, 1964). Examining students for academic achievement emphasizes the specific role of testing in education, but generally apart from the broader question of the student's motivations. The *n*-achievement technique is concerned with a highly generalized trait, usually measured by means of a type of projective test. The subject is requested to make up stories interpreting a number of standard pictures. These stories are then analyzed for their achievement-related content and numerical scores are assigned. Although each of these efforts has merit, neither directly tackles the central problem of the student's motivation to learn specific educational materials. From the present point of view, it may be presumed that unless there is in the student a reasonably serious and deep-seated motivation to learn, classroom learning like all other learning will be at best meager and transitory.

2. *The emphasis upon the student's motivation is an especially critical one if education rather than training is involved.* One of the major objectives of education, as contrasted with those of training, is to build in the pupil a strong and persistent motivation to learn—one that will carry over to his everyday activities outside of the classroom as well as into his future classrooms. Transfer of this kind of learning motivation may

be considered as important as transfer of the actual knowledge acquired in the classroom. This point is one that is unfortunately lost by teachers preoccupied with the maintenance of classroom control and the dispensing of information.

3. *In the primary grades, a major objective of the teacher should be to avoid stunting that natural curiosity and interest which the normal child brings with him to school.* It is a great national tragedy that so much of this natural resource should be wasted in the early grades. To renew a pupil's interest in learning is very often an impossibly difficult task for the secondary teacher because of faulty attitudes and habits already strongly formed in the earlier school situation.

4. *In secondary grades, especially, an effort should be made to encourage independence of thought rather than conformity—or divergence rather than convergence in problem solving.* The divergent problem solver is one who is motivated to think for himself rather than to conform without independent thought. In view of the tremendous pressures toward conformity in our culture, this is indeed a challenging problem for the teacher.

5. *The personality and training of the teacher are the most critical determinants of the establishment of persistent motivation to learn in the pupil.* This kind of consideration should receive more attention than it typically does in teacher selection and preparation. While this factor appears to be important at all levels of learning, it is probably more critical in the early formative years.

6. *The multiplicity of motivations in the pupil is something that needs more recognition in practice.* While there may be stated recognition of diverse and contradictory motives, teachers typically receive little training in how they are to be handled. Solution of this problem would allow teaching objectives to be more reasonably determined and teacher success more accurately assessed.

7. *There is a desperate need for well-controlled research directly attacking the problem of classroom motivation.* Such applied research should utilize the standard methodological tools of behavioral science, but must deal directly with classroom

materials in a classroom setting. There have been some striking advances within recent years in research utilizing various types of automated teaching devices, and this research certainly has implications for motivation. But what is needed is more research emphasis on the typical motivational problems of pupils in ordinary learning situations.

8. *The motivational conditions adventitiously imposed by the school comprise a hidden curriculum.* That is, the student is always learning, but not exactly what the teacher intends. To judge from the number of dropouts and the attitudes of many students, the educational system does a masterful job of generating avoidance behavior. Unfortunately, many of the reward and punishment contingencies of the typical school appear to be aimed at teaching the student that learning is aversive. If this chapter does no more than succeed in alerting school personnel to the motivational implications of their system, it will have performed a very useful function.

Elaboration of these general propositions will be attempted throughout the remaining pages of this chapter. It is our hope and expectation that the presentation of a variety of points of view will help the education student as well as others to understand better some of the basic problems that face our educational system. Fundamental to most of these problems is the question of motivating the student. While much of what we are here stressing will be apparent to many teachers and educators, the glaring absence of anything like a similar stress in the educational literature strengthens our impression that there is a real need for it. There is, of course, stress on such matters as curriculum reforms, technology of teaching, and achievement testing. All of these have value. However, the technology of education could be more meaningfully applied if we knew more about the motivational dynamics in the education process.

EDUCATIONAL OBJECTIVES

It should be recognized at the outset that formal education has a variety of divergent objectives. Which of these objectives are held, implicitly or explicitly, will very largely determine the kind of procedures that are favored.

TRAINING AND EDUCATION

A fundamental distinction which we think critical to this problem is that between training and education. Training may be distinguished in terms of its much greater degree of specificity. That is to say, in training there is no question at all as to what is to be learned. In our society we train an amazing number of persons—athletes, stenographers, proofreaders, dancers, factory workers, and even children in schoolrooms. In all these forms of training, there is a special attempt to impress into the learner a particular response or set of responses, an identifiable skill of some sort.

TRAINING

Although there are wide differences among training programs with regard to the number and complexity of response patterns involved, they are alike in two fundamental respects. First, they have relatively clear objectives. The trainer knows exactly what he wants learned and because he does, his outcomes can be assessed with relative precision. Second, they utilize mainly extrinsic motivation. That is to say, the responses that are to be learned are ones which are instrumental to some particular objective—in work or sports or even in the classroom. Since the motivation is in this sense "external" to the task learned, it is particularly important that the pupil shall understand the reason for his training, that he shall see the responses to be learned as instrumental to previously valued activities and objectives. While most such reasons are perfectly obvious in the case of work and sports, for example, they are not always so clear in the classroom. For this reason, the teacher needs to do all that he can to demonstrate the reasons for learning such traditional material as the "three R's," learning which may be regarded as closer to training than to education. These skills are primarily "tools" which come to serve the pupil in a great variety of other motivated behaviors that he will need to perform. While an alert and capable learner may develop real pleasure in these skills—and so have some degree of intrinsic motivation for performing them—the fact remains that they are, fundamentally, behaviors that serve as instrumental functions.

EDUCATION

The ultimate goal of education is in certain respects very different from that of training. The difference mainly revolves around the fact that education is much less specific with regard to its objectives, at least as these can be related to concrete activities. In other words, it is difficult for a teacher to show a pupil how the material learned, say history or geography, will be instrumental to other activities.

Education provides *knowledge* and *information* about the world. Some of it comes through lectures, books, and discussions, some of it through experience in laboratories and in living. All of these convey to the individual some knowledge of the vast cultural heritage of our society. This provision may be recognized as the first objective of education.

Education also provides a *general sophistication* about the world. To some extent this sophistication rsults from the accumulation of specific knowledge and information that the student receives, but, more generally, it tends to transcend such specific material and is concerned with more fundamental understanding of the "why's" and "how's."

Finally, and perhaps most importantly, education makes an individual want to continue to learn things for himself. It is this *motivational* objective with which we are particularly concerned in the present chapter.

Obviously, it is difficult in many situations to separate training from education. The differences are mainly in their varying objectives, but it is important to keep these differences in mind when one considers those cases in which training and education are intimately related.

TRANSFER OF MOTIVATION

The ultimate test of any training or education effort is how well the learner performs outside of the learning situation. Since performance always depends upon motivation as well as on learning (see Chapter 6), an important objective of education should be to develop in the student the kind of motivation to learn and to perform that will transfer to extraclassroom situations. Such transferred motivation will help to insure the continued effective performance of old habits and skills as well as the acquisition of new ones. It is not safe to assume that when habits and skills are to be transferred to a new situation sufficient independent motivation to use them will be present. Consider, for instance, the Cub Scout who needs to use his recently learned reading skills to understand pamphlets in connection with obtaining special badges. The persistence and effectiveness of his reading performance will depend not only upon how strongly motivated he is by the desire to earn the badges, but also upon how much intrinsic motivation to read is transferred from the school situation.

An important part of early elementary education is clearly training; that is, the acquisition of a set of responses in reading, writing, arithmetic. Achievement tests are designed to answer the question of whether a student has acquired an appropriate set of responses. Evaluation should also be made of whether the student has learned to want to learn more. Or has he learned merely to want an "A" on his report card, or to want a smile from the teacher? Quite normally, teachers do not have the information necessary to answer these questions. Thus during the child's early formative years it is especially important for the teacher to maintain two concerns: (1) that aversive properties not be developed in the learning situation, and (2) that the acquisition of basic tools be accepted by the pupil as necessary for future goals.

CLASSROOM REINFORCEMENT CONTINGENCIES

An analysis of classroom reinforcement contingencies might reveal five that frequently work against education:

1. *The student quickly learns that going beyond the assignment does not pay off.* In fact, extra work soon becomes identified with punishment; witness, "Write the words you missed 100 times." (In this teaching procedure, the teacher reveals his own attitude towards study—it is tedious and to be avoided.)

2. *The student learns that the rewards of the school may be obtained in easier ways than by academic performance* (as by verbalizing the "right" things: "I study every night," "This is interesting," and the like). The student may offer many forms of subtle rewards to the teacher; interest and attention are obvious ones. This sort of behavior, of course, requires intelligence; if the rewards of the school were arranged in the proper way, the same perceptive individual would devote his energies to learning other things—not how to manipulate the teacher but how to manipulate symbols and ideas.

3. *The student learns to avoid excellence.* The student with an obviously high motivation to learn may be singled out by both teachers and peers as suspect. If the teacher has never known the excitement of learning, he is unable to attribute genuineness to his students. Furthermore, if the teacher is favorably impressed, he may administer a negative reinforcer by calling favorable attention to the exceptional student. To the bright and high-achieving student who is hoping that his deviancy will pass unnoticed by his peers, this sort of attention can be a personal disaster.

4. *The student learns that conformity is rewarded.* The student who conforms is meeting the demand characteristics of the environment. The term "demand characteristics" refers to the repertory of behaviors which are acceptable (rewarded) or not acceptable (punished) by either member of an interaction. One such demand characteristic in the school environment might be, "You shall not ask the teacher questions about the subject matter for which he is inadequately prepared."

5. *The student learns that curiosity is irrelevant.* Departing from the lesson plan takes too much time and the material might not be "covered." Therefore, no matter how exciting an idea may appear, it is to be handled, if at all, "tomorrow" or "next semester."

Many more such contingencies could be mentioned. The point is that students—even low achievers or the dropouts—learn what the school teaches. They may learn to avoid, withdraw, manipulate—and they may even learn history or mathematics. More importantly and hopefully, they may learn how to learn and, in the process, learn that learning can be rewarding. That these desirable goals are not more frequently obtained is an indictment of the system, not of the student. The focus should be upon behaviors learned by the student; the fact that he may have read so many pages of European History is, in the context of this argument, irrelevant. It is a symptom; it is an intermediate behavior that should simply provide the mechanism whereby a student's desire to learn can be converted into knowledge.

AVERSIVE MOTIVATION

The pervasiveness of an essentially negative sort of motivation in the classroom—the fear of failure and associated social punishment—has been emphasized by Skinner (1954) and Alpert (1962) among others.

Alpert's point of view is fundamentally similar to that expressed here. He has identified the *long-term* goal of education (1962, p. 126) as the "development or maintenance of attitudes and motives that are supportive of continued learning in order that the child might move eagerly ahead in his education." Alpert makes an important contrast between this kind of objective and *short-term* motives, such as curiosity, competition, achievement—and, above all, fear of social punishment. Of these, he says (on the same page) : "It is not at all clear that the motives which keep a child in school are the same motives which would support his being intellectually alert as an adult. It may, in fact, turn out that some of the best short-term motivators are the most unfortunate in their long-term effects."

This last comment refers directly to the negative motivation mentioned above. In this respect, Alpert agrees with Skinner, who has argued convincingly for the need to shift emphasis away from this kind of condition and toward more wholesome types of positive motivators and reinforcers.

The secondary school and college are or should be concerned more particularly with instilling internal motivation to continue learning and inquiring. In these schools, students expect and get information and training, but no longer the basic skill training that was necessary in the primary grades. High schools and colleges therefore have better opportunities to help the student reach the ultimate goal of formal education—a continued interest in learning and inquiring. But reaching this goal will be very difficult indeed unless the student has been curious and inquiring in the elementary school. If his behavior has been maintained by some sort of aversive schedule, there will be much negative emotional conditioning to overcome.

There should certainly be less emphasis on the control of behavior through aversive contingencies and more upon the shaping of desirable behavior by the judicious use of positive reinforcement. But remote rewards, such as grades (with very long delays of reinforcement), are terribly ineffective. Humans are able, fortunately, to mediate long delays by means of learned chains of verbalization; nevertheless, the more immediate the reward, the better.

VARIETIES OF STUDENT MOTIVATION

In this section we present a summary of what we see as the major motivations for the student at various age and grade levels. This material is included in the hope that it will emphasize the multiplicity of motivational factors and encourage a more widespread concern with this problem. It is particularly important that the student of education look closely at the actual motivating factors in the classroom because of the great discrepancy between what the child's motives are and the teacher's or parent's conception of what these motives are. Such conceptions too often consist more of what the adult thinks the child's motives should be, from an adult viewpoint, than of what they actually are; it is extremely difficult for an adult to see the world from the child's point of view. Moreover, the difficulty is compounded by the adult's failure to recognize the difficulty. As Hilgard and Russell (1950, p. 40) have aptly said, "Overemphasis upon verbally acknowledged motives leads to moralizing about behavior instead of making a more penetrating psychological analysis."

In presenting an account of what seem to us to be some of the more critical motives of children—and, in the following section, of adults—we will not attempt to spell out the various dimensions on which motives may be ordered (see Chapter 1). Nevertheless, the reader should keep in mind that certain of these dimensions are particularly relevant in the educational setting. For example, consider the temporal dimension. Much classroom motivation can be categorized as distinctly short-term, for teachers as well as for pupils. That is to say, these motives are specific to immediate problems, such as learning to spell some particular words. But it is quite clear that even such short-term motives and associated behaviors are influenced, and sometimes quite markedly, by long-term motivational factors—for example, the underprivileged Negro's realization that further schooling will be of small value to him in regard to a future occupation.

THE PRESCHOOL CHILD

THE CURIOSITY MOTIVE

The normal child's natural curiosity must be recognized as the major factor in his early motivation. Within recent years, a great deal of experimental evidence for the potency of the curiosity motive in mammals has been amassed (see Fowler, 1965). The rapidly developing recognition of this motive is largely due to the efforts of Harlow (1953), who persistently inveighed against the nearly exclusive concern in learning and behavior theory with such biologically based drive factors as hunger, thirst, and sex.

R. W. White (1959) also impressively documented the wide range of behaviors associated with exploration of the environment. White's postulation of a so-called "effectance" activation is relevant to the learning behavior of preschool children. By this term, White refers to an intrinsic motivating tendency in organisms to use and develop their sensory and motor capacities, independent of any instrumental function these capacities may serve (such as in the acquisition of food and the like). Whether or not one accepts this particular theoretical interpretation, the validity of the fundamental behavioral observations remains. There is in the normal developing mammal a strong tendency to exercise and improve his sensorimotor skills. This sort of tendency at least in part underlies the play activities of young mammals. While we recognize the danger of generalizing from infrahuman mammalian behavior to human behavior, anyone who has observed many children is aware of the strength of this motivating factor. Adults working with preschool children should encourage and channel this kind of behavior and thereby not only increase the knowledge and sensorimotor skills of the child but also develop in him desirable motivations to experience and learn more of his rapidly enlarging world.

Unfortunately, guided preschool experience is least likely to be available to those many children from relatively impoverished environments who need it most. In this respect, the so-called "head-start" program recently introduced by the federal government is a particularly promising effort. Approximately half a million children who entered the first grade in 1966 were involved in the 1965 program. Designed to offer preschool children from impoverished home environments an opportunity for intellectual stimulation and so avoid having them fall behind in learning from the first grade on, this project should help to alleviate some of the retrogression that normally occurs when a child's curiosity is blunted. Unfortunately, the problem is so massive that unless this program, or one like it, is applied on a very wide scale its effectiveness will be slight indeed; but it is important that at least a start has been made.

The preschool child certainly responds to social-motivational factors such as adult approval and peer approval, but in less obvious ways than older children. Achievement motivation is probably also present, but in the absence of experimental evidence its strength can only be guessed. It is interesting, however, that the preschool child tends to choose a task which insures success (Sears and Levin, 1957). There can be little doubt that even at this age the fear of social censure—or at least the absence of social approval—is beginning to be an effective motivating factor.

KINDERGARTEN AND ELEMENTARY SCHOOL

BLOCKING OF CURIOSITY

Again in kindergarten and elementary school, the child's natural curiosity is the most important positive motive that can be utilized for formal learning, and it is particularly important at this time that it not be blocked. Some of the ways in which such blocking may occur are:

1. Deprivation of sensorimotor and verbal stimulation.
2. Overemphasis on purely rote learning of uninteresting material without adequate interpretation or explanation or effort to arouse the child's interest.
3. Overemphasis on housekeeping and discipline; for example, forcing the normally restive child to remain quite still while others recite.
4. Boredom, which is a serious factor in the large classroom and is often interpreted by the teacher as inattentiveness.
5. Interruption of more highly valued play activities, again in the absence of adequate explanatory efforts.
6. Long periods of physical inactivity.
7. Lack of recognition of the child's short attention span; his inattentiveness may be mistakenly attributed to mischievousness.
8. Presentation of material on a level which the child cannot understand.
9. Perceived failure in competition, especially in a culture where competitive success tends to be highly valued. Just as success tends to feed upon success, so failure tends to feed upon failure. The child who gets a bad start, for whatever reason, is severely handicapped (see Frankel, 1961).
10. Response to peer approval of a negative sort. A child tends not to do well if there is strong peer pressure in this direction.

When one thinks about how many of these adverse factors actually operate in a classroom, it should be evident that primary difficulties are not child-determined but situational. The child's behavior simply reflects the reward contingencies which are present. It is, therefore, important to consider possible alternatives either in classroom structure or technological innovations. Such techniques as have been developed by Montessori and by Moore, described in detail in the next chapter, allow the child enough freedom and enough challenge to alleviate many of the above problems.

Apart from the problem of curiosity and related motives, the primary-grade pupil has other major motivations. As a matter of fact, this is the period during which there is at least an initiation of most of the motivational conditions which will persist throughout the remainder of his educational career. Some of the more prominent of these motives should be mentioned.

ENVIRONMENTAL CONTROL

Closely related to the development of curiosity, and of exploratory behavior, is the maturing of what may be called "control" or "mastery" of the environment. That is to say, the primary-grade child really begins to recognize the kind of power that he has, and can obtain, over his environment—social as well as physical. While he may have been actively manipulating people—his parents, siblings, baby-sitters—for some time, recognition of this power and more active utilization of it now emerge, and on a growing scale. The same thing occurs, and in a more obvious manner, with regard to manipulation of the physical environment, as knowledge and skills develop. In a sense, this kind of development is an extension of what White (1959) has called "effectance" motivation, but it does not take long for the child to recognize the instrumental value of his skills—how they can be used, not merely for their own sake, but in ways that will serve his other motives and needs.

The kind of environmental manipulation which we have been describing is that which relates directly to the real world. At some time during the primary-grade period the normal child discovers how it is also possible to manipulate the world vicariously, particularly through reading. As a result, his interest in reading typically grows rapidly, and, as his reading skills develop, the amount of time he spends in this activity often increases spectacularly. While this kind of motivation obviously has great value, because reading serves to improve his direct as well as his indirect or vicarious control of the environment, there are also certain risks involved. One is that reading can serve as an escape, especially for the child whose real world is all too bleak and unpromising. A balance between such escapist use of reading and direct experience with the world is important in education, and for this reason it is considered important to expose the child to as many facets of his society as possible—the business, industrial, and social aspects as well as the laboratory.

REINFORCEMENT BY SUCCESS

It is generally agreed that success in itself is a potent motivating factor. Its importance as reinforcement is probably greatest in the primary classes, before formal examinations have come to exercise their stranglehold on academic performance. But even for teachers with the best of intentions there are problems associated with the use of successful performance as a reinforcer.

For example, in the large and crowded classroom that is typical of our primary grades, how is it possible for a teacher to insure that each child will have his share of success? Individual attention to children is practically impossible, at least on anything like an adequate basis, simply because there isn't time enough for it. Not really knowing the achievement level of a child, the teacher will not be able to estimate the kind of task that will give reasonable assurance of success, yet at the same time offer some challenge. Because of the great individual differences present, among children and across subject matter, the use of averaged expectations derived from ability tests can be very misleading.

Moreover, we are lacking in the kind of developmental standards that would serve as the basis for evaluation of progress in such areas as mathematics. According to Piaget (1953), the child does not attempt to understand mathematical concepts in the same way as an adult, so that evaluation on adult standards is not appropriate. Recognition of the need for reasonable norms is one of the factors underlying the recent increase in attention to Piaget's developmental research. It also supports the interest in the "new" mathematics using modular arithmetic.

PRAISE AND BLAME

Praise and blame are closely associated with and instrumental to success and failure. The extensive literature on this problem, as it can be separated from success as such and from formal grading procedures, has been reviewed by Hilgard and Russell (1950) and more recently by Kennedy and Willcutt (1964). To sum up a very complex situation, praise most generally acts to facilitate learning and performance.

Another analysis of the effects of praise and blame has been made by Johanneson. He found that performance was influenced by both praise and blame but that the net effect depended upon the combination of the two, and also upon the type of task. Johanneson (1962, p. 196) concluded that "Praise seems to be of great importance to highly anxious pupils, to pupils with a low self-reliance, and to pupils with negative attitudes towards the teacher." Repeated blame, he found, tended to lower the pupil's self-rating. The potential long-lasting effects of the use of blame for reinforcement require that it be used judiciously.

PUNISHMENT

An especially good treatment of the use of punishment is provided by Hilgard and Russell (1950), who emphasize not only its undesirable aspects but also what the teacher can do to prevent some of these, such as being sure that positive behaviors are available to the child. If they are not, the child will turn to other avoidance behaviors, such as withdrawal.

Other motivations that develop during this period are competition—scholastic as well as athletic—and, generally, what McClelland and his collaborators have called "achievement motivation." The latter differs from competition in being a more generalized and long-term factor. Competitive standards are internalized so that the presence of actual competitors is not necessary to motivate performance.

PEER APPROVAL

Finally, we may point to the variety of social conditions that play an ever increasing role during the primary grades. While parent and teacher approval also play an important role, peer approval becomes of relatively greater importance. Parents and teachers would like to think that their judgment is important to the child—as indeed it is to some extent, especially in certain children. Nevertheless, it has become distressingly evident that the judgment of one's peers is a most pervasive and in many cases an overwhelmingly powerful motivating factor.

Peer groups have a subculture of their own and use their own means of enforcing adherence to group standards. The standards of the peer group are often at variance with the parental standards and with school standards. Since children insist on conformity among themselves, it becomes very important that somehow they become interested in valuing scholastic and intellectual pursuits if they are to become educated in the full sense of the term. Unfortunately, the fear of social disapproval, whether by peers, parents, or teachers and other supervisors, continues to operate as a kind of negative reinforcement. It accounts for a disproportionately great amount of the immediate motivation in the classroom. This is a persistent and difficult but nevertheless highly important problem that needs to be faced realistically by parents and teachers and not simply shunted aside.

JUNIOR-SENIOR HIGH SCHOOL
SOCIAL MOTIVATION, PEER APPROVAL

The predominant motivational factor that enters the child's life in the junior-high-school situation is the new social incentives reflected in peer relationships. Social development is a very important aspect of child health, but it is also quite true that it can easily get out of hand, for example in the formation of cliques and gangs with questionable value systems. Because of the strong development of peer-acceptability motivation at the secondary-school stage, it is very important that educationally adequate peer standards obtain. Here the role of parents and teachers is critical, and those who manage to instill in the peer groups standards of educational excellence have taken a giant stride forward.

Interference with academic learning becomes more severe at the time a child reaches secondary school. There are the various social pressures and, in some cases, the need to work for money. Unhappy home conditions also tend to interfere with study.

MINORITY GROUPS

Certain minority groups in the American culture are especially handicapped motivationally as well as otherwise. The most visible of these is the American Negro. It is impossible for a person from a middle-class white subculture to understand the extent of this handicap. A recent article by Battle (1966) provides a dramatic account of the motivational difficulties involved in attempts to educate the Negro. The Negro boy in a large city ghetto is a particular problem, mainly because of the greater scarcity of jobs for Negro men. As Battle observes (p. 17), "he knows that job programs are rigged against him—that vocational schools are seldom integrated, and the ones with mostly Negro students teach dry cleaning while white schools teach electronics and data processing." It is hardly surprising that three times as many Negro girls as boys achieve honors in high school. Indeed, it is surprising that any such children emerge as scholars and intellectual achievers. A more academic treatment of these problems, with some of the same conclusions drawn, may be found in G. B. Watson's *No Room at the Bottom—Autoinstruction and the Reluctant Learner* (1963).

THE ROLE OF EXAMINATIONS AND GRADES

Another new source of motivation enters during the high-school period. This is emphasis on good grades for college entrance.

Historically, school examinations have been the classic techniques used to insure appropriate application by the student and presumably, achievement of a certain level of learning. Recently a number of critical questions have been raised concerning the efficacy of this technique. Here we comment on three of them.

First, simply forcing a student to "put time in" on a subject is no guarantee of effective learning. This proposition is especially true if the only motivational conditions are strictly extrinsic to the task, as Hilgard and Russell (1950) have pointed out in their comprehensive review of educational incentives.

Second, the side effects of the motivation produced by examinations in some cases are extremely deleterious. One of them is inducing students to cheat. Another is markedly raising the student's anxiety level.

Third, and most important, serious questions are being raised as to the adequacy of the typical tests of achievement, with regard to their narrowness of scope (among others, see Thelen, 1963; Fishman and Clifford, 1964). The major point here is that, at best, examinations measure and grades evaluate only a restricted range of an individual's abilities—and both are especially likely to ignore the very critical problem of creativity (see Torrance, 1965a, 1965b). As Fishman (above, p. 78) has said of objective examinations, "They are seemingly objective mechanisms, but as such they exemplify all of the unconscious fortifications of the status quo . . . They are addressed to a world of talent which is only one facet of the total repertoire of intellective talent demonstrable via current and normal school channels."

In spite of the ferment evidenced over this problem, examinations and grades will be with us until more effective means of evaluation have been developed. The reason, entirely apart from their questionable motivating role, is that most educational systems require some method of assessing progress and no satisfactory substitute for the examination system has yet been devised. Here the problem is particularly acute with regard to college-entrance requirements. Secondary-school grades correlate so well with college grades that they will surely continue to be used as major predictors of college success, and hence also as selectors in college-entrance procedures. Grades therefore remain powerful incentives for the college-bound high-school student.

COLLEGE AND UNIVERSITY

VARIETY OF MOTIVATIONS

College students obviously have a great variety of motivations. On the one hand, there are some very strong positive motivations to learn and to better oneself. Such genuine learning motivation appears to be stronger in certain of the smaller liberal-arts colleges, although this difference may to some extent be a function of the selection of better students, or at least of students from better academic backgrounds.

Unfortunately, these positive attractions seem to be playing a very minor role for many students. Negative factors—such as the avoidance of the military draft, the postponement of work responsibilities, or the desire to leave home and yet not have to undertake full economic responsibility for oneself—are often predominant. Some college students enter and remain in college primarily because of family pressures or traditions—college is simply something expected of them—or for essentially social reasons, such as making a "good" marriage or forming the most desirable social relationships for eventual utilization in business.

Other common motivations of college students appear to be a mixture of positive and negative factors. Thus, some students are primarily motivated by a desire to better themselves, educationally, and so make possible a higher social and economic status (as by means of a higher-paying job than is otherwise likely). Other students appear to be motivated by a need to "find" themselves, and such searching obviously has negative as well as positive motivational aspects.

INAPPROPRIATE MOTIVATION

The motivational confusion shown by many college students is to a certain degree a reflection of a basic confusion in our educational system between training and education. Our society gives strong lip service to higher education for all and fails to recognize the greater utility, for many students who are forced to remain in college, of good vocational-training programs. The shortage of such programs at the high-school level is especially unfortunate. To a great extent the necessity of college appears to have been oversold. Graduation from college has become vital to the self-esteem of many students, not to mention their job ambitions. If they fail, they are unable to see themselves as personally effective or worthy. Many of these students have neither the intrinsic motivation for learning nor the interests characteristic of people who find academic types of learning enjoyable. Yet, these students try desperately to stay in a situation that holds few rewards for them.

SOCIAL AFFAIRS; CHEATING

There are two particularly troublesome kinds of motivation— troublesome, that is, from the standpoint of effective learning. First, as is quite apparent to any observer of the college scene, social affairs use up a tremendously high proportion of the energies of many students. Study and learning take a very poor second place, with efforts along these lines deliberately maintained at the minimal level that will keep the student in school. Second, there is the powerful motivation to cheat, shown not only by the inferior student but also by the one who is more capable but is beset by motives that conflict with adequate study. Although there is need for an evaluative system of some sort, the great overemphasis upon grades is the fundamental *immediate* source of cheating motivation. From a long-range point of view, cheating occurs because of the great influence of motivations other than learning for its own sake.

COMPLEXITY OF MOTIVES

The complexity as well as the multiplicity of these various motivational factors needs to be emphasized. Overemphasis by adults on one or the other aspect of student motivation, perhaps in accordance with the adult's own biases and perceptual predispositions, can have unfortunate consequences on the student's academic development. The full range of motivational factors operating in each individual needs to be appreciated.

Much of an individual's behavior is the product of extremely complex interactions among a variety of motivational and learning factors. Such complexity makes the analysis of individual behavior very difficult. In addition, no situation is precisely the same for different individuals—or even for the same individual from day to day. These factors result in the uniqueness of behavior.

PROFESSIONAL TRAINING

There is at the higher-education stage a reemphasis on training as distinguished from education. Although there are certainly educational aspects involved in any professional training, nevertheless most of the effort tends to be of a training sort. The same may be said of graduate education in the sciences, since much of what a scientist needs to learn involves relatively factual materials, the majority of which must be committed to memory—statistics, microscopy, and the like. Family obligations quite obviously play a major role in diverting the attention of the professional and graduate student from his studies. In recent years, the presence of substantial numbers of predoctoral fellowships has aided enormously in this respect by releasing the superior student from the necessity of earning a living for his family while involved in his professional study.

ADULT EDUCATION

Except for specialized, distinctly vocational types of training and retraining, most of the continued educational efforts made by adults tend to be motivated by a genuine desire to learn or by a recognition of the desirability of further education to better their social or occupational status. Unfortunately, many obstacles are placed in the way of the adult who wishes to improve his educational background. Enlargement of university centers of continuing education has helped, however, to ease some of these obstacles.

VARIETIES OF ADULT MOTIVATION

Certainly the student's motivation is the central problem in education. But student motivation is complex. It reflects the motivations—and the related behaviors—of many others, and especially those of the parents and the teachers. The teacher's motives in turn are partly, and often largely, a function of the motives of operating and controlling personnel (parents, teachers, school administrators). In this section, therefore, we will briefly review the major motivational patterns exhibited by these other participants in the educational process.

This survey of the motives of "significant others" is essentially the sort of knowledge that many observers of our school systems will already have. Explication of these points is necessary, however, in any thorough consideration of the educational process. Effective solutions to pressing educational problems cannot be developed unless there is explicit concern with the variety and diversity of motivations which operate in educational processes. Better understanding of the often contradictory motives is a prerequisite for lasting improvement in educational endeavors.

MOTIVES OF PARENTS

We may assume that most parents in our culture, and particularly in the broad "middle-class" spectrum, have a genuine and deep-seated interest in fostering the continued intellectual and social development of the child. Even with this motivation, however, parents have difficulty in translating their wishes into effective deeds. Merely wishing the child to do well in school is, of course, no guarantee of behavior that will help the child to achieve such an objective. This disparity is particularly likely if the parent himself is limited in knowledge or has strong conflicting motives. Doubtless, a child's parents have mixed motives about his education, especially as he progresses through the system and work possibilities begin to emerge as competitors with further education. These often become overriding considerations when combined with such fundamental facts as financial need.

PARENTAL NEEDS

Among the many types of motives commonly shown by parents in regard to their child's education are some that relate more to parents' personalities and needs than to the child's. For one instance, observers have long noted the pressures exerted by parents on their children, mainly their male children, to take advanced professional training of one kind or another. Thus the third-generation physician will often have strong and quite evident motives for encouraging his son to continue in the medical tradition. Another instance is the rapidly developing tendency for children's grades, and other achievements, to be used by parents as status symbols, serving much in the way that Cadillacs and mink coats have served in days past. This characteristic often tends to be indistinguishable from the genuine pride that parents feel in connection with children's achievements; nevertheless, when this trend is accentuated it can become a serious problem. Parental pressure for high grade performance is particularly unfortunate for a child who is already achieving at a level commensurate with his abilities. As a matter of fact, a study by Haggard (1957) indicates that "socialization pressure" may have deleterious effects even upon the intellectually gifted.

A concrete indication of how serious and extensive this sort of influence can be is provided by the following personal comment by a professional colleague of ours:

During a period of internship in a child clinic, I observed that the tremendous identification of fathers with the academic performance of their children was often a significant factor in the child's emotional disturbance. The disturbance was often manifest in school work which was below expectance for the measured ability of the child. Most of these children were the offspring of professionals, such as college professors and medical doctors. The child's failure was somehow their failure—not their failure as a parent, but a failure which was taken as a reflection of their own abilities. The logic seemed to be, "If I am an intelligent, achieving person, then my children will be intelligent and achieving also." The child's failure (which might be not making A's) appeared to constitute a personal threat and the parent would respond with punishment. This was sometimes overt (e.g., verbal punitiveness), sometimes covert (e.g., withdrawal of affection). The parent is at this point both discouraged and bewildered: "What on earth is *wrong* with the child?" In the verbally punitive parent, this is likely to be said in the presence of the child who eventually accepts the verdict of his parent and, perhaps, of the school that there is, indeed, "something" wrong with him. The seeking of support or self-gratification through one's children can be one of the more educationally disruptive of parental motives. One would suspect in such cases that the parent has some insecurity in regard to his own abilities.

MOTIVES OF TEACHERS

Many teachers are, fortunately, motivated by a sincere desire to educate their pupils—to see them develop to the limits of their potential in learning and performance. This motivation, combined with a reasonable amount of ability and training, appropriate personality traits, and adequate support from the school system, obviously produces the optimal arrangement for effective teaching.

But while the teaching of the student is considered a primary goal, the teacher's concern will also be directed toward pleasing the principal and parent. Therefore, he must see to it that his students do well on achievement tests and that discipline is kept. Sarason's description of a day in the classroom clearly shows how much of a teacher's attention is directed toward the latter problem (Sarason, Davidson, and Blatt, 1962).

PERSONALITY FACTORS

Teachers, along with all other people, have conflicting motives—personal problems, financial problems, and the like which affect them. There is no question but that the teacher's personality is a significant factor as he introduces the material to the classroom, evaluates behavior, reinforces by praise or blame, and otherwise does his work. Travers, in considering a variety of commonly used incentives, notes (1965, p. 68) that "What is significant is that the teacher understands the artificial nature of incentives and utilizes them only as they relate to the unique needs of the student."

Sears and Hilgard (1964), in a comprehensive review of the teacher's role, point out (p. 199) that evaluative "activities go far beyond marking papers; they include attention to many experiences of success and failure, of expanded or restricted autonomy, of immediate and long-term goal-setting, of recognition of individual progress, and of attitudinal response to divergent behavior. These evaluative behaviors have the characteristics of positive and negative reinforcers, and as such, are motivationally relevant to learning."

Two other important facets of teacher-children relationships are "affective interaction" and "cognitive interaction" (Sears and Hilgard, 1964). In the affective area the teacher sets the tone of the class by the way in which he handles situations involving disciplinary problems, the creative child, competition, conflict, or the like. In the cognitive area he sets the tone by the way in which he approaches the learning task and by the methods he uses. The teacher's personality, as reflected in his classroom behaviors, is thus of critical importance in the teacher-pupil interaction. This factor must not be overlooked as educational researchers and theorists plan various innovations and reforms. Teacher selection and training are factors of critical significance. Some of the problems attendant to the training of effective teachers are thoroughly and provocatively discussed in recent books by Koerner (1963) and by Sarason, Davidson, and Blatt (1962).

ATTITUDINAL FACTORS

Part of the motivational problem in students is the fact that many teachers have little faith in the motivational properties of learning. They appear skeptical of the idea that a student can find the use of his own intellect and the acquisition of knowledge rewarding; therefore, they must surround the learning process with all sorts of positive and negative consequences. They appear to have embraced some concept like original sin—students are inherently bad and must be forced to do what is good for them. Corollaries are: (1) there's something wrong with anything that is enjoyed, and (2) human nature is essentially unmodifiable. This latter point of view is particularly strange when held by a person who has been trained expressly as a specialist in behavior modification.

An important source of conflicting motives in teachers may be the great diversity that exists in our culture in regard to educational techniques, objectives, and underlying philosophies of education. Teachers vary widely in the kind of procedures and notions that they gain in their training, and these factors often interact with the teacher's own background. The role of discipline, for example, is a particularly important problem whose solution is vigorously disputed. Thus, the teacher who comes from a family with a strong tradition of personal discipline is likely to have difficulty in adjusting to the more permissive role stressed for the teacher in some schools—and vice versa.

MOTIVES OF SCHOOL ADMINISTRATORS
PRINCIPALS AND SUPERINTENDENTS

The motives of supervisory personnel may be basically similar, in most respects, to those of teachers, but since they generally have less direct contact with pupils their influence is mainly by means of their relationships with the teachers. Also supervisory personnel are more likely to be concerned with special educational problems, such as the curriculum or housekeeping details, as well as with a desire to please their own superiors, the school-board members. This is not to say, of course, that principals and superintendents are exclusively concerned with matters such as these, but it is nonetheless quite true that to some extent they need to be so concerned—or many will soon find themselves in new occupational roles. This fact must be considered in any evaluation of the interaction of motivational processes that underlie the overt behaviors exhibited in educational situations.

Recent interesting appraisals of the problems of supervisory personnel may be found in Callahan's *Education and the Cult of Efficiency* (1962) and Koerner's *The Miseducation of American Teachers* (1963).

BOARD MEMBERS

Remote as boards of education or college trustees tend to be from the student, they nevertheless play an important determining role in setting the stage for the success or failure of the educational enterprise. As holders of the purse strings, they determine the physical environment and the quality and quantity of the faculty. Their motives, in most cases, tend very strongly to reflect the motivations of the majority in their subculture, which is frequently that of the business community.

Apart from the financial and business aspects of their motivation, board members may attempt to exert undue pressures upon personnel in the educational establishment in connection with political and socioeconomic matters. This pressure tends to interfere with the development of free inquiry and discourages independence of thought.

Suggested Readings

Nielsen, G. S., ed. 1962. *Child and education.* Proceedings of the Fourteenth International Congress of Applied Psychology. Copenhagen: Munksgaard, 3.

Sarason, S. B., K. S. Davidson, and B. Blatt. 1962. *The preparation of teachers: An unstudied problem in education.* New York: John Wiley and Sons.

Watson, G. B., ed. 1963. *No room at the bottom—autoinstruction and the reluctant learner.* National Education Association.

Chapter 8

MOTIVATION IN EDUCATION: METHODS AND RESEARCH

Of the multitude of special educational programs and methods which have been attempted within the United States within recent years, only a relatively small number have clear relevance for the motivation of students. In this section we shall review a selected few of these, beginning with the progressive-education movement, now mainly of historical import, and ending with the contemporary and yet informal stress upon creativity. In between, we shall consider the Montessori method, two examples of curriculum reform (the Dual Progress Plan and the Trump Plan), the vigorous and still actively developing movement of programed learning, and the remarkable laboratory school developed by O. K. Moore, utilizing his so-called "talking typewriter" in a specially designed responsive environment.

THE PROGRESSIVE-EDUCATION MOVEMENT

Developing in this country during the nineteenth century and having only loose and informal relationships with similar but older trends in European education, the progressive-education movement was throughout the first half of the twentieth century a tremendously influential force. Because of its relevance for motivational problems, although its role was not always described in these terms, it is here reviewed. As a formal movement, it has now been officially "dead" for more than a decade. The Progressive Education Association was dissolved in the conservative aftermath of World War II in 1955 and its journal publication was suspended in 1957.

DEWEY'S ROLE

The relationship between man and society was the general concern of the movement. As its effective head for most of the first half of this century, John Dewey has most cogently expressed the specific educational objectives. In his book *Experience and Education,* Dewey (1938) described the traditional education imposed from above and outside the child as being based upon adult standards, adult subject matters, and adult methods. Progressive education, on the other hand, has the following specific objectives:

1. Expression and cultivation of the child's individuality.
2. Allowing of free activity, as opposed to externally imposed discipline.
3. Learning from experience rather than from tests and teachers.
4. Acquisition of skills as a means of attaining important objectives.
5. Making the most of opportunities of the present life, as opposed to preparation for a more or less future goal.
6. Acquaintance with a changing world rather than the static one that is typically portrayed in traditional tests and teaching methods.

The reader will note the similarity between many of these objectives, as here summarized in general terms, and much of what is said in the remainder of this chapter. Dewey also emphasized the desire *to continue to learn* as being the most important attitude to be formed in school—a theme that has been emphasized throughout Chapter 7.

It is important to recognize that the leading progressive educationists, and especially John Dewey himself, were fully aware of the limitations of the movement and of the problems involved in its implementation. Dewey, for example, emphasized that the weakest part of the program was in relation to the selection and organization of "intellectual" subject matter (1938, p. 66) and that the difficulties of the method were not to be overlooked. With respect to the latter point, he said (1938, p. 115) of the movement: "The greatest danger that attends its future is, I believe, the idea that it is an easy way to follow, so easy that its own course may be improvised."

THE MOVEMENT'S CONTRIBUTION

Although it has become popular, in certain circles, to criticize the progressive-education movement and to point to its official demise as evidence of its essential failure, such criticism by and large misses the point. Perhaps the difficulties of the movement have not been so much with the basic ideas, especially Dewey's, as with their misinterpretations by school personnel as well as laymen. The progressive-education movement died, if that is the proper way to describe the dissolution of the Association, not only because of the opposition from traditionalists but also because of its own internal divisions. Nevertheless, the movement largely accomplished its general objectives. It had effected an enormous change in the American school system, even if it had not succeeded perfectly in remodeling the system according to its own tenets. And in one way or another, each of the more recent programs and methods next to be described has built upon the enduring groundwork provided by the progressive-education movement.

THE MONTESSORI SYSTEM

MARIA MONTESSORI

Maria Montessori was an Italian educator who initiated a most influential system of primary education in Europe. Although her own professional training was in medicine—in 1894 she was the first woman to receive the M.D. degree in Italy—her early professional work involved the education of retarded children. The techniques which she developed, following the lead of Séquin, were so effective that she became interested in applying them also to normal children. She had continued success. As a result of her active lecturing throughout Europe and Asia, Montessori schools were established in many countries, and, at the present time, a number of such privately financed institutions operate in major cities in the United States.

Montessori began her intensive work with children from underprivileged areas, three to six years old. She had observed that the traditional methods of discipline forced children to sit in classrooms, immobilized "like rows of butterflies transfixed with pins." This traditional discipline she replaced with what amounted to a voluntary system. Her objective was to enlist the interest of the child by showing him exactly what to do on some specific task and then allowing him freedom to do what he had been shown. As far as possible, the teacher concentrated on precise movements and emphasized the correct sequence of movements in relatively circumscribed tasks. Children so taught learned to count and work simple sums, as well as to read and write, before the age of six. Moreover, they would typically spend from 15 to 60 minutes in concentrated effort on a single task before turning to some other.

Later, Montessori worked with older children, in the six- to ten-year age range, emphasizing similar types of individually paced practice on such topics as grammar, geometry, and advanced arithmetic.

THE METHOD

Montessori's method is based upon certain assumptions similar to those held by the progressive educationists. She believed that the fundamental problem in education is a social one in that adults tend to oppress children unintentionally. They do not understand the child's right to independence, to activity, or to exploration of the world for himself. To alleviate these restrictions, the Montessori school, as described by Standing (1957),

1. Is constructed for the child and his needs.
2. Attempts to take advantage of the child's love of order.
3. Utilizes materials with striking sensory characteristics, mainly involving different colors, shapes, sizes, and textures.
4. Makes the teacher the link between the child and the environment.

In addition to the above account, Montessori's own works (1912, 1917) are also available. An indication of the recent influence of this movement may be seen in the fact that six Montessori books, four by Montessori herself and two by the noted author Dorothy Canfield Fisher, were reprinted by a single publisher (Robert Bentley) in 1965.

The apparent success of the Montessori method, especially with younger children, demands that a thorough evaluation be made not only of the techniques themselves but also of the assumptions upon which they were based. Pitcher (1963, p. 26) has noted that many of the basic tenets of this once revolutionary method "have been incorporated in modern schools and then modified in a way that lessens their rigidity."

This conclusion apparently applies most directly to the pre-school situation. Equipment has been specifically constructed for the needs of the child at this age, which emphasizes sensory and motor characteristics that engage the attention of the child. It is apparent that a host of questions in this area need researching. For example, there is the whole problem of the rigid sequence of movements required. An additional problem concerns the manner in which the sensorimotor characteristics of equipment should be manipulated. It is unfortunate indeed that such questions have been in the main answered by the kind of commercial "research" that occurs in a toy factory when these manufacturers put such products on the market!

Another particularly important problem demanding research concerns the role of the teacher. How does a Montessori-trained teacher compare with a traditionally trained teacher? What is the most effective role of the teacher in the classroom environment? A comment by Standing (1957, p. 259) is relevant and interesting; he notes that the Montessori teacher "must make her presence felt by those who are seeking and hide from those who have already found." Other questions concern the exact manner in which such a teacher "links" the environment and the child, and in what manner a direct effort is made to utilize techniques of positive and negative reinforcement.

There is evident need for careful observation of the Montessori system followed by specifically designed research projects, since this method appears to be effective with young children.

MORE RESTRICTED REFORMS IN EDUCATIONAL METHODS

The Dual Progress Plan and the Trump Plan will be briefly described as examples of contemporary efforts to improve the staffing of the schools, the physical environment, and the curriculum, all of which have motivational implications.

DUAL PROGRESS PLAN

The Dual Progress Plan (Stoddard, 1961) has been devised for use with primary grades. It is based on an assumption of the critical importance of individual differences in children and in teachers. Since children vary in their abilities, their progress in one subject should not be based upon their progress in another. Teachers, also, vary in their level of competence in subject matter; therefore, Stoddard suggests, mathematics, science, music, art, English, and social studies, should be taught by teachers who are proficient in those subjects and the students should be grouped according to ability in these subject areas.

While this technique categorizes pupils according to certain kinds of individual differences and therefore has merit, the teachers' handling of these individual differences remains a critical problem (see Sarason, Davidson, and Blatt, 1962).

TRUMP PLAN

Another reform, developed by a commission headed by J. Lloyd Trump (Trump and Baynham, 1961), is directed toward reorganization of the secondary schools. As the plan is summarized by Woodring (1964, p. 295), "Class periods of the standard length are to be replaced by periods of varying length. The standard class size of 30 pupils is to be replaced by some very large lecture and demonstration classes and some small discussion groups. Laboratory activities and a considerable amount of individual work are provided. Use will be made of educational television and teaching machines. New buildings will be designed to facilitate the new organization, and the teaching staff will be organized on the team basis."

This plan, now in effect in about fifty schools, would appear to have some advantage over traditional types of classes in that it allows for individual differences and places students in small groups where there is more opportunity for discussion and individual attention.

PROGRAMED LEARNING

The movement called "programed learning" is one of the more vigorous contemporary educational innovations with direct implications for motivation. In essence, programed learning is a procedure whereby the student instructs himself, using such aids as a programed text or a teaching machine. This kind of informal procedure permits the learner to test himself and to set his own pace.

Although the first teaching machine was introduced by Pressey in 1926, the major impetus for the contemporary movement has come from the work of Skinner (1954, 1959). He developed his principles largely on the basis of his operant-conditioning research with lower animals, especially the rat and the pigeon.

TYPES OF PROGRAMS

In the simplest kind of program, the linear or straight-line program, responses that approach some specified terminal behavior are immediately reinforced by knowledge of results, and all others are nonreinforced. This "shaping" process is thus aimed at bringing the student gradually and with a minimum of error from simple to complex behaviors. (An interesting account of how this same principle is used in training animals is provided in the recent [1966] book by Breland and Breland.) Thus the linear program emphasizes a sequence of behaviors in which the response units are kept very small, so that learning proceeds by successive mastery of the parts of the program, rather than by an effort to master larger units of the material all at one time.

All programs prepared for this kind of learning are intended to be "psychologically" rather than merely logically or chronologically coherent sequences, and they all require some kind of differential response by the learner (such as writing the answer for a programed text, or pushing a button for a teaching machine).

The so-called branching type of program is somewhat more

complicated than the linear. It involves telling the student who has made an error why he was wrong, so that there is in this variation a more important role for errors and their explicit correction. Recent developments in computer technology have greatly facilitated the use of this type of programing. One of its more dramatic uses is in the training of medical students in diagnosis (Swets and Feurzeig, 1965).

CRITICAL EVALUATION

The Montessori system and the programed-learning technique, arising from totally diverse initial problems and theoretical bases, nevertheless have much in common. Each emphasizes the importance of small and carefully ordered behavioral steps, with the learner providing his own motivation and his own pacing. The former characteristic, while, in the view of its proponents, responsible for much of the success of each technique, is also the focus of most of the criticism that has been directed against the two methodologies.

This kind of attack upon programed learning is well exemplified by some comments by Cronbach (1962). Emphasizing the motivational values of learning by discovery and documenting his arguments with evidence from the classical Gestalt psychologists as well as more recent work by such investigators as Piaget (1953) and White (1959), Cronbach contrasts these important methods with programed learning. He observes (1962, p. 145): "A striking antithesis to the emphasis on discovery is presented in proposals for programmed instruction. The followers of Skinner are also inheritors of Thorndike; they are skeptical of transfer, and view knowledge as consisting of correct responses to specifiable stimuli." Cronbach proceeds to elaborate this argument by pointing out that the programer "makes no place for the pupil to develop preverbal experiences or to form intuitive hypotheses and trace them to their inevitable erroneous conclusions . . . The moment the pupil does deviate from the desired line of thought, he is stopped and given the desired answer." J. S. Bruner's *The Process of Education* (1960) may be mentioned as a good source for further arguments of this general sort.

Ignoring the fact that the latter comments apply only to linear programing and not to the branching type, we find ourselves in essential agreement with this line of reasoning. Improperly used, the teaching machine or the programed text can certainly stifle creativity and discourage discovery. Nevertheless, we feel that programed learning does have an important place in academic work. Our acceptance of these two apparently contradictory positions can be explained, very simply, by acknowledging that each emphasis represents an effective approach to a *different* kind of educational problem. In other words, we are reluctant to accept either discovery or sequential-rote behavior as the sole kind of learning necessary in education. Each has its place, and an important place, and in a complete educational program both must be included.

ADVANTAGES OF PROGRAMING

Programed learning, when properly administered, has several distinct advantages. First, programed instruction maximizes individual differences among pupils, rather than minimizes them as the traditional system tends to do. More specifically, the superior student is permitted to save time in reaching a high level of proficiency. The slow student is not pressured to keep up with a particular group or left completely behind. The teacher's time is released for giving students a greater amount of individual attention; in contrast, when an entire class is taught as a unit, the teacher must compromise in distribution of time allowed because of the quick achievement of the more gifted children. That is, in the traditional technique, the teacher spends more time on a particular unit than the better pupils need but less time than the inferior ones require.

Second, programed learning is broadly applicable to educational and training materials. It has proven to be especially valuable in subject matter where the rote-learning component is predominant—for instance, foreign languages and certain kinds of mathematics—but it has also proved effective in various other subjects, such as social studies. It is particularly important in the learning of rote materials that errors not be reinforced. In less straightforward subject matter it is important that the various alternatives be clearly presented. Viewed in this manner, the teaching machine, as the major vehicle of programed learning, is a teaching aid and *not* a replacement of the classroom teacher.

Programed learning has the great merit of primarily utilizing positive reinforcement. There is little question, whatever one's theoretical bias, that there has been an extreme imbalance in our traditional system between positive and negative reinforcement. It has been estimated (G. B. Watson, 1963, p. 90), for example, that 75 per cent of the time spent in the classroom of a school in a disadvantaged neighborhood consists of essentially negative reinforcement, such as verbal punishment or threat of punishment. Anything that helps to redress this imbalance is almost certain to have salutary effects upon the educational process.

Finally, apart from its intrinsic merit as a teaching procedure, the programed-learning movement has been of great value in forcing a careful evaluation and reworking both of educational objectives and of the content and organization of educational materials. These reforms, if any are made, must be regarded as a highly desirable by-product of programed learning.

O. K. MOORE'S "TALKING TYPEWRITER" AND THE RESPONSIVE ENVIRONMENT

Perhaps the most promising—and certainly one of the most fascinating—of all of the special programs is that devised by O. K. Moore (1963). Deliberately restricting the role of the teacher and minimizing as far as possible external reinforcements, either positive or negative, Moore has succeeded in training children three to six years old, of all levels of intellectual capacity, to read and write within a relatively short time. Together with Richard Kobler, an engineer, he has invented an automated and computerized learning situation called the responsive environment which is designed to facilitate the kind of direct responsiveness that is emphasized in the program.

The original laboratory was established at the Hamden Hall Country Day School, in Hamden, Connecticut. At the time of the 1963 report, a total of 250 children had participated in the project. Some idea of the success of the program may be gained from the fact that first-grade children who have gone through the learning laboratory publish their own newspaper, samples from which are shown in Moore's report (1963) . After two years in the program, children completing the first grade were able to read, on the average, at the beginning sixth-year level. Case histories of educable retardates as well as of gifted children in the Moore report (1963) are impressive documentations of the effectiveness of the program.

PROCEDURE

During the first session, the responsive environment is set for "free exploration." The child is placed in the chair before the typewriter keyboard and told to enjoy himself and to raise his hand if he wants anything. Before he enters the booth the child's nails are painted with nontoxic water colors corresponding to the typewriter keys, as an aid to correct fingering. The assistant leaves the booth and goes to a control panel from which he watches the child through a one-way window. When the child strikes a key, the responsive environment types the letter and pronounces its name. The child remains alone in the booth for 30 minutes unless he asks to be removed before this time is up.

A second phase begins when in the judgment of the assistant and other staff, who keep records on the child's behavior in the booth at the daily sessions, the child is ready. He is then moved to the "search and match" phase without warning. Now the responsive environment is set so that typewriter characters appear in a rectangular exhibitor window before the child touches a key. The machine locks the keyboard, with the exception of the appropriate matching key, and pronounces the name of the character. As soon as the child finds the right key, the machine repronounces the name of the character and then covers it up before exposing a new one. The assistant can make allowances for individual differences by means of various adjustments in the matching.

When the child no longer needs to search in order to match, he is moved to the "word-construction" phase, again without warning. He is confronted with a situation in which several letters appear. After the child has struck the appropriate letter, the name of the letter is pronounced. When a word is completed, the word is pronounced. This is the reading part of the word-construction phase, symbolized as WC-R.

A second part of the word-construction phase is writing (WC-W). An attempt is made to have the child write on the typewriter his own words or ones that have meaning for him. To prepare for this activity, he may be taken into a different room where he is encouraged to talk. His recorded words are then programed into the responsive environment. Or a child may talk directly into a microphone to make a recording which is reproduced so that he can actually write his own dictation.

In the fourth phase, "reading and writing," the responsive environment can read a sentence or a paragraph or ask a question or tell a story, either before or after a child types, as well as respond to individual characters in the manner previously described. As Moore points out, the method "must come to terms with the traditional school curriculum" (1963, p. 26). Material is chosen for presentation so as to encourage imaginative interpretations and, at the same time, be appropriate for children of widely varying intellectual capacity. Moore cites "Alice in Wonderland" as a story which all children begin to read with enjoyment but which permits the gifted child to go beyond the manifest content.

A better idea of the procedure can be obtained from an account, here excerpted, of the initial experiences of an educable retardate with an IQ of 65, who had been dismissed from public-school kindergarten the previous year because of disruptive behavior tendencies (Moore, 1963, pp. 31–32).

Billy's introductory session was calm—he quietly followed the guide around—he could not be drawn into conversation. Once in a while he smiled and in general was wide-eyed. In his second introductory session he explored some on his own but spent most of the time holding the guide's hand. By the end of this session he was becoming curious about the equipment and seemed quite relaxed—and so he was scheduled for the automated booth the following day. The third day he came in— noisy and confident—he permitted the booth assistant to help him into the elevated chair, he watched her leave and then turned his attention immediately to the keyboard. What happened next is best described as an attack upon the instrument. In 30 minutes he typed 1302 characters. The booth assistant had to turn off the instrument and lead him out of the booth when his time was up. For the next nine sessions he continued to "machine gun" the instrument at a gradually slowing pace. In his eleventh session there was a sharp drop in strokes—the booth assistant wrote, "He seems to be getting interested in looking at what he has typed." The laboratory supervisor shifted him from Phase 1, Free Exploration, to Phase 2, Search and Match. Billy was startled and angry—he put up his hand over and over to call the booth assistant in—he evidently thought the instrument was broken and that the assistant would not fix it. All previous sessions had lasted 30 minutes but Billy stopped this one after 9 minutes. He had made five matches by accident (he had not come up with a way of systematically trying all keys). The laboratory supervisor switched him back to Phase 1 for his next session and he was very pleased, although he proceeded more cautiously than he had before—looking, listening, and occasionally repeating what was said. After another five days his time dropped to 15 minutes and the supervisor again switched him to Phase 2 for the following session.

This time he was calmer about the change. After five minutes he was pressing every key with his thumb—he clapped his hands when he made a match. At the end of this 30-minute session he said he wanted to take the "typewriter" home. For the next 60 days he played Search and Match in its increasingly difficult versions. There seemed to be no diminution in his interest. This was the game for Billy—he made it more complex for himself by shutting his eyes while finding keys, by "dive bombing" the keyboard, by first using one hand and then the other. He was still not using the color coding of fingers to keys, however. The supervisor switched him to Phase 3, Word Construction, R and W, even though his interest had not waned. He could find the characters to make words but he did not want the words—he told the instrument to "shut up." His time dropped down to 3 minutes after five days. He was shifted back to Phase 2. In WC-W he had been nearly mute—he kept mumbling something about "it's not broken." Billy continued in Phase 2 for another 30 days, still eager and interested. His refusal to go on to words was perplexing because by this time he was very expert at finding all characters and was using the color-coding system. Also, he had learned to print all the characters in the handwriting booth (this included the ampersand which most booth assistants have to learn, too) .[1]

[1] Reprinted by permission from Omar Khayyam Moore, *Autotelic Responsive Environments and Exceptional Children,* Hamden, Connecticut: Responsive Environments Foundation. Copyright © 1963 by Responsive Environments Foundation.

At the time of Moore's (1963) report, Billy had returned to public school and successfully completed the first grade. Moreover, his IQ at retest had risen to 79 and his social adjustment at home as well as at school was reported to be much improved.

THE RESPONSIVE ENVIRONMENT

Although the initial work of Moore's laboratory has been concerned with the learning of linguistic skills, he points out that other subject matters involving complex conceptualizations can also be taught in the same general manner. He sees the key feature as the "autotelic responsive environment." "Autotelic" refers to intrinsic motivating and reinforcing properties. Moore explains that external reinforcements should not be introduced while the basic skills are being learned, because they complicate matters by distracting the learner. A "responsive environment," for Moore, is one which (1) permits free exploration, (2) gives immediate knowledge of results, (3) allows the learner to pace himself, (4) permits discovery of various kinds of relationships, and (5) is structured so as to facilitate a series of interconnected discoveries.

Certain of these characteristics, and of the related procedures in the laboratory, are obviously very similar to those in the Montessori system and programed learning. The combination of all of them, however, is unique to the Moore program. Furthermore, his emphasis on discovery by the child blunts the point of the major criticism of programed learning. In this respect, it is similar to the branching type of machine program.

The success of Moore's laboratory program is all the more impressive because participation is limited to a thirty-minute daily session and is strictly on a voluntary basis. With regard to the latter point, it is interesting that introduction to the laboratory is by another child, prepared in the responsive environment, who acts as a guide and explains to the newcomer that (1) he comes to the laboratory only if he wants to do so, (2) he may leave whenever he wishes, (3) he must leave when his time is up, (4) he need not explain or justify his coming or his going, (5) he must go to the booth assigned for that day, and (6) once he says he wants to leave, or actually leaves, he can come back the *next* day but not that same day.

The extremely strong motivational attraction of this program is suggested by Moore's observation (1963, p. 11) that "One of the most remarkable things about this environment is that, day in and day out, children elect to come to it—sometimes several months go by without one child of the current group (which number 60) refusing his turn."

One of the most interesting features of the laboratory school, and one that very likely helps to account for its success in training children as well as in strengthening motivation, is the way in which diversions are discouraged. The thirty minutes of each daily session are play—but play with a very businesslike purpose and with a high degree of efficiency. Thus, all "significant" adults in a child's life, such as parents, are kept out of the environment. Parents are permitted a single visit to the laboratory each school year, but this is arranged so that they neither see their child nor are seen by him. Furthermore, the decor of the laboratory is kept as simple and uncomplicated as possible. The laboratory booths have no windows (which, according to Moore, invite digression).

One last advantage of this laboratory-school program should be emphasized. This concerns the manner in which individual differences in socialization and intellectual abilities are adjusted to and utilized. For example, gifted children are given special roles such as guides, coordinators of the newspaper, and the like. In this way they are not isolated from the normal and dull-normal or retarded children, as they tend to be when placed in separate educational groups; and neither are they allowed to become bored by tasks that are much too easy for them. It should be apparent that this skillful use of individual variations serves a most useful educational purpose and helps to maintain the motivation of the learner (who is permitted to progress at his own pace in the actual learning) at an extremely high level.

One major disadvantage of this program is the relatively elaborate and expensive equipment that has been developed. It is probable that much of the value of the program can be achieved without that expense, as evidenced by similar laboratory research of Staats (1964), utilizing much less elaborate equipment.

We are hopeful that unique and promising experimental programs such as these can be given a thorough trial on a wide basis. These programs represent the kind of attention to motivational problems that is necessary in education.

CREATIVITY

We include the problem of creativity not because there has been any very formalized movement in support of a particular technique, as in the case of the methods previously reviewed in this section, but rather because within recent years educators and investigators have felt an increasing concern with the encouragement of creativity in the classroom and because creativity raises serious questions bearing on motivation.

THE PRIMARY GRADES

Let us initiate our discussion by looking at the situation in the typical classroom in the primary grades. Here we follow the well-developed analysis presented by Torrance (1965a, 1965b), who has spearheaded the recent emphasis on this problem.

Creative thinking is inhibited by a complex of factors (Torrance, 1965b). First, there is an essentially repressive environment. Not merely is creativity not directly rewarded; it is actively discouraged. The pupil who asks an unusual question or makes an extraordinary comment tends to be felt as a threat by the ordinary teacher. For one thing, the teacher will probably not know the answer, since the question is not one for which he has been prepared. Worse still, allowing such questions may be a serious threat to class discipline. Other students, equally unable to appreciate the question, may interpret it, perhaps correctly, as a threat to the teacher and may thereby be encouraged to try their own unusual or "funny" questions or comments.

Second, schoolwork evaluation procedures, from the earliest grades on, are geared not to creativity but rather to achievement. The creative child is not likely to be also a highly achieving student, at least by the ordinary standards of achievement. This discrepancy is especially serious at the high-school level, because college admission practices utilize achievement measures and so tend to eliminate the creative but nonconforming student. A certain fraction of high-school and college dropouts may be attributed to this condition. While this fraction is certainly a very small one, nevertheless in absolute numbers the total is important. It should be apparent that what happens educationally to even a small number of highly talented children is very important from the standpoint of their possible contributions to society.

Third, there are important social stereotypes, existing in the classroom as well as in other places, that tend to discourage creativity. For example, the creative person tends to be thought of in terms of art and music—not of science or politics. But these latter areas are precisely the ones in which creativity is especially needed. Occupational selections, which determine educational choices in high school and beyond, need to be based upon an improved picture of this situation. It is impossible, of course, even to estimate how many talented, creative students are lost to the sciences by this sort of misinformation, but the number must be considerable.

Another type of social stereotype involves the fact that whole areas of experience are taboo in certain respects. Thus, girls are not expected to be interested in science or engineering. Further, at an even earlier level of education, there is the predominant notion that girls are not supposed to do well in mathematics—a notion that no doubt helps to account in very large measure for their actually lower performance level in mathematics and related subjects.

Finally, there is the problem of how the schools evaluate creativity, as a special kind of ability. Alpert (1962) makes the important point that the school provides for the emergence of the "good student"—that is, the high academic achiever—as well as of the "good mixer and/or athlete," but there is no corresponding role for the "creative-original" student. Moreover, individual teachers tend to value the high-achieving but not the high-creative child. Until this situation is improved, to the extent that there is recognition of a social role for the creative child more commensurate with his potential importance, there is not likely to be a marked improvement in his own self-image. The fostering of such an improvement should certainly be an important objective of educational change.

Torrance has indicated, on the basis of observations of pupils and teachers as well as questionnaire responses, how creative behavior may be more effectively reinforced in the classroom. He suggests that the teachers be encouraged to show respect for unusual questions and imaginative ideas and to let such questioners know that their ideas have value. Further, pupils should be allowed practice time without strict evaluation and should be encouraged to proceed with self-initiated activities. Perhaps it would be even better to reinforce the questioning attitude for its own value. Although these suggestions may often conflict with orthodox school practices, their implementation would assuredly help to improve the treatment of potentially creative pupils. Such pupils should certainly be permitted to develop more fully than is at present generally possible within our school systems.

One of the more distressing aspects of our present educational system is the tragic waste of so much talent. Such waste is by no means restricted to highly gifted or especially creative children. There is more than ample evidence that even our average children can learn at a far more rapid rate than they commonly show, given appropriate opportunities and reasonable motivation. Demonstration of this fact has been provided by our discussion of the success of the Montessori system and by Moore's (1963) dramatic results with extremely young children. Further illustrations abound. For one example, McNeil and Keisler (1961) have reported the learning by thirteen first-grade pupils of abstract scientific principles and terminology. As Bruner has observed (1960, p. 12), "Experience over the past decade points to the fact that our schools may be wasting precious years by postponing the teaching of many important subjects on the ground that they are too difficult."

THE GIFTED CHILD

Thus far we have been discussing the problems of the creative child without regard for his over-all intellectual level. As a matter of fact, we have implied that there is no very high correlation between creativity and intellectual level, as measured by the ordinary intelligence test. That is to say, creative ideas may well be produced by children who have less than brilliant IQ ratings. Beyond an IQ of approximately 120, measures of intelligence and creativity appear to be relatively independent. It is nevertheless true that intellectually gifted children do tend to be more creative than others, and also that they encounter a special set of problems in the usual school. For these reasons we conclude this section with a consideration of the problem of motivating the highly gifted child.

Torrance (1965a) has analyzed the classroom situation for the gifted child. He finds that the learning of gifted children tends to be far below their potential because in the ordinary classroom they are given too little opportunity to use what they can learn, are not allowed to learn in their own way (which may be quite different from that of the average student), and generally are unable to utilize their superior abilities. They tend to develop an interest in grades. This helps to blunt such creative tendencies as they might have, which is hardly surprising under the circumstances that have been described. Also, when special attention is paid to them, too much may be expected in too short a time—so that they are frequently presented with tasks and expectations that are either too easy or too hard. Correction of these unfortunate conditions, perhaps by providing special scheduling and special teachers, is essential if we are to realize more of the potential provided by our gifted children.

EDUCATIONAL RESEARCH

The great need for more research, and more effective research, on the role of motivational processes in education should be quite apparent to the reader of this and the preceding chapter. It would certainly seem that a fraction of the research effort spent, say, on the curriculum or the class structure could be diverted to the problems of motivation. One may well inquire as to what good any changes will do if the fundamental motivations of the students—and their corresponding behaviors—are left unaffected. There is simply no justification for assuming that once the appropriate curriculum or class-structure changes are made the relevant motivational changes will also occur. And the only way in which the direction and extent of any motivational changes produced by curriculum or class modification can be properly assessed is by means of the kind of research on motivation that we are emphasizing.

It is necessary to introduce a further word of caution. In research on motivation, as well as on other educational problems, halfway measures will not do. It will be necessary, for example, to utilize adequate experimental controls. In other words, this research must meet at least minimum standards of scientific rigor. As should be evident from our preceding discussion, the problems of motivation and learning, as they exist in the classroom, are complexly intertwined, and their separation will require much careful effort. They must be abstracted, first conceptually and then experimentally, to permit development of adequate analysis and sound conclusions upon which wise policy decisions can be based.

RESISTANCE TO IMPROVEMENTS

One of the problems associated with improving research on learning and motivation in the classroom is the resistance shown by some of the vested interests in the educational establishment. This situation was graphically pictured by Trow (1948) almost two decades ago, and unfortunately, it does not appear to have changed markedly since then. Trow comments (p. 130) that "a visit to a school is still a saddening experience to an educational psychologist. With due respect to the many exceptions, so many things are wrong. After a few moments of silent meditation he talks to some of the teachers. He shortly discovers that he is a mere theorist, that what he is talking about, if it is comprehended at all, 'won't work out in practice.' The ego protection of some of the older teachers . . . sets up a deflecting screen which his words do not penetrate. The principal or superintendent is open-minded in conversation, but his autocratic control may be such that one wonders that the teachers are doing as well as they are."

The need for better research on educational processes has been well stated by Brownell (1948, p. 181), who says: "It is time that we raise the level of our research. We have had too many fragmentary, superficial investigations which purport to show that this or that needs to be done to modify classroom teaching. . . . Too often we have been content at the close of periods of learning to measure rate and accuracy of performance in the function taught. We have not felt it necessary to go beyond these criteria and to secure additional measures of process level. . . . Nor have we concerned ourselves enough about the retention of what is learned or about its transferability in useful ways to new learning tasks."

HILGARD'S ANALYSIS

An especially useful and provocative treatment of the relationship between learning theory and educational practice has recently been made by Hilgard (1964). Since learning theory is very closely related to motivation theory, we would like to look closely at his salient points and then add some comments of our own on the general problem.

Hilgard initiates his discussion by attacking what he calls "some faulty conjectures." Using the term *theory* to apply to both learning and motivation, we may present his argument in terms of the following six major propositions, here stated as the negations of the commonly held but essentially erroneous beliefs:

1. *Scientifically based instruction is not dependent upon agreement among theorists.* This proposition follows from the fact that much of the disagreement among theorists concerns points that are not relevant to practical matters. Moreover, there is a very large, and ever increasing, core of propositions upon which the majority of theorists tend to agree, even while violently

disagreeing upon various refinements. To a great extent it is this seldom emphasized area of agreement from which practical implications may be drawn.

2. *Satisfactory principles of instruction will not directly flow from even the best-ordered theory.* There is no direct relationship between theory and technology. As we discuss below, a great deal more needs to be done in the way of trimming theoretical principles to practical problems.

3. *Knowledge of sound experimental results, considered apart from theoretical arguments, is not sufficient as a base for instruction.* Such an assumption ignores the very intimate relationship between experimentation and theory. Empirical data have relevance for science primarily in terms of the way in which they do relate to theory.

4. *There is no reason to ignore the theorist merely because he is not finished and his knowledge cannot be directly translated into instructional principles.* It would be foolish indeed to ignore the aid that soundly established theory can provide merely because final solutions cannot be obtained all at once.

5. *Merely getting together knowledgeable psychologists, who know about theory, and educators, who know about instructional problems, will not in itself produce solutions of the practical problems.* The problems are too difficult to solve by brief and essentially superficial interactions (such as week-end conferences). Hilgard's suggested procedure is close collaboration in long-range investigations. We do not feel that this prospect is as promising or feasible as an alternative suggested below.

6. *Although it is true that we can learn much from the observation of good teaching, it is also true that improvements can be made on the basis of research.* Hilgard (1964, p. 404) draws the following analogy: "to throw away all the possibility of improving instruction through carefully designed studies would be like returning medical practice to the prescientific physician because we still value the bedside manner."

Hilgard then presents a very detailed and instructive analysis of the relationship between pure research, directed at discovery and confirmation of fundamental scientific principles, and what he calls "technological research and development," more often called "applied research" because it is directed primarily at the production of principles immediately applicable to specific problems of a technical sort. Each of these major categories is divided into three subcategories. Considered with reference to school-related problems, the three types of pure research are (1) the remotely relevant (as animal mazes) ; (2) the generally relevant (as human concept formation or verbal learning) ; and (3) the directly relevant (as learning of mathematics, reading, and the like). The three stages in technical research and development, considered with reference to the locus of the research, are (1) the laboratory or special classroom (for example, programed instruction) ; (2) the normal classroom (for example, trying out the results obtained in [1]) ; and (3) advocacy and adoption in policy situations (for example, preparation of appropriate manuals and textbooks). Hilgard's discussion of these various stages, in terms of concrete projects, should be consulted by anyone seriously interested in these problems.

As Hilgard's treatment indicates, there is no easy road from theory to practice; transformation of theoretical principles into practical policies requires an intense and continuing interaction in which the principles are fitted into new molds in accordance with practical needs. Better still, new principles will be developed in accordance with practical problems of the classroom. But in this process, casual acquaintance with either the principles of psychology or the needs of education is not by itself sufficient as a substitute for more thorough understanding of the other field.

A PROGRAM FOR RESEARCH TRAINING

Our own preference for practical steps directed at solving educational problems more effectively would be along lines somewhat different from those suggested by Hilgard, but by no means incompatible. It is unrealistic to expect the typical "pure" researcher to become very closely concerned with more strictly applied problems (although under special circumstances, such as those that obtain in wartime, many necessarily do so and frequently with considerable success). It is equally unrealistic to expect the person who is well established in more practical pursuits to train himself, methodologically and substantively, in the manner of his pure-scientist counterpart. Each man is much too apt to be so thoroughly engaged in his own endeavors that, even granting some motivation to take on some new task, he is unlikely to have much opportunity to do so.

A much more feasible procedure is to encourage, on as large a scale as possible, intensive training in experimental psychology for graduate students and postdoctoral fellows who are themselves primarily interested and trained in educational practices. Young graduate students should be more amenable than their more established colleagues to undertaking these new and different kinds of training. Moreover, they will often find the experimentalists with whom they train to be sympathetic and helpful. Our own experience with graduate education students of this sort has confirmed our view that the interaction can be a most fruitful one.

It is also possible that some progress can be made in interesting the experimentalist in the practical problems of the classroom, but we are certainly not very hopeful about this possibility. One way to stimulate such an interest is for the student experimentalist to utilize school children as subjects in his learning and motivation research, as Hilgard suggests. Such a procedure will tend to pay dividends, not only in interesting the experimental-research supervisor in these problems but also, and perhaps more likely, in permitting the close and systematic observation of the subject by the experimenter. There are few better ways to encourage the kind of insightful discoveries that are so badly needed in psychology as well as education.

Some examples of the kind of research that we have in mind are reviewed in the Sears and Hilgard article (1964), to which we have already referred on several occasions. A somewhat different kind of research effort, prominent in the Soviet school system, has been reviewed by Boguslavsky (1957). As his report clearly shows, educational research in the Soviet Union has involved the close and continuous participation of psychologists and has utilized behavioral principles in a much more direct manner than is customary in this country. This vigorous research program should be looked into by anyone seriously interested in developing our own research capabilities in the classroom.

Finally, certain suggestions previously made (Marx, 1960) may be repeated. The following procedures are among those which offer promise for improving the student's motivation and which need to be more intensively investigated in classroom research: (1) whetting the appetite (for instance, through taking advantage of the incentive value of prizes and the like by allowing adequate sampling of them before the learning session); (2) emphasizing instrumental behaviors (as by spreading external motivators as widely as possible over a class early in learning and removing them as skills are developed so that intrinsic motivation has an opportunity to develop also); (3) utilizing suspense and discovery (as by allowing the student to complete his work on problems with a minimum of guidance); (4) avoiding initial discouragement (as by giving partial assignments early in learning so that a child is not forced to go through the motions of practice or study when he is not adequately prepared); and (5) preventing extinction of effort (for instance, offering a variety of new secondary reinforcers and motivators in the latter phases of practice so that interest in a subject is maintained).

The prospect of a sound body of research on motivation in education is a very exciting one. The suggestions offered in the above paragraph, while derived from experimental studies of learning, demand an intensive research effort if their relevance to the problems of education is to be established and techniques for their implementation developed. A research effort of this magnitude, however, will in turn demand either men who can apply the principles of psychological research to the problems of education or a far closer collaboration between experimentalist and educationalist than is usually observed. Few problems are of more practical importance than those of education. A democratic society, in particular, depends for its survival upon an educated electorate. It is in a way surprising that such vast investments of money and manpower have been devoted to solving the applied problems of physics (because we want to get to the moon) and biochemistry (because we wish to preserve life) whereas so little, relatively, is being done to produce an adequate educational technology. In this day of technological "miracles," our waste of human resources seems inexcusable. Surely an enlightened and rational system of education is within our grasp. It is our hope that these preliminary suggestions for collaboration between experimentalist and educationalist will help to stimulate interest in this exciting prospect.

Suggested Readings

Bruner, J. S. 1960. *The process of education*. Cambridge: Harvard University Press.

Hilgard, E. R., ed. 1964. *Theories of learning and instruction*. Yearbook of the National Society for the Study of Education, 63, Part I.

Montessori, Maria. 1964. *Spontaneous activity in education*. Translated by Florence Simmonds. Cambridge: Bentley (reprint of 1917 publication) .

Gagné, R. M. 1965. *The conditions of learning*. New York: Holt, Rinehart and Winston.

REFERENCES

Adolph, E. F. 1939. Measurements of water drinking in dogs. *American Journal of Physiology*, 125: 75–86.

Allport, G. W. 1937. *Personality*. New York: Henry Holt and Co.

Allport, G. W. 1947. Scientific models and human morals. *Psychological Review*, 54: 182–192.

Allport, G. W. 1954. *The nature of prejudice*. Reading, Mass.: Addison-Wesley.

Allport, G. W. 1955. *Becoming: Basic considerations for a psychology of personality*. New Haven: Yale University Press.

Alper, Thelma G. 1952. The interrupted task method in studies of selective recall: a reevaluation of some recent experiments. *Psychological Review*, 59: 71–88.

Alpert, R. 1962. Modifying personality in a school setting. In G. S. Nielsen, ed., *Child and Education*. 14th International Congress of Applied Psychology, Vol. 3. Copenhagen: Munksgaard.

Amsel, A., and F. K. Cole. 1953. Generalization of fear-motivated interference with water intake. *Journal of Experimental Psychology*, 46: 243–247.

Anand, B. K., and J. R. Brodbeck. 1951. Hypothalamic control of food intake in rats and cats. *Yale Journal of Biological Medicine*, 24: 123–140.

Anand, B. K., and S. Dua. 1955. Feeding responses induced by electrical stimulation of the hypothalamus in cats. *Indian Journal of Medical Research*, 43: 115–122.

Anderson, O. D., R. Parmenter, and H. S. Liddell. 1939. Some cardiovascular manifestations of the experimental neurosis in the sheep. *Psychosomatic Medicine*, 1: 93–100.

Andersson, B. 1952. Polydipsia caused by intrahypothalamic injections of hypertonic NaCl-solutions. *Experientia* 8: 157–158.

Andersson, B. 1953. The effect of injections of hypertonic NaCl-solutions into different parts of the hypothalamus of goats. *Acta Physiologica Scandinavica*, 28: 186–201.

Andersson, B., and S. M. McCann. 1955. A further study of polydipsia evoked by hypothalamic stimulation in the goat. *Acta Physiologica Scandinavica,* 33: 333–346.

Aronson, E., and J. Mills. 1959. The effect of severity of initiation on liking for a group. *Journal of Abnormal and Social Psychology,* 59: 177–181.

Atkinson, J. W. 1958. *Motives in fantasy, action, and society.* Princeton: D. Van Nostrand Company.

Atkinson, J. W. 1964. *An introduction to motivation.* Princeton: D. Van Nostrand Company.

Austin, V. T., and F. R. Steggerda. 1936. Congenital dysfunctions of the salivary glands with observations on the physiology of thirst. *Illinois Medical Journal,* 69: 124–127.

Ausubel, D. P., and H. M. Schiff. 1955. A level of aspiration approach to the measurement of goal tenacity. *Journal of General Psychology,* 52: 97–110.

Bailey, P., and F. Bremer. 1921. Experimental diabetes insipidus. *Archives of Internal Medicine,* 28: 773–803.

Bandura, A. 1961. Psychotherapy as a learning process. *Psychological Bulletin,* 58: 143–159.

Bandura, A., and R. H. Walters. 1959. *Adolescent aggression.* New York: Ronald Press.

Battle, M. 1966. The white man can't help the black ghetto. *The Saturday Evening Post,* 239 (3) : 10–17.

Beach, F. A. 1940. Effects of cortical lesions upon the copulatory behavior of male rats. *Journal of Comparative and Physiological Psychology,* 29: 239–244.

Beach, F. A. 1941. Copulatory behavior of male rats raised in isolation and subjected to partial decortication prior to the acquisition of sexual experience. *Journal of Comparative and Physiological Psychology,* 31: 457–470.

Beach, F. A. 1942a. Copulatory behavior in prepuberally castrated male rats and its modification by estrogen administration. *Endocrinology,* 31: 679–683.

Beach, F. A. 1942b. Male and female mating behavior in prepuberally castrated female rats treated with androgens. *Endocrinology,* 31: 673–678.

Beach, F. A. 1942c. Sexual behavior of prepuberal male and female rats treated with gonadal hormones. *Journal of Comparative Psychology,* 34: 285–292.

Beach, F. A. 1943. Effects of injury to the cerebral cortex upon the display of masculine and feminine mating behavior by female rats. *Journal of Comparative and Physiological Psychology,* 36: 169–199.

Beach, F. A. 1951. Instinctive behavior: Reproductive activity. In S. S. Stevens, ed., *Handbook of experimental psychology.* New York: John Wiley and Sons.

Beach, F. A. 1955. The descent of instinct. *Psychological Review,* 62: 401–410.

Beach, F. A. 1956. Characteristics of masculine "sex drive." In M. R. Jones, ed., *Nebraska symposium on motivation,* pp. 1–31. Lincoln: University of Nebraska Press.

Beach, F. A., M. W. Conovitz, F. Steinberg, and A. C. Goldstein. 1956. Experimental inhibition and restoration of mating behavior in male rats. *Journal of Genetic Psychology,* 89: 165–181.

Beach, F. A., and A. Marie Holtz. 1946. Mating behavior in male rats castrated at various ages and injected with androgen. *Journal of Experimental Zoology,* 101: 91–142.

Beach, F. A., A. Zitrin, and J. Jaynes. 1956a. Neural mediation of mating in male cats. I. Effects of unilateral and bilateral removal of the neocortex. *Journal of Comparative and Physiological Psychology,* 49: 321–327.

Beach, F. A., A. Zitrin, and J. Jaynes. 1956b. Neural mediation of mating in male cats. III. Contributions of occipital, parietal, and temporal cortex. *Journal of Comparative Neurology,* 105: 111–125.

Beaumont, W. 1833. *Experiments and observations on gastric juice and the physiology of digestion.* Plattsburg, N.Y.: F. P. Allen.

Berkowitz, L. 1962. *Aggression, a social psychological analysis.* New York: McGraw-Hill Book Co.

Bernard, C. 1856. *Leçons de physiologie expérimentale appliquée a la médecine,* Vol. 2. Paris: Baillieré.

Bernard, L. L. 1924. *Instinct, a study in social psychology.* New York: Henry Holt and Co.

Bernhaut, M., E. Gellhorn, and A. T. Rasmussen. 1953. Experimental contributions to the problem of consciousness. *Journal of Neurophysiology,* 16: 21–36.

Bettelheim, B., and M. Janowitz. 1950. *Dynamics of prejudice.* New York: Harper and Bros.

Bidder, F., and C. Schmidt. 1852. *Die Verdauungssaefte und der Stoffwechsel.* Mittau und Leipzig: Reyher.

Binder, A., D. McConnell, and N. A. Sjoholm. 1957. Verbal conditioning as a function of experimenter characteristics. *Journal of Abnormal and Social Psychology,* 55: 309–314.

Bindra, D. 1959. *Motivation: A systematic reinterpretation.* New York: Ronald Press.

Bitterman, M. E., and W. H. Holtzman. 1952. Conditioning and extinction of the galvanic skin response as a function of anxiety. *Journal of Abnormal and Social Psychology*, 47: 615–623.

Blodgett, H. C. 1929. The effect of the introduction of reward upon the maze performance of rats. *University of California Publications in Psychology*, 4: 113–134.

Boguslavsky, G. W. 1957. Psychological research in Soviet education. *Science*, 125: 915–918.

Boling, J. L., W. C. Young, and E. W. Dempsey. 1938. Miscellaneous experiments on the estrogen-progesterone induced heat in the spayed guinea-pig. *Endocrinology*, 23: 182–187.

Bower, G. H., and N. E. Miller. 1958. Rewarding and punishing effects from stimulating the same place in the rat's brain. *Journal of Comparative and Physiological Psychology*, 51: 669.

Brady, J. V. 1957. An experimental approach to the analysis of emotional behavior. In P. Hoch and J. Zubin, eds., *Experimental Psychopathology*. New York: Grune and Stratton.

Brady, J. V. 1960. Temporal and emotional effects related to intracranial electrical self-stimulation. In E. R. Ramey and D. S. O'Doherty, eds., *Electrical studies on the unanesthetized brain*. New York: Hoeber.

Brady, J. V., J. Boren, D. Conrad, and M. Sidman. 1957. The effect of food and water deprivation upon intra-cranial self-stimulation. *Journal of Comparative and Physiological Psychology*, 50: 134.

Brady, J. V., and D. Conrad. 1960. Some effects of brain stimulation on timing behavior. *Journal of Experimental Analysis of Behavior*, 3: 93.

Breland, K., and Marian Breland. 1966. *Animal Behavior*. New York: Macmillan Co.

Bremer, F. 1935. Cerveau isolé et physiologie du sommeil. *Comptes rendus de la Société de Biologie*, 118: 1235–1241.

Breuer, J., and S. Freud. [1895.] *Studies in hysteria*. New York: Nervous and Mental Disease Publications, 1937.

Bridgman, P. W. 1927. *The logic of modern physics*. New York: Macmillan Co.

Brill, A. A. [1924.] *Lectures on psychoanalytic psychiatry*. New York: Vintage, 1956.

Brownell, W. A. 1948. Criteria of learning in educational research. *Journal of Educational Psychology*, 39: 129–132.

Bruner, J. S. 1960. *The process of education*. Cambridge: Harvard University Press.

Bruner, J. S. 1964. The course of cognitive growth. *American Psychologist*, 19: 1–15.

Butler, R. A. 1957. The effect of deprivation of visual incentives on visual exploration motivation in monkeys. *Journal of Comparative and Physiological Psychology,* 50: 177–179.

Callahan, R. E. 1962. *Education and the cult of efficiency.* Chicago: University of Chicago Press.

Campbell, B. A., and Doris Kraeling. 1954. Response strength as a function of drive level during training. *Journal of Comparative and Physiological Psychology,* 47: 101–103.

Cannon, W. B. 1918. The physiological basis of thirst. *Proceedings of the Royal Society of London,* 90: 283–301.

Cannon, W. B. 1939. *The wisdom of the body,* 2nd ed. New York: W. W. Norton and Co.

Cannon, W. B., and A. L. Washburn. 1912. An explanation of hunger. *American Journal of Physiology,* 29: 441–454.

Capehart, J., W. Viney, and J. M. Hulicka. 1958. The effect of effort upon extinction. *Journal of Comparative and Physiological Psychology,* 51: 505–507.

Carlson, A. J. 1916. *The control of hunger in health and disease.* Chicago: University of Chicago Press.

Carpenter, C. R. 1942. Sexual behavior of free ranging rhesus monkeys (macaca mulatta). *Journal of Comparative Psychology,* 33: 113–162.

Carr, H. A. 1925. *Psychology: A study of mental activity.* New York: Longmans, Green and Co.

Chapman, D. W., and J. Volkmann. 1939. A social determinant of the level of aspiration. *Journal of Abnormal and Social Psychology,* 34: 225–238.

Chasdi, E. H., and M. S. Lawrence. 1955. Some antecedents of aggression and effects of frustration in doll play. In D. McClelland, ed., *Studies in motivation.* New York: Appleton-Century-Crofts.

Chow, K. L., W. C. Dement, and E. R. John. 1957. Conditioned electrocorticographic potentials and behavioral avoidance response in cat. *Journal of Neurophysiology,* 20: 482–493.

Clark, R. A. 1955. The effects of sexual motivation on phantasy. In D. McClelland, ed., *Studies in motivation.* New York: Appleton-Century-Crofts.

Cohen, A. R. 1955. Social norms, arbitrariness of frustration, and status of the agent of frustration in the frustration aggression hypothesis. *Journal of Abnormal and Social Psychology,* 51: 222–226.

Collier, G., and M. H. Marx. 1959. Changes in performance as a function of shifts in the magnitude of reinforcement. *Journal of Experimental Psychology,* 57: 305–309.

Cotton, J. W. 1953. Running time as a function of amount of food deprivation. *Journal of Experimental Psychology,* 46: 188–198.

Cowen, E., J. Londes, and P. E. Schaet. 1959. The effects of mild frustration on the expression of prejudiced attitudes. *Journal of Abnormal and Social Psychology,* 58: 33–38.

Cowles, J. T. 1937. Food-tokens as incentives for learning by chimpanzees. *Comparative Psychological Monographs,* 14: No. 71.

Crespi, L. P. 1942. Quantitative variation of incentive and performance in the white rat. *American Journal of Psychology,* 55: 467–517.

Cronbach, L. J. 1962. Psychological issues pertinent to recent American curriculum reforms. In G. S. Nielsen, ed., *Child and education.* Copenhagen: Munksgaard.

Crum, Janet, W. L. Brown, and M. E. Bitterman. 1951. The effect of partial and delayed reinforcement on resistance to extinction. *American Journal of Psychology,* 64: 228–237.

D'Amato, M. R. 1955. Secondary reinforcement and magnitude of primary reinforcement. *Journal of Comparative and Physiological Psychology,* 48: 378–380.

Davidson, J. R., and E. Douglass. 1950. Nocturnal enuresis: A special approach to treatment. *British Medical Journal,* 1: 1345–1347.

Davis, K. B. 1929. *Factors in the sex life of twenty-two hundred women.* New York: Harper and Bros.

Deese, J. 1958. *The psychology of learning.* New York: McGraw-Hill Book Co.

Dembo, Tamara. 1931. Der Ärger als dynamisches Problem. *Psychologische Forschung,* 15: 1–144.

Deutsch, J. A. 1960. *The structural basis of behavior.* Chicago: University of Chicago Press.

Dewey, J. 1938. *Experience and education.* New York: Macmillan Co.

Dinsmoor, J. A. 1950. A quantitative comparison of the discriminative and reinforcing functions of a stimulus. *Journal of Experimental Psychology,* 40: 458–472.

Dollard, J., L. Doob, N. E. Miller, O. Mowrer, and R. Sears. 1939. *Frustration and aggression.* New Haven: Yale University Press.

Dollard, J., and N. E. Miller. 1950. *Personality and psychotherapy: An analysis in terms of learning, thinking and culture.* New York: McGraw-Hill Book Co.

Duncan, C. P. 1949. The retroactive effect of electroshock on learning. *Journal of Comparative and Physiological Psychology,* 42: 32–44.

Dunlap, K. 1919. Are there any instincts? *Journal of Abnormal Psychology,* 14: 307–311.

Elliott, M. H. 1929. The effect of appropriateness of rewards and of complex incentives on maze performance. *University of California Publications in Psychology,* 4: 91–98.

English, H. B., and A. C. English. 1958. *A comprehensive dictionary of psychological and psychoanalytical terms.* New York: Longmans, Green and Co.

Epstein, A. N. 1960. Reciprocal changes in feeding behavior produced by intrahypothalamic chemical injections. *American Journal of Physiology,* 199: 969–974.

Estes, W. K. 1943. Discriminative conditioning: I. A discriminative property of conditioned anticipation. *Journal of Experimental Psychology,* 32: 150–155.

Estes, W. K. 1948. Discriminative conditioning: II. Effects of a Pavlovian conditioned stimulus upon a subsequently established operant response. *Journal of Experimental Psychology,* 38: 173–177.

Farber, I. E. 1954. Anxiety as a drive state. In M. R. Jones, ed., *Current theory and research on motivation.* Lincoln: University of Nebraska Press.

Farber, I. E. 1955. The role of motivation in verbal learning and performance. *Psychological Bulletin,* 52: 311–327.

Farber, I. E., and K. W. Spence. 1953. Complex learning and conditioning as a function of anxiety. *Journal of Experimental Psychology,* 45: 120–125.

Fay, J. C., J. D. Miller, and H. F. Harlow. 1953. Incentive size, food deprivation, and food preference. *Journal of Comparative and Physiological Psychology,* 46: 13–15.

Ferster, C. B., and B. F. Skinner. 1957. *Schedules of reinforcement.* New York: Appleton-Century-Crofts.

Festinger, L. 1942. Wish, expectation, and group standards as factors influencing level of aspiration. *Journal of Abnormal and Social Psychology,* 37: 184–200.

Festinger, L. 1957. *A theory of cognitive dissonance.* Evanston, Ill.: Row, Peterson and Co.

Festinger, L. 1961. The psychological effects of insufficient rewards. *American Psychologist,* 16: 1–11.

Filler, W., and N. Drezner. 1944. Results of surgical castration in women over forty. *American Journal of Obstetrics and Gynecology,* 47: 122–124.

Fishman, J. A., and P. I. Clifford. 1964. What can mass-testing programs do for-and-to the pursuit of excellence in American education. *Harvard Educational Review,* 34 (1) : 63–79.

Fowler, H. 1965. *Curiosity and exploratory behavior.* New York: Macmillan Co.

Frank, J. D. 1935. Individual differences in certain aspects of aspiration. *American Journal of Psychology,* 47: 119–128.

Frank, J. D. 1936. A comparison between certain properties of the level of aspiration and random guessing. *Journal of Psychology,* 3: 43–62.

Frankel, E. 1961. The gifted academic underachiever. *Science Teacher,* 28: 49–51.

Freedman, F. S. 1962. *Theory and practice of psychological testing.* New York: Holt, Rinehart and Winston.

French, J. D. 1957. The reticular formation. *Scientific American,* 196: 2–8.

French, J. D., F. K. Amerongen, and H. W. Magoun. 1952. Ascending reticular activating system in brain stem of monkeys. *Archives of Neurology and Psychiatry,* 68: 577–590.

French, J. D., and H. W. Magoun. 1952. Effects of chronic lesions in central cephalic brain stem of monkeys. *Archives of Neurology and Psychiatry,* 68: 591–604.

French, J. D., M. Verzeano, and H. W. Magoun. 1952. Contrasting features of corticopetal condition in direct and indirect sensory systems. *Transactions of the American Neurological Association,* 77: 44–47.

Freud, S. [various dates]. *The complete psychological works of Sigmund Freud.* J. Strachey, ed. and trans. London: Hogarth Press, 1955.

Galambos, R., G. Sheatz, and V. C. Vernier. 1956. Electrophysiological correlates of a conditioned response in cats. *Science,* 123: 376–377.

Garafolo, Loranze, and R. C. Davis. 1957. Gastrointestinal activity in hunger and after food: The question of hunger pangs. *Proceedings of the Indiana Academy of Science,* 67: 298.

Gardner, J. W. 1940. The relation of certain personality variables to level of aspiration. *Journal of Psychology,* 9: 191–206.

Gianturco, C. 1934. Some mechanical factors in gastric physiology. *American Journal of Roentgenology,* 131: 735–744.

Gilman, A. 1937. The relation between blood osmotic pressure, fluid distribution and voluntary water intake. *American Journal of Physiology,* 120: 323–328.

Goodrich, K. P. 1959. Performance in different segments of an instrumental response chain as a function of reinforcement schedule. *Journal of Experimental Psychology,* 57: 57–63.

Gould, R. 1939. An experimental analysis of "level of aspiration." *Genetic Psychology Monographs,* 21: 1–116.

Gould, R. 1941. Some sociological determinants of goal strivings. *Journal of Social Psychology*, 13: 461–473.

Graham, F. K., W. A. Charwat, A. S. Honig, and P. D. Weltz. 1951. Aggression as a function of the attack and the attacker. *Journal of Abnormal and Social Psychology*, 46: 512–520.

Greenspoon, J. 1954. The effect of two non-verbal stimuli on the frequency of members of two verbal response classes. *American Psychologist*, 9: 384.

Greer, M. A. 1955. Suggestive evidence of a primary "drinking center" in hypothalamus of the rat. *Proceedings of the Society of Experimental Biology, N.Y.*, 89: 59–62.

Grice, C. R. 1948. The relation of secondary reinforcement to delayed reward in visual discrimination learning. *Journal of Experimental Psychology*, 38: 1–16.

Grindley, G. C. 1929. Experiments on the influence of the amount of reward on learning in young chickens. *British Journal of Psychology*, 20: 173–180.

Grossman, S. P. 1960. Eating or drinking elicited by direct adrenergic or cholinergic stimulation of hypothalamus. *Science*, 132: 301–302.

Guthrie, E. R. 1935. *The psychology of learning*. Revised edition. New York: Harper and Bros., 1952.

Guttman, N. 1953. Operant conditioning extinction, and periodic reinforcement in relation to concentration of sucrose used as reinforcing agent. *Journal of Experimental Psychology*, 46: 213–224.

Haggard, D. F. 1959. Acquisition of a simple running response as a function of partial and continuous schedules of reinforcement. *Psychological Record*, 9: 11–18.

Haggard, E. A. 1957. Socialization, personality and academic achievement in gifted children. *The School Review*, 1957 volume: 388–414.

Hall, C. S. 1954. *A primer of Freudian psychology*. Cleveland: World Publishing Co.

Hall, C. S., and G. Lindzey. 1957. *Theories of personality*. New York: John Wiley and Sons.

Hall, J. F. 1951. Studies in secondary reinforcement: II. Secondary reinforcement as a function of the strength of drive during primary reinforcement. *Journal of Comparative and Physiological Psychology*, 44: 462–466.

Harker, G. S. 1956. Delay of reward and performance of an instrumental response. *Journal of Experimental Psychology*, 51: 303–310.

Harlow, H. F. 1953. Mice, monkeys, men and motives. *Psychological Review*, 60: 23–32.

Heath, R. G., and W. A. Micklé. 1960. Evaluation of seven years' experience with depth electrode studies in human patients. In E. R. Ramey and D. S. O'Doherty, eds., *Electrical studies on the unanesthetized brain*. New York: Hoeber.

Hebb, D. O. 1955. Drives and the C.N.S. (conceptual nervous system). *Psychological Review*, 62: 243–254.

Herb, F. H. 1940. Latent learning—non-reward followed by food in blinds. *Journal of Comparative Psychology*, 29: 247–256.

Hernandez-Peon, R., H. Sherrer, and M. Jouvet. 1956. Modification of electric activity in cochlear nucleus during attention in unanesthetized cats. *Science*, 123: 331–332.

Heron, W., B. K. Doane, and T. H. Scott. 1956. Visual disturbances after prolonged perceptual isolation. *Canadian Journal of Psychology*, 10: 13–18.

Hertz, R., R. K. Meyer, and M. A. Spielman. 1937. The specificity of progesterone in inducing receptivity in the ovariectomized guinea pig. *Endocrinology*, 21: 533–535.

Herzberg, A. 1941. Short treatment of neuroses by graduated tasks. *British Journal of Medical Psychology*, 19: 36–51.

Hetherington, A. W., and S. W. Ranson. 1940. Hypothalamic lesions and adiposity in the rat. *Anatomical Record*, 78: 149.

Hildum, D. C., and A. W. Brown. 1956. Verbal reinforcement and interviewer bias. *Journal of Abnormal and Social Psychology*, 53: 108–111.

Hilgard, E. R. 1948. *Theories of learning*. Revised edition. New York: Appleton-Century-Crofts, 1956.

Hilgard, E. R. 1964. A perspective on the relationship between learning theory and educational practices. In *Theories of learning and instruction*. Yearbook of the National Society for the Study of Education, 63: Part I, 402–418.

Hilgard, E. R., and D. H. Russell. 1950. Motivation in school learning and instruction. In *Theories of learning and instruction*. Yearbook of the National Society for the Study of Education, 49: Part I, 36–68.

Hoebel, B. G., and P. Teitelbaum. 1962. Hypothalamic control of feeding and self-stimulation. *Science*, 135: 375–377.

Hovland, C., and R. Sears. 1940. Minor studies in aggression: VI. Correlation of lynchings with economic indices. *Journal of Psychology*, 9: 301–310.

Howarth, C. I., and J. A. Deutsch, 1962. Dissipation of a drive process as the cause of apparently fast extinction in ESB habit. *Science*, 137: 35–36.

Hull, C. L. 1933. Differential habituation to internal stimuli in the albino rat. *Journal of Comparative Psychology,* 16: 255–273.

Hull, C. L. 1943. *Principles of behavior.* New York: Appleton-Century-Crofts.

Hull, C. L. 1952. *A behavior system.* New Haven: Yale University Press.

Hulse, S. H. 1958. Amount and percentage of reinforcement and duration of goal confinement in conditioning and extinction. *Journal of Experimental Psychology,* 56: 48–57.

Humphreys, L. G. 1939. Acquisition and extinction of verbal expectation in a situation analogous to conditioning. *Journal of Experimental Psychology,* 25: 294–301.

Hutt, P. J. 1954. Rate of barpressing as a function of quality and quantity of food reward. *Journal of Comparative and Physiological Psychology,* 47: 235–239.

Jenkins, M. 1928. The effect of segregation on the sex behavior of the white rat as measured by the obstruction method. *Genetic Psychology Monographs,* 3: 455–571.

Jenkins, W. O., and J. C. Stanley, Jr. 1950. Partial reinforcement: A review and critique. *Psychological Bulletin,* 47: 193–234.

Johannesson, K. 1962. Effects of praise and blame upon achievement and attitudes of school children. In G. S. Nielsen, ed., *Child and Education.* 14th International Congress of Applied Psychology, Vol. 3. Copenhagen: Munksgaard.

Jones, E. E. 1953, 1955, 1957. *The life and work of Sigmund Freud.* New York: Basic Books, Vol. I., 1953; Vol. II., 1955; Vol. III., 1957.

Jones, E. E., S. L. Hester, A. Farina, and K. E. Davis. 1959. Reactions to unfavorable personal evaluations as a function of the evaluator's perceived adjustment. *Journal of Abnormal and Social Psychology,* 59: 363–370.

Jones, M. C. 1924. A laboratory study of fear: The case of Peter. *Journal of General Psychology,* 31: 308–315.

Jucknat, M. 1937. Leistung. Anspruchsniveau und Selbstbewusstsein. *Psychologische Forschung,* 22: 89–179.

Jung, C. G. 1953. Two essays on analytic psychology. R. F. C. Hull, trans. *Collected works,* vol. 7. New York: Pantheon Press.

Kennedy, W. A., and H. C. Willcutt. 1964. Praise and blame as incentives. *Psychological Bulletin,* 62: 323–353.

Kimble, G. A. 1961. *Hilgard and Marquis' conditioning and learning.* 2nd ed. New York: Appleton-Century-Crofts.

King, R. A. 1959. The effects of training and motivation on the components of a learned instrumental response. Unpublished Ph.D. dissertation. Duke University.

Koch, S. 1954. Clark L. Hull. In W. K. Estes and others, *Modern learning theory*. New York: Appleton-Century-Crofts.

Koch, S. 1959. Epilogue. In S. Koch, ed., *Psychology: A study of a science*, vol. 3. New York: McGraw-Hill Book Co.

Koerner, J. D. 1963. *The miseducation of American teachers*. Boston: Houghton-Mifflin.

Krasner, L. 1958. Studies of the conditioning of verbal behavior. *Psychological Bulletin*, 55: 148–170.

Krasner, L., and L. P. Ullman. 1965. *Research in behavior modification*. New York: Holt, Rinehart and Winston.

Kuo, Z. Y. 1930. The genesis of the cat's response to the rat. *Journal of Comparative and Physiological Psychology*, 11: 30–35.

Kuo, Z. Y. 1932a. Ontogeny of embryonic behavior in Aves, I. The chronology and general nature of the behavior of the chick embryo. *Journal of Experimental Zoology*, 61: 395–430.

Kuo, Z. Y. 1932b. Ontogeny of embryonic behavior in Aves, II. The mechanical factors in the various stages leading to hatching. *Journal of Experimental Zoology*, 62: 453–489.

Kuo, Z. Y. 1932c. Ontogeny of embryonic behavior in Aves, III. The structure and environmental factors in embryonic behavior. *Journal of Comparative Psychology*, 13: 245–272.

Kuo, Z. Y. 1932d. Ontogeny of embryonic behavior in Aves, IV. The influence of embryonic movements upon the behavior after hatching. *Journal of Comparative Psychology*, 14: 109–122.

Kuo, Z. Y. 1932e. Ontogeny of embryonic behavior in Aves, V. The reflex concept in the light of embryonic behavior in birds. *Psychological Review*, 39: 499–515.

Lawrence, D. H., and L. Festinger. 1962. *Deterrents and reinforcement: The psychology of insufficient reward*. Stanford: Stanford University Press.

Lawson, R. 1957. Brightness discrimination performance and secondary reward strength as a function of primary reward amount. *Journal of Comparative and Physiological Psychology*, 50: 35–39.

Lawson, R. 1960. *Learning and behavior*. New York: Macmillan Co.

Leeper, R. 1935. The role of motivation in learning: A study of the phenomenon of differential motivational control of the utilization of habits. *Journal of Genetic Psychology*, 46: 3–40.

Lehrman, D. S. 1953. Problems raised by instinct theories. *Quarterly Review of Biology*, 28: 337–365.

Lewin, K. 1935. *A dynamic theory of personality*. K. E. Zener and D. K. Adams, trans. New York: McGraw-Hill Book Co.

Lewin, K. 1936. *Principles of topological psychology*. F. Heider and Grace Heider, trans. New York: McGraw-Hill Book Co.

Lewin, K. 1954. In W. K. Estes and others, *Modern learning theory*. New York: Appleton-Century-Crofts.

Lewin, K., T. Dembo, L. Festinger, and Pauline S. Sears. 1944. Level of aspiration. In J. McV. Hunt, ed., *Personality and the behavior disorders*. New York: Ronald Press.

Lewis, D. J. 1960. Partial reinforcement: A selective review of the literature since 1950. *Psychological Bulletin,* 57: 1–28.

Li, C. L., and H. H. Jasper. 1953. Microelectrode studies of the electrical activity of the cerebral cortex in the cat. *Journal of Physiology,* 121: 117–140.

Liddell, H. S. 1951. The influence of experimental neuroses on respiratory function. In H. A. Abramson, ed., *Somatic and psychiatric treatment of asthma*. Baltimore: Williams and Wilkins Co.

Liddell, H. S. 1954. Conditioning and emotions. *Scientific American,* 190: 48–57.

Liddell, H. S. 1955. The natural history of neurotic behavior. In I. Goldston, ed., *Society and medicine: Lectures to the laity*. New York: International Universities Press.

Liddell, H. S. 1956. *Emotional hazards in animals and man*. Springfield, Ill.: Charles C Thomas.

Lilly, J. C. 1958. Learning motivated by subcortical stimulation: The start and stop patterns of behavior. In H. Jasper and others, eds., *Reticular formation of the brain*. Boston: Little, Brown, and Co.

Lindesmith, H. S. 1947. *Opiate addiction*. Bloomington, Ind.: Principia Press.

Lindsley, D. B., L. H. Schreiner, W. B. Knowles, and H. W. Magoun. 1950. Behavioral and EEG changes following chronic brain stem lesions in the cat. *EEG and Clinical Neurophysiology,* 2: 483–498.

Lindsley, O. R. 1956. Operant conditioning methods applied to research in chronic schizophrenia. *Psychiatric Research Reports,* 5: 140–153.

Lippitt, R. 1940. An experimental study of the effect of democratic and authoritarian group atmospheres. *University of Iowa Studies in Child Welfare,* 16: 43–105.

Logan, F. A. 1952. The role of delay of reinforcement in determining reaction potential. *Journal of Experimental Psychology,* 43: 393–399.

Logan, F. A., E. M. Beier, and R. A. Ellis. 1955. Effect of varied reinforcement on speed of locomotion. *Journal of Experimental Psychology*, 49: 260–266.

Logan, F. A., E. M. Beier, and W. D. Kincaid. 1956. Extinction following partial and varied reinforcement. *Journal of Experimental Psychology*, 51: 57–61.

Lorenz, K. Z. 1956. *King Solomon's ring*. London: Methuen and Co.

Lundin, R. W. 1961. *Personality: An experimental approach*. New York: Macmillan Co.

McCandless, B. R. 1961. *Children and adolescents*. New York: Holt, Rinehart and Winston.

McClelland, D. C. 1965. Toward a theory of motive acquisition. *American Psychologist*, 20: 321–333.

McClelland, D. C., and F. S. Apicella. 1945. A functional classification of verbal reactions to experimentally induced failure. *Journal of Abnormal and Social Psychology*, 40: 376–390.

McClelland, D. C., J. W. Atkinson, R. W. Clark, and E. L. Lowell. 1953. *The achievement motive*. New York: Appleton-Century-Crofts.

MacCorquodale, K. 1955. Learning. *Annual Review of Psychology*, 6: 29–62.

McDougall, W. 1908. *An introduction to social psychology*. 30th ed., London: Methuen and Co., 1950.

McDougall, W. 1912. *Psychology, the study of behavior*. London: Williams and Norgate.

McDougall, W. 1923. *Outline of Psychology*. New York: Charles Scribner's Sons.

McNeil, J. D., and E. R. Keisler. 1961. Individual differences and effectiveness of auto-instruction at the primary grade level. *California Journal of Educational Research*, 12: 160–164.

Mahut, H. 1957. Personal communication to Samuels (1959).

Margolin, S. E., and M. E. Bunch. 1940. The relationship between age and the strength of hunger motivation. *Comparative Psychological Monographs*, 16, No. 4: 1–34.

Martin, W. G., and H. S. Morton. 1952. Clinical studies with the electrogastrograph. *Archives of Surgery*, 65: 382–396.

Marx, M. H. 1951. Experimental analysis of the hoarding habit in the rat: II. Terminal reinforcement. *Journal of Comparative and Physiological Psychology*, 44: 168–177.

Marx, M. H. 1957. Experimental analysis of the hoarding habit in the rat: III. Terminal reinforcement under low drive. *Journal of Comparative and Physiological Psychology*, 50: 168–171.

Marx, M. H. 1960. Motivation. In C. W. Harris, ed., *Encyclopedia of Educational Research*, 3rd ed. New York: Macmillan Co.

Marx, M. H., ed. 1963. *Theories in contemporary psychology.* New York: Macmillan Co.

Marx, M. H. 1966. The activation of habits. *Psychological Reports,* 19: 527–550.

Marx, M. H., and A. J. Brownstein. 1957. Experimental analysis of the hoarding habit in the rat: IV. Terminal reinforcement followed by high drive at test. *Journal of Comparative and Physiological Psychology,* 50: 617–620.

Marx, M. H., and W. A. Hillix. 1963. *Systems and theories in psychology.* New York: McGraw-Hill Book Co.

Marx, M. H., and W. W. Murphy. 1961. Resistance to extinction as a function of the presentation of a motivating cue in the startbox. *Journal of Comparative and Physiological Psychology,* 54: 207–210.

Marx, M. H., and W. A. Pieper, 1962. Acquisition of instrumental response as a function of incentive contrast. *Psychological Reports,* 10: 635–638.

Marx, M. H., and W. A. Pieper. 1963. Instrumental acquisition and performance on fixed-interval reinforcement as a function of incentive contrast. *Psychological Reports,* 12: 255–258.

Masserman, J. H. 1943. *Behavior and neurosis: An experimental psychoanalytic approach to psychobiologic principles.* Chicago: University of Chicago Press.

Masserman, J. H., and K. S. Yum. 1946. An analysis of the influence of alcohol on experimental neurosis in cats. *Psychosomatic Medicine,* 8: 36–52.

Mednick, M. T., and O. R. Lindsley. 1958. Some clinical correlates of operant behavior. *Journal of Abnormal and Social Psychology,* 57: 13–16.

Melton, A. W., ed. 1964. *Categories of human learning.* New York: Academic Press.

Miles, R. C. 1956. The relative effectiveness of secondary reinforcers throughout deprivation and habit-strength parameters. *Journal of Comparative and Physiological Psychology,* 49: 126–130.

Miller, G. A., E. Galanter, and K. H. Pribram. 1960. *Plans and the structure of behavior.* New York: Holt, Rinehart and Winston.

Miller, N. E. 1939. Experiments relating Freudian displacement to generalization conditioning. *Psychological Bulletin,* 36: 516–517.

Miller, N. E. 1941. The frustration-aggression hypothesis. *Psychological Review,* 48: 337–342.

Miller, N. E. 1944. Experimental studies of conflict. In J. McV. Hunt, ed., *Personality and the behavior disorders,* vol. I., 431–465. New York: Ronald Press.

Miller, N. E. 1948. Studies of fear as an acquirable drive. I. Fear as motivation and fear reduction as reinforcement in the learning of new responses. *Journal of Experimental Psychology,* 38: 89–101.

Miller, N. E. 1959. Liberalization of basic S-R concepts: Extensions to conflict behavior, motivation and social learning. In S. Koch, ed., *Psychology: A study of a science.* vol. 2. New York: McGraw-Hill Book Co.

Miller, N. E. 1961. Implications for theories of reinforcement. In D. E Sheer, ed., *Electrical stimulation of the brain.* Austin: University of Texas Press.

Miller, N. E., and J. Dollard. 1941. *Social learning and imitation.* New Haven: Yale University Press.

Miller, N. E., and D. Kraeling. 1952. Displacement: Greater generalization of approach than avoidance in generalized approach-avoidance conflict. *Journal of Experimental Psychology,* 43: 217–221.

Montemurro, D. G., and J. A. F. Stevenson. 1955–1956. The localization of hypothalamic structures in the rat influencing water consumption. *Yale Journal of Biological Medicine,* 28: 396–403.

Montessori, M. 1912. *The Montessori method.* A. E. George, trans. 4th ed. New York: Frederick A. Stokes Co.

Montessori, M. 1917. *The advanced Montessori method.* A. E. George, trans. New York: Frederick A. Stokes Co.

Moore, C. R., and D. Price. 1938. Some effects of testosterone and testosterone propionate in the rat. *Anatomical Record,* 71: 59–78.

Moore, O. K. 1963. *Autotelic responsive environments and exceptional children.* Hamden: Responsive Environments Foundation, Inc.

Moreno, J. L. 1946. *Psychodrama.* New York: Beacon House.

Morgan, Christiana D., and H. A. Murray, 1935. A method for investigating fantasies: The thematic apperception test. *Archives of Neurology and Psychiatry,* 34: 289–306.

Morgane, P. J. 1961. Distinct "feeding" and "hunger motivating" systems in the lateral hypothalamus of the rat. *Science,* 133: 887.

Morrell, F., and H. H. Jasper. 1956. Electrographic studies of the formation of temporary connections in the brain. *EEG and Clinical Neurophysiology,* 8: 201–215.

Moruzzi, G., and H. W. Magoun. 1949. Brain stem reticular formation and activation of the EEG. *EEG and Clinical Neurophysiology,* 1: 455–473.

Mowrer, O. H., and W. M. Mowrer. 1938. Enuresis—a method for its study and treatment. *American Journal of Orthopsychiatry,* 8: 436–459.

Muenzinger, K. F. 1942. *Psychology: The science of behavior.* New York: Harper and Bros.

Mundy-Castle, A. 1953. An analysis of central responses to photic stimulation in normal adults. *EEG and Clinical Neurophysiology,* 5: 1–22.

Murray, H. A. 1943. *Thematic apperception test manual.* Cambridge, Mass.: Harvard University Press.

Murray, H. A. 1953. Thematic appreciation test. In A. Werder, ed., *Contributions toward medical psychology,* vol. II. New York: Ronald Press.

Myers, Nancy A. 1957. Extinction of an operant response in children following partial and regular primary and secondary reinforcement procedures. Unpublished doctoral dissertation, University of Wisconsin.

Nissen, H. W. 1929. The effects of gonadectomy, vasotomy, and injections of placental and orchic extracts on the sex behavior of the white rat. *Genetic Psychology Monographs,* 5: 451–457.

Notterman, J. M. 1951. A study of some relations among aperiodic reinforcement, discrimination training and secondary reinforcement. *Journal of Experimental Psychology,* 41: 161–169.

Nuthmann, A. M. 1957. Conditioning of a response class on a personality test. *Journal of Abnormal and Social Psychology,* 54: 19–23.

Olds, J. 1955a. Physiological mechanisms of reward. In M. R. Jones, ed. *Nebraska symposium on motivation.* Lincoln: University of Nebraska Press.

Olds, J. 1955b, "Rewards" from brain stimulation in the rat. *Science,* 122: 878.

Olds, J. 1958a. Adaptive functions of the paleocortex. In H. F. Harlow and C. N. Woolsey, eds., *Biological and biochemical bases of behavior.* Madison: University of Wisconsin Press.

Olds, J. 1958b. Effects of hunger and male sex hormone on self-stimulation of the brain. *Journal of Comparative and Physiological Psychology,* 51: 320.

Olds, J. 1962. Hypothalamic substrates of reward. *Psychological Review,* 42: 555–604.

Olds, J., and D. Milner. 1954. Positive reinforcement produced by electrical stimulation of septal region and other regions of the rat brain. *Journal of Comparative and Physiological Psychology,* 47: 419–427.

Olds, J., R. P. Travis, and R. C. Schwing. 1960. Topographic organization of hypothalamic self-stimulation functions. *Journal of Comparative and Physiological Psychology,* 53: 23.

Otis, N. B., and B. McCandless. 1955. Responses to repeated frustrations of young children differentiated according to need area. *Journal of Abnormal and Social Psychology,* 50: 349–353.

Ovsiankina, Maria. 1928. Die Wiederaufnahme von unterbrochenen Handlungen. *Psychologische Forschung,* 11: 302–379.

Patton, R. A. 1951. Abnormal behavior in animals. In C. P. Stone, ed., *Comparative psychology.* 3rd ed. New York: Prentice-Hall.

Pavlov, I. P. 1906. The scientific investigation of the psychical faculties or processes in the higher animals. *Science,* 24: 613–619.

Pavlov, I. P. 1927. *Conditioned reflexes.* G. V. Anrep, trans. London: Oxford University Press.

Pelz, E. B. 1958. Some factors in "group decision." In Eleanor Maccoby, T. M. Newcomb, and E. L. Hartley, eds., *Readings in social psychology.* 3rd ed. New York: Holt, Rinehart and Winston.

Pereboom, A. C. 1957. An analysis and revision of Hull's theorem 30. *Journal of Experimental Psychology,* 53: 234–238.

Perkins, C. C., Jr. 1947. The relation of secondary reward to gradients of reinforcement. *Journal of Experimental Psychology,* 37: 377–392.

Peters, H. N., and R. L. Jenkins. 1954. Improvement of chronic schizophrenic patients with guided problem-solving motivated by hunger. *Psychiatric Quarterly Supplement,* 28: 84–101.

Pettigrew, T. F., and M. R. Cramer. 1959. The demography of desegregation. *Journal of Social Issues,* 15: 61–71.

Piaget, J. 1953. How children form mathematical concepts. *Scientific American,* 189: 74–79.

Pieper, W. A., and M. H. Marx. 1963. Effects of within-session incentive contrast on instrumental acquisition and performance. *Journal of Experimental Psychology,* 65: 568–571.

Pitcher, Evelyn G. A revolution in education. Review of E. M. Standing, *A revolution in education. Harvard Educational Review,* 33 (2) : 259–264.

Pubols, B. H., Jr. 1960. Incentive magnitude, learning, and performance in animals. *Psychological Bulletin,* 57: 89–115.

Ramond, C. K. 1954. Performance in instrumental learning as a joint function of delay of reinforcement and time of deprivation. *Journal of Experimental Psychology,* 47: 248–250.

Renner, K. E. 1964. Delay of reinforcement: A historical review. *Psychological Bulletin,* 61: 341–361.

Riddoch, G. 1917. The reflex functions of the completely divided spinal cord in man, compared with those associated with less severe lesions. *Brain,* 40: 264–402.

Ripple, R. E. 1964. *Readings in learning and human abilities.* New York: Harper and Row.

Robinson, E. A., and E. F. Adolph. 1943. Pattern of normal water drinking in dogs. *American Journal of Physiology,* 139: 39–44.

Rosenzweig, M. R. 1962. The mechanism of hunger and thirst. In L. Postman, ed., *Psychology in the making.* New York: Alfred A. Knopf.

Rothballer, A. B. 1956. Studies of the adrenaline sensitive component of the reticular activating system. *EEG and Clinical Neurophysiology,* 8: 603–622.

Rubenstein, L. 1931. The treatment of morphine addiction in tuberculosis by Pavlov's conditioning method. *American Review of Tuberculosis,* 24: 682–685.

Ryans, D. G. 1942. Motivation in learning. In *The psychology of learning,* Yearbook of the National Society for the Study of Education, 41, Part II: 289–331.

Saltzman, I. J. 1949. Maze learning in the absence of primary reinforcement: A study of secondary reinforcement. *Journal of Comparative and Physiological Psychology,* 42: 161–173.

Salzinger, K., and S. Pisoni. 1957a. Reinforcement of affect responses of schizophrenics during the clinical interview. Paper read at Eastern Psychological Association, New York, April.

Salzinger, K., and S. Pisoni. 1957b. Reinforcement of verbal affect responses of schizophrenics during the clinical interview: the effect on conditioning of placement of the period of reinforcement. Paper read at American Psychological Association, New York, August.

Samuels, I. 1959. Reticular mechanisms and behavior. *Psychological Bulletin,* 56: 1–25.

Sarason, I. G. 1960. Empirical findings and theoretical problems in the use of anxiety. *Psychological Bulletin,* 57: 403–415.

Sarason, S. B., K. S. Davidson, and B. Blatt. 1962. *The preparation of teachers: An unstudied problem in education.* New York: John Wiley and Sons.

Schwartz, M. 1956. Instrumental and consummatory measures of sexual capacity in the male rat. *Journal of Comparative and Physiological Psychology,* 49: 328–333.

Sears, Pauline S. 1941. Level of aspiration in relation to some variables of personality: Clinical studies. *Journal of Social Psychology,* 14: 311–336.

Sears, Pauline S. 1951. Doll play aggression in normal young children. *Psychological Monographs,* 65, No. 6.

Sears, Pauline S., and E. R. Hilgard. 1964. The teacher's role in the motivation of the learner. In *Theories of learning and instruction,* Yearbook of the National Society for the Study of Education, 63, Part I: 182–209.

Sears, Pauline S., and H. Levin. 1957. Levels of aspiration in preschool children. *Child Development,* 28: 317–326.

Sears, R. R. 1944. Experimental analysis of psychoanalytic phenomena. In J. McV. Hunt, ed., *Personality and the behavior disorders,* vol. I. New York: Ronald Press.

Sears, R. R., and Pauline S. Sears. 1940. Minor studies of aggression. V. Strength of frustration-reaction as a function of strength of drive. *Journal of Psychology,* 9: 297–300.

Sem-Jacobsen, C. W., and A. Torkildsen. 1960. Depth recording and electrical stimulation in the human brain. In E. R. Ramey and D. S. O'Doherty, eds., *Electrical studies on the unanesthetized brain.* New York: Hoeber.

Seward, J. P., and R. J. Weldon. 1953. Response latency as a function of change in delay of reward. *Journal of Comparative and Physiological Psychology,* 46: 184–189.

Sgro, J. A., and S. Weinstock. 1963. Effects of delay on subsequent running under immediate reinforcement. *Journal of Experimental Psychology,* 66: 260–263.

Sharpless, S., and H. H. Jasper. 1956. Habituation of the arousal reaction. *Brain,* 79: 655–680.

Sidman, M., J. V. Brady, D. G. Conrad, and A. Schulmann. 1955. Reward schedules and behavior maintained by intracranial self-stimulation. *Science,* 122: 830–831.

Skinner, B. F. 1938. *The behavior of organisms: An experimental analysis.* New York: Appleton-Century-Crofts.

Skinner, B. F. 1948. "Superstition" in the pigeon. *Journal of Experimental Psychology,* 38: 168–172.

Skinner, B. F. 1954. The science of learning and the art of teaching. *Harvard Educational Review,* 24: 86–97.

Skinner, B. F. 1959. *Cumulative record.* New York: Appleton-Century-Crofts.

Skinner, B. F., H. C. Solomon, and O. R. Lindsley. 1954. A new method for the experimental analysis of the behavior of psychotic patients. *Journal of Nervous and Mental Disorders,* 120: 403–406.

Spence, K. W. 1956. *Behavior theory and conditioning.* New Haven: Yale.

Spence, K. W. 1960. *Behavior theory and learning.* Englewood Cliffs, N. J.: Prentice-Hall.

Spence, K. W. 1964. Anxiety (drive) level and performance in eyelid conditioning. *Psychological Bulletin,* 61: 129–139.

Spence, K. W., and I. E. Farber. 1953. Conditioning and extinction as a function of anxiety. *Journal of Experimental Psychology,* 45: 116–119.

Spence, K. W., I. E. Farber, and Elaine Taylor. 1954. The relation of electric shock and anxiety to level of performance in eyelid conditioning. *Journal of Experimental Psychology,* 48: 404–408.

Spence, K. W., and Janet T. Spence. 1966. Sex and anxiety differences in eyelid conditioning. *Psychological Bulletin,* 65: 137–142.

Spence, K. W., and Janet A. Taylor. 1953. The relation of conditioned response strength to anxiety in normal, neurotic, and psychotic subjects. *Journal of Experimental Psychology,* 45: 265–272.

Staats, A. W. 1964. *Human learning (Studies extending conditioning principles to complex behavior).* New York: Holt, Rinehart and Winston.

Stagner, R., and C. S. Congdon. 1955. Another failure to demonstrate displacement of aggression. *Journal of Abnormal and Social Psychology,* 51: 695–696.

Standing, E. M. 1957. *Maria Montessori, her life and work.* London: Hollis and Carter.

Steisel, I. M., and B. D. Cohen. 1951. The effects of two degrees of failure on level of aspiration and performance. *Journal of Abnormal and Social Psychology,* 46: 79–82.

Stoddard, G. D. 1961. *The dual progress plan.* New York: Harper and Row.

Stone, C. P. 1927. The retention of copulatory ability in male rats following castration. *Journal of Comparative Psychology,* 7: 369–387.

Stotland, E. 1959. Peer groups and reactions to power figures. In D. Cartwright, ed., *Studies in social power.* Ann Arbor: Institute for Social Research.

Swets, J. A., and W. Feurzeig. 1965. Computer-aided instruction. *Science,* 150: 572–576.

Szasz, T. S. 1961. *The myth of mental illness.* New York: Hoeber.

Tanner, J. M., and B. Inhelder. 1956. *Discussion on child development,* vol. II. London: Tavistock Publications.

Taylor, Janet A. 1951. The relationship of anxiety to the conditioned eyelid response. *Journal of Experimental Psychology,* 41: 81–92.

Taylor, Janet A. 1953. A personality scale of manifest anxiety. *Journal of Abnormal and Social Psychology,* 48: 285–290.

Taylor, Janet A. 1956. Drive theory and manifest anxiety. *Psychological Bulletin,* 53: 303–320.

Taylor, Janet A., and K. W. Spence. 1952. The relationship of anxiety level to performance in serial learning. *Journal of Experimental Psychology,* 44: 61–64.

Terman, L. M. 1938. *Psychological factors in marital happiness.* New York: McGraw-Hill Book Co.

Thelen, H. A. 1963. Discovery and inquiry: A dynamic approach to teaching and learning. In G. B. Watson, ed., *No room at the bottom.* National Education Association.

Thibaut, J. W., and J. Coules. 1952. The role of communication in the reduction of interpersonal hostility. *Journal of Abnormal and Social Psychology,* 47: 770–777.

Thibaut, J. W., and H. W. Riecken. 1955. Authoritarianism, status, and the communication of aggression. *Human Relations,* 8: 95–120.

Thorndike, E. L. 1898. Animal intelligence: An experimental study of the associative processes in animals. *Psychological Monographs,* 2: No. 8.

Thorndike, E. L. 1911. *Animal intelligence.* New York: Macmillan Co.

Tinbergen, N. 1951. *A study of instinct.* Oxford: Clarendon Press.

Tolman, E. C. 1932. *Purposive behavior in animals and man.* New York: D. Appleton Co.

Tolman, E. C. 1959. Principles of purposive behavior. In S. Koch, ed., *Psychology: A study of a science.* New York: McGraw-Hill Book Co.

Tolman, E. C., and L. H. Honzik. 1930. "Insight" in rats. *University of California Publications in Psychology,* 4: 215–232.

Tombaugh, T. N. 1965. The effects of delay of reinforcement during acquisition and extinction upon runway performance. Unpublished doctoral dissertation. University of Missouri.

Tombaugh, T. N., and M. H. Marx. 1965. The effects of ordered and constant sucrose concentrations on nonreinforced performance. *Journal of Experimental Psychology,* 69: 630–636.

Torrance, E. P. 1965a. *Gifted children in the classroom.* New York: Macmillan Co.

Torrance, E. P. 1965b. *Rewarding creative behavior.* Englewood Cliffs: Prentice-Hall.

Travers, J. F. 1965. *Learning: Analysis and application.* New York: David McKay Co.

Trow, W. C. 1948. How educational psychology and child development can contribute to the preparation of teachers. *Journal of Educational Psychology,* 39: 129–132.

Trump, J. L., and D. Baynham. 1961. *Guide to better schools: Focus on change.* Chicago: Rand McNally and Co.

Ullman, L. P., and L. Krasner. 1965. *Case studies in behavior modification.* New York: Holt, Rinehart and Winston.

Verplanck, W. S. 1955. Since learned behavior is innate, and vice versa, what now? *Psychological Review,* 62: 139–144.

Wagensteen, O. H., and H. A. Carlson. 1931. Hunger sensations in a patient after total gastrectomy. *Proceedings of the Society of Experimental Biology and Medicine,* 28: 545–547.

Wagner, A. R. 1961. Effects of amount and percentage of reinforcement and number of acquisition trials on conditioning and extinction. *Journal of Experimental Psychology,* 62: 234–242.

Walker, K. C. 1942. The effect of a discriminative stimulus transferred to a previously unassociated response. *Journal of Experimental Psychology,* 31: 312–321.

Warden, C. J., and E. L. Haas. 1927. The effect of short intervals of delay in feeding upon speed of maze learning. *Journal of Comparative Psychology,* 7: 107–115.

Watson, G. B., ed. 1963. *No room at the bottom—autoinstruction and the reluctant learner.* National Education Association.

Watson, J. B. 1925. *Behaviorism.* New York: W. W. Norton and Co.

Weinstock, S. 1958. Acquisition and extinction of a partially reinforced running response at a 24-hour intertrial interval. *Journal of Experimental Psychology,* 56: 151–158.

White, R. K., and R. Lippitt. 1960. *Autocracy and democracy: An experimental inquiry.* New York: Harper and Bros.

White, R. W. 1959. Motivation reconsidered: The concept of competence. *Psychological Review,* 66: 297–333.

Wike, E. L., and W. Kintsch. 1959. Delayed reinforcement and runway performance. *Psychological Record,* 9: 19–28.

Wike, E. L., and H. J. McNamara, 1957. The effects of percentage of partially delayed reinforcement on the acquisition and extinction of an instrumental response. *Journal of Comparative and Physiological Psychology,* 50: 348–351.

Wike, E. L., J. R. Platt, and J. M. Knowles. 1962. The reward value of getting out of a starting box: Further extension of Zimmerman's work. *Psychological Record,* 12: 397–400.

Wikler, A., and J. H. Masserman. 1943. Effects of morphine on learned adaptive responses and experimental neurosis in cats. *Archives of Neurology and Psychiatry,* Chicago, 50: 401–404.

Williams, C. D. 1955. The elimination of tantrum behaviors by extinction procedures. *Journal of Abnormal and Social Psychology,* 39: 269.

Witt, D. M., A. D. Keller, H. L. Batsel, and J. R. Lynch. 1952. Absence of thirst and resultant syndrome associated with anterior hypothalamectomy in the dog. *American Journal of Physiology,* 171: 780.

Wolf, A. V. 1950. Osmometric analysis of thirst in man and dog. *American Journal of Physiology,* 161: 75–86.

Wolf, A. V. 1958. *Thirst: Physiology of the urge to drink and problems of water lack.* Springfield, Ill.: Charles C Thomas.

Wolfe, J. B. 1934. The effect of delayed reward upon learning in the white rat. *Journal of Comparative Psychology,* 17: 1–21.

Wolfe, J. B. 1936. Effectiveness of token-rewards for chimpanzees. *Comparative Psychological Monographs,* 12: No. 60.

Wolpe, J. 1958. *Psychotherapy by reciprocal inhibition.* Stanford: Stanford University Press.

Woodring, P. 1964. Reform movements from the point of view of psychological theory. In *Theories of learning and instruction,* Yearbook of the National Society for the Study of Education, 63, Part I: 286–305.

Woodworth, R. S. 1918. *Dynamic psychology.* New York: Columbia University Press.

Woodworth, R. S. 1947. Reinforcement of perception. *American Journal of Psychology,* 60: 119–124.

Yamaguchi, H. G. 1951. Drive (D) as a function of hours of hunger (h) . *Journal of Experimental Psychology,* 42: 108–117.

Yerkes, R. M., and J. D. Dodson. 1908. The relation of strength of stimulus to rapidity of habit-formation. *Journal of Comparative and Neurological Psychology,* 18: 459–482.

Yerkes, R. M., and J. H. Elder. 1936. The sexual and reproductive cycles of chimpanzees. *Proceedings of the National Academy of Science,* 22: 276–283.

Young, P. T. 1961. *Motivation and emotion: A survey of the determinants of human and animal activity.* New York: John Wiley and Sons.

Zeaman, D. 1949. Response latency as a function of the amount of reinforcement. *Journal of Experimental Psychology,* 39: 466–483.

Zeigarnik, Bluma. 1927. Über das Behalten von erledigten und unerledigten Handlungen. *Psychologische Forschung,* 9: 1–85.

Zimmerman, D. W. 1957. Durable secondary reinforcement. *Psychological Review,* 64: 373–383.

Zimmerman, D. W. 1959. Sustained performance in rats based on secondary reinforcement. *Journal of Comparative and Physiological Psychology,* 52: 353–358.

Zotterman, Y. 1956. Species differences in the water taste. *Acta Physiologica Scandanavica,* 37: 60–70.

INDEX